Dear Pop –

Continually flowing are the rivers
toward their source, as water's
smooth traverse does forever
change the course.

Great writers, men of vision, emerge
along the way, providing passage for
those to follow, and like the river's
surge, form what will be tomorrow.

Happy 80th Birthday Dad. This poem
was written while I was at Cal
in 1985, but has never been so
relevant!

The San Joaquin
A River Betrayed

Updated Second Edition

The San Joaquin
A River Betrayed

Updated Second Edition

by
Gene Rose

Word
Dancer
Press

Clovis, California

Printed in the United States of America

Published by Quill Driver Books/Word Dancer Press, Inc.
8386 N. Madsen Avenue • Clovis, CA 93611
559-322-5917 / 800-497-4909

Word Dancer Press books may be purchased for educational, fund-raising, business or promotional use. Please contact Special Markets,
Quill Driver Books/Word Dancer Press, Inc. at the above address or phone numbers.

ISBN 1-884995-20-9

To order a copy of this book, please call
1-800-497-4909

Other books by Gene Rose published by Quill Driver Books/Word Dancer Press, Inc.:
Reflections of Shaver Lake

Other books on California published by Quill Driver Books/Word Dancer Press, Inc.:
From Mud-Flat Cove to Gold to Statehood: California 1840-1850, by Irving Stone
California's Geographic Names: A Gazetteer of Historic and Modern Names of the State, compiled by David L. Durham
California Desperadoes: Stories of Early California Outlaws in Their Own Words, by William B. Secrest
Black Bart: Boulevardier Bandit, by George Hoeper
San Juan Bautista: The Town, The Mission & The Park, by Charles W. Clough
The Valley's Legends & Legacies (series), by Catherine Morison Rehart

---

Front cover photo by Gene Rose
Quill Driver Books/Word Dancer Press project cadre:
Doris Hall, Dave Marion, Stephen Blake Mettee

Publishing made possible in part by a sponsorship from The San Joaquin River Parkway and Conservation Trust, a non-profit land trust with offices located in Fresno, California. Its mission is to preserve and restore San Joaquin River lands having ecological, scenic or historic significance, to educate the public on the need for stewardship, to research issues affecting the river, and to promote educational, recreational, and agricultural uses consistent with the protection of the environment. For additional information, please contact them at 559-248-8480.

Contents

Preface

The Mississippi, the Columbia, the Colorado, and the Missouri rivers: few natural features of this planet have dominated people's lives like its rivers. Rivers form the larger arteries of life, sustaining every living thing with the miracle of water. Indeed, rivers are life itself.

The San Joaquin River of California was once such a river. From its pristine source in the High Sierra to its conclusion in the San Joaquin-Sacramento Delta, the heartland river of the Golden State was once a great river; yet today it flows as one of the most controversial rivers in America, used and abused like no other.

More than a solitary river, the San Joaquin represents a vast river system, embracing half a dozen tributaries—all rivers unto themselves. Nearest the delta enters the Mokelumne River, bringing with it the flows of the Cosumnes River. Farther upstream at Stockton comes the Calaveras River whose Spanish name—the skulls—suggests some of its magic, or its mysteries. The Stanislaus enters next, to be followed by the Tuolumne and Merced Rivers, bearing the liquid grandeur of Yosemite National Park. During the wet winters a collection of secondary streams, such as the Chowchilla and Fresno Rivers, and a host of west side streams show their ephemeral heads. Upstream, the main stem of the San Joaquin channel wends its way to the foothills, eventually fanning out into a network of forks and rivulets that reach the eternal snowfield of the majestic Sierra.

Draining an area of nearly 20,000 square miles—larger than the states of New York and New Jersey—the San Joaquin River is the sister to the even larger Sacramento River which drains the northern section of the sprawling Central Valley. At its genesis, the main fork flows eastward from the Ritter Range to Thousand Island Lake; then it turns south, west and, finally, north—a route that forms something of a crude shaped question mark. Such a configuration is perhaps fitting for the San Joaquin River, so steeped in conflict and controversy.

The landscape through which the San Joaquin flows shows a similar diversity, from towering mountains, deep canyons and undulating foothills to the vast plains and deltas. From its birthplace on high, it flows through some of the most beautiful country in America—the headwaters of the American conservation and parks movement. By the time the river reaches the delta nearly 400 miles and 10,000 vertical feet later, it is little more than a public sewer, a fouled, controlled drain for agricultural and municipal waste water.

At its midsection, the river has served as the womb and cradle of hydroelectric development in America, powering what has become the world's leading "nation state," California. In this mode, the river reinforces the slogan that here are the "hardest working waters in the world," powering industry and homes up and down the state. At the last count the main stem contained a dozen major dams and twice that number of powerhouses. The larger basin counted nearly sixty dams, storage facilities that add their muscle, providing still more electrical power to the Golden State.

Still other enigmas or dimensions go with the river.

By some measure, there is a little bit of the San Joaquin River in most of us. In various ways the river sustains millions of Americans, irrigating nearly 200 different crops—a cornucopia of foods and fibers that make their way around the world.

As it is now "plumbed," into the massive Central Valley Project—that is, manipulated—the river's natural hydrology has been destroyed. Today the San Joaquin flows as one of the nation's most controlled rivers, moving more in man-made canals, tunnels and penstocks than it does in its own natural channel. Today the riverboats are gone, as are the fish and wildlife. In the forty-one-mile stretch downstream of Gravelly Ford, the river doesn't flow at all until it reaches the Mendota Pool, where it is artificially revived by the Delta-Mendota Canal, so it can be diverted and defiled further downstream.

The river's great natural diversity also reflects much of its vast and varied human history despite its relatively brief time span. The San Joaquin gave rise to land baron and cattle king Henry Miller, whose vast holdings made him the largest landowner this country has ever known—only because the crafty Miller realized that "he who controls the water also controls the wealth." And control it he did, fathering some of the first and largest irrigation projects the world had ever seen.

Today, the San Joaquin is a troubled river. Some see it as a river betrayed, a river corrupted—"diverted by the Friant-Kern Canal to distant Kern County rather than to flow its own way," as one river veteran reflected. For others it appears as the dead river, the "ex-river," no longer able to flush itself clean. And for those in the San Francisco Bay area, it is a public sewer, so fouled that it is no longer perceived as a source of life and sustenance; rather it is something to be feared.

While nearly all of America's major rivers have been compromised, few have been so misused as the San Joaquin. In its comparatively brief history it has been dammed, diverted and depleted beyond comprehension.

In *The Living River* (Winchester Press), author Charles E. Brooks observed that "rivers do not return to the sea; they return to their headwaters in the form of rain and snow to start their long run to the sea, nourishing and sustaining all life in the process.

"Rivers are thus the lifeblood of the land, running over instead of through it; wetting, nourishing, tearing down and rebuilding, shaping and destroying, they are life itself in raw, living, always changing, but never-ending repetition. Without them, no other life can survive.

"Without the circulation of fresh water down the arteries of streams to the ocean, and water's return by evaporation and air movement to the capillaries, all things on earth would soon cease to exist, and the land would become barren. If the rivers die, so does the whole world."

Such may be the scenario for the San Joaquin Valley or other irrigated areas of the country. By greed, ignorance and the apparent quest for power, the once mighty San Joaquin, the heartland river has been killed; its artery severed.

This book is not an academic history; rather, it is the story of a real river—its people, its places and its past—based on the lives and letters of those who have known it firsthand. More than anything, it seeks to identify the forces and figures who have shaped, altered—and corrupted—the course of a once mighty river. To this end we have looked at its history in a regional or hydrologic context, rather than in the traditional approach of using politically drawn boundaries. By no means does this book contain the complete story of the river so washed by time and subverted by man. Some might perceive this account as an environmental history; more likely, it is the river's epitaph—the story of a river wronged.

So come, step back in time and travel along; there's one of the old river steamers now. Let's hop onboard and journey up the river. Let's see how far we can get. We'll look at the river's rich and colorful past. Along the way we'll visit its backwaters and byways. We'll also stop and examine those places where the water barons and power brokers left their mark—and those spots where the government went wrong. Even if there is not enough water, we can at least explore the territory. I hope you find the trip interesting and engaging. All aboard!

Acknowledgments

A lot of water has flowed over the dams since the San Joaquin River became an integral part of California life.

In tracing the course of this tremendous yet troubled river, I have been aided by an exceptional group of friends and associates—besides an inordinate number of relative strangers whose ties to the river run deep. Others have contributed their records or remembrances or assisted in some other way in bringing this project to completion.

At the headwaters of helpers stand the librarians, curators and special assistants from the half-dozen counties that constitute the greater San Joaquin River basin. Their ranks include the Fresno City and County Historical Society, the Fresno County Free Library, the Madera County Historical Society, the Merced County Historical Society, the Stanislaus County Historical Society and the San Joaquin County Historical Society.

The other institutions include the Woodward Section of Madden Library, California State University Fresno; the Miliken Museum of Los Banos; the McHenry Library at Modesto; the Newman Museum of Newman; the California State Library at Sacramento; the National Maritime Museum of San Francisco, and the Wells Fargo Bank Archives, also of San Francisco; and the Bancroft Library, Water Resources Archives and the Lowie Museum of Anthropology, all within the University of California at Berkeley.

Assistance has also come from Gretchen Temple of the Stockton-San Joaquin County Public Library; Bill Myers, historian for Southern California Edison Company; Ed Steen, veteran stream gauger and retired ranger from the Sierra National Forest; Ken Choy of Pacific Gas and Electric Company; Jim Snyder, historian for Yosemite National Park; Grant Allen Anderson, manager, Library Services for the Church of Jesus Christ of Latter-Day Saints; Claude Delphia of the Patterson Township Historical Society; Earl J. Hohlmeyer, past president of the Antioch Historical Society; Alex Hildebrand of the San Joaquin River Flood Protection Association; Dr. King N. Huber of the U.S. Geological Survey; and various representatives of the U.S. Forest Service. Fellow members of the Westerners also offered up tidbits of information.

I am also indebted to those who had the San Joaquin River in the blood—those who are no longer with us. They lived and loved the real river—in flood and drought. I am particularly appreciative of the vast information provided by the late J. Martin Winton of Fresno, an often crusty curmudgeon, whose outspokenness was exceeded only by his firsthand knowledge of the river and its resources. Ed Steen, veteran stream gauger, provided others gems of upper San Joaquin River. Glenn Burns, Tony Imperatrice, Carl Hobe and Evelyn Rank also shared their days along the river, before they went with the final flow.

To Helen Mott of Fresno, who shared the extensive records and interviews of her late husband, Tom Mott—a man of many talents and whose knowledge of the West Side ran deeper than perhaps any other person—I am especially indebted. His records were especially helpful in providing a more exacting picture of early life along the river.

Similarly, the editorial library of the *Fresno Bee*, with its exceptional staff and files, provided a volume of information, particularly as it involved the evolution of the Central Valley Project and Friant Dam.

Finding vintage photos was a major problem. Sharon Hiigel of the Fresno City and County Historical Society; Dr. Catherine Julienne, formerly of the Merced County History Department; Jerry Laval of Graphic Technology, Fresno; Margaret Collins of the Newman Museum; Kerman postcard collector Ben Georgeson; Ron Mahoney of the Madden Library, California State University, Fresno; Don Cobb of Fresno; Harry Pederson of Kerman; the Central California Irrigation District at Los Banos; Meera Hawkins of the Modesto Irrigation District all helped as did the U.S. Bureau of Reclamation which supplied photographs of the river.

Finally, I am indebted to my wife, Doris, without whose patience and understanding this book would not have seen print.

To all, thank you.

The Setting

Born in the Alpine snowfields of the High Sierra, the main fork of the San Joaquin River begins life high on the slopes of the towering 13,000-foot Ritter Range. Here among the ridges and ramparts of the ancestral Sierra the first glimmer of the river emerges as tiny drops of snowmelt, delivered months, even years ago by storms from the distant Pacific. At not distant locations, the north and south forks, as well as other tributaries, are undergoing a similar metamorphosis. These molecules of magic do not linger long in this often hostile world of snow and ice. Slowly at first, they seep downward, gathering force and form along the way. The fledgling San Joaquin River is on the move.

Within the first embrace of Thousand Island, Garnet or Shadow lakes—some of the sparkling gems of the John Muir Trail country—the collected droplets gather. At this first resting spot, the waters stand clear and cold. When scientists tested the water in the 1960s, they found its quality equivalent to distilled water in purity; but now there are fears of acid rain or of a devilish microorganism known as giardia. Yet the molecules move on, eastward now, dropping through boulder-lined canyons dotted by an increasing number of aspens and pines. On it flows, dancing its way down the mountain side of the Ansel Adams Wilderness—a landscape of beauty and boldness. Gradually the river swings south, slowing for a moment, entering an area of lush mountain meadows lined with willows and still more aspen. On it surges, passing a unique geological formation of basalt known as Devils Postpile, a unit of the National Park Service. Contained here by the walls of the canyon, the river plunges over the 101-foot lip of Rainbow Falls, highest waterfall on the river.

Below, the mist and spray regroup, only to plunge into a no-man's-.land of deep canyons and cataracts where towering granite walls soar to the sky. For miles the river rumbles its way through this chasm, echoing its wildness. Until 1981, when a trio of adventurers using kayaks and climbing ropes forced their way down the chasm, the river corridor was impenetrable; early travel through the canyon was confined to Indian or miners' trails along the upper rims. Within the depths of this remote and rugged gorge, the river runs free and wild. During the spring runoff, it shouts its freedom in wild abandon—a bejeweled stream of dancing waters—crashing and thrashing its way through the length of the canyon. In late summer, however, particularly in dry years, the receding river reveals yet another world, one of sculptured grottos and deep pools, etched by sands of time and the cycle of rivers unending.

Downstream, a host of smaller streams and creeks join the fray. Near Junction Butte, the north fork links up, having garnered its flows from the Madera Crest and the western slope of the Minarets. More side streams link up, pouring forth their bounty and beauty into the main fork. At the spot where explorer and geologist William Brewer spotted and named a huge "Balloon Dome" in 1864, the south fork makes its entrance, adding force and fury with a liquid heritage that reaches all the way back to the towering ramparts of Evolution Basin in Kings Canyon National Park.

At Thousand Island Lake, high in the Sierra, the main fork of the San Joaquin River begins its rugged journey to the valley below.

By some measure, the San Joaquin River gorge represents one of those "out-of-this-world" places. Down the years, at a few of the accessible river crossings, some of the early pioneers attempted to span the river with small bridges. The indomitable Henry Miller, famed land and cattle king, left his legacy in the form of a bridge known as "Miller's Crossing." While Miller was able to manipulate nearly all the human institutions of the day, his stout bridge was no match for the river's spring runoff, and the river has continued to have its way here in this inner-sanctum.

The river plunges downward, sounding its descent with a roar heard along canyon's rim. Snaking its way past Hells Half Acre—a name befitting the gorge's grim or glorious dimensions—the river finally brakes to a halt at Mammoth Pool Reservoir, the first of many man-made impoundments along the way and the first spot accessible by car since Devils Postpile. Dammed and diverted here, the river is shunted into a ten-mile-long tunnel where it will spin the giant hydroelectric turbines below.

Downstream, within the tributary Big Creek drainage to the east, stands a larger network of dams and powerhouses with all the power its name implies—the first major hydroelectric project of its kind—a development that took the modern world out of the dark ages. More dams and power plants line the main channel and secondary streams. By any measure, this is "hydro country," dominated by the giant utilities, Southern California Edison Company, and Pacific Gas and Electric Company. So, consumed by penstocks and powerhouses, the canyon's complexion undergoes a marked industrial transformation, off limits to the casual visitor. At Stevenson Creek, for example, the vanquished remains of a once great waterfall trickle over the eastern escarpment of the canyon, denying modern-day viewers the appreciation of that earlier wonder.

Downstream, more dams and diversions appear as the river moves on. They bear names of Redinger and Kerckhoff—giants, pioneers in the development of modern day hydropower, sustaining the slogan that here are the "hardest working waters in the world." For one brief stretch below Redinger Lake the river comes to life again, only to be impounded once more. Again and again, spent waters are returned to the relicted channel so they can be diverted to spin yet more turbines and generate more electrical power. At Kerckhoff One, PG&E takes over where SCE has left off, with huge underground tunnels diverting much of the flow to streamside and underground power plants. The river's remains flow on through the foothills, its natural channel forming giant oxbow turns, skirting tabletop mountains that form the foothill canyon.

At the tailrace or discharge of Kerckhoff Two, the waters return to the natural channel, only to be impounded again. Here behind the massive concrete barrier known as Friant Dam—often billed as the fifth largest concrete dam in the world—an eleven-mile-long man-made reservoir forms the southern anchor for the vast Central Valley Project, one of the world's most ambitious irrigation and flood control projects. To this point, all the power projects have been "flow-through" facilities; that is, the impounded water is eventually returned to the main channel so it can be used again. But here, within the embrace of 520,000-acre-foot Millerton Lake, the once mighty San Joaquin River comes to an abrupt halt.

For thousands of years before the dam builders came along, the San Joaquin ran free and wild, yielding to nothing except climatic forces even more powerful than itself. Drought and flood years were its way. In dry years the runoff could be as low as 362,000 acre feet, and a succession of dry years now spell disaster. But the flood years represent the other side of the fickle two-faced river, sending an angry animal down the canyon—a tenfold difference—with up to 4.6 million acre feet having surged through the canyon in the peak years. In a normal weather year, over 95 percent of the 1.7 million acre feet flow will be diverted into the mammoth Friant-Kern or Madera canals to irrigate distant farmlands, confirming, as one observer lamented, that the San Joaquin did not flow to the sea, but to distant Tulare and Kern counties.

For the thirsty water user in the valley, the San Joaquin River's liquid gold means money—big money for some, little for others. For the electrical utilities above, a flow-through acre foot of water is worth $87 alone. So precious are its flows that in the early 1980s, generators were finally retrofitted to the discharge ports of Friant Dam, squeezing out even more revenues and garnering additional power. On the farming side of the equation, growers using subsidized CVP water pay from as little as $3.00 an acre-foot to many times that figure when left to their own, as is the case for most small farmers.

Below Friant Dam a remnant river struggles on, carrying a scant 166 cubic feet per second, an allocation reached only after years of legal fighting. This trickle glides by the Lost Lake Recreation Area, washing the bedrock mortar holes—visible reminders of the ancient ones, those natives who lived in harmony with the land not so long ago. Moving westerly along its southern most arc, the trickle creeps past Fort Washington Beach, past fading landmarks such as Pumpkin Center and Lane's Ferry, historic place-names that evoke little or no recognition from today's multitude.

Almost due north of downtown Fresno, the wisp of a river passes under Highway 41, unrecognized as a true river by many of the motorists bound to Yosemite National Park. Here on the floor of the valley, within the urban sprawl of Fresno, the river's remains skirt sand-and-gravel mines, river-bluff homes, golf courses, and the first of many farms and orchards. Along this section, the river is little more than a "step-across" stream, dotted by an occasional pond, crossed by a couple of railroad bridges and, finally, Freeway 99, a main north-south route of the Golden State. In 1937, before Friant Dam was in place, the runoff swollen river reached within a few feet of the ninety-foot-high bridge, spreading out from bank to bank. Today, no one knows the river of old. Few of the passing motorists ever see a real river anymore. Only its remains struggle on, following a channel carved by time and torrents, past Skaggs Bridge and Highway 145, eking out the barest existence as a series of "pumping ponds." Here lies a strange mixture of ambiguous water law and "government-gone-wrong" clashes with history and heritage. The river's remains testify that this is the most litigated river in the United States. It is difficult to imagine that commercial river steamers and barges once made their way to Sycamore Point, the upper point of defined navigability on the river. Today, time has masked the transformation; no one knows that precise location.

At Gravelly Ford the flow has dwindled to five cubic feet a second, the defined limit of government's responsibility to maintain a so-called "live stream." The river's final resting place stands far removed from earlier times when the cliff-dwelling Indians found the river a source of life, abundant with fish and game. And it was here that the early Spanish explorers, fortunate enough to find a shallow bed of gravel, forded the river en route to their journeys of discovery. For most years now, only a dry river channel bears witness to its demise.

Below Gravelly Ford a dry channel of sand and silt marks the river's route. The once majestic San Joaquin River appears only as an apparition—a ghost river—its exposed bottom standing in marked contrast to the waning willows that still line its once proud path. Occasionally a jack rabbit scurries across this barren wasteland, a dry wash and fleeting reminder that this was once a riparian landscape rich in fish and wildlife. The salmon, the eagles and the elk have disappeared also—a

sad commentary on man's stewardship to the larger artery of life. At several locations, and as a further insult, the dewatered channel has become the local dumping ground, its sandy bottom littered with wrecked cars, rusting refrigerators, beer cans and other trappings of a throwaway society.

About once every eight years—but only after a particularly wet winter and only when Friant Dam is unable to accommodate the additional snowmelt—does any semblance of the "real" river return. As a result, silt and vegetation now choke the relicted channel; the sands of the Sierra have backfilled the channel, reducing its overall depth of eight feet. For a few days during the winter of 1985–86, the San Joaquin River scared the daylights out of downstream residents, when a relatively meager 7,000 cubic foot per second flow, about one-tenth of its record historic peak, came down the channel. Without sufficient venue, the surge tore through the old levees, flooding homes and farmlands, recalling for a moment the river of old.

For mile after mile the dry channel wanders across the valley's vast landscape, pushing its woeful route westward. At Mendota, however, the river undergoes yet another strange metamorphosis. Here at the aging, silt-clogged Mendota Pool, the river reemerges, "reconstituted" with the distant waters of the Sacramento Delta, delivered through another engineering marvel of the CVP project known as the Delta-Mendota Canal. Supplemented by the spent Kings River waters, which have made their way down Fresno Slough, the reincarnated river moves on again, supplying a network of irrigation canals and more farmlands that fan out from Mendota Pool.

Thus revived, the river resumes its historic path, making a marked turn northward on its troubled and enigmatic journey. Eventually it reaches the historic community of Firebaugh, famed for its cantaloupes, cotton and varied crops, added reminders of the river's transformation. East of town, a modern bridge whisks today's traveler across the tainted river with little reflection of Andrew Firebaugh, the early settler who ferried many of the pioneers across the once formidable waterway. Downstream, more ditches and diversions again define the revived but manipulated waterway. As it goes, a more insidious and unseen threat flows by; the waters introduced by the Delta Mendota Canal leave nearly 1.6 million tons—300 pounds an acre—of salt a year. The land is being poisoned.

By the time the river reaches Highway 152 east of Los Banos, it is dry once more. Only on maps does the river exist; but on it goes, through the grasslands, skirting the San Luis and Kesterson national wildlife refuges, names that belie the environmental disaster lurking here. One of the ditches ending at Kesterson bears the dubious name of the San Luis Drain. Over the past few years, the drain has carried agricultural wastewater and naturally occurring selenium into the refuge.

In 1983, the United States Fish and Wildlife Service determined that selenium was responsible for the death or deformation of thousands of birds and waterfowl at the refuge. While essential to life in small amounts, the element has been working its way into the food chain in greater concentrations, posing even greater concerns. Efforts to abate the problem have been expensive and largely ineffective. However, seepage back into the historic river channel has been further contaminated by agricultural wastewater. These meager flows preclude dilution or flushing; higher concentrations of selenium and heavy metals are also showing up downstream, threatening the very future of valley agriculture and the Bay Area.

Farther downstream near Newman, at the confluence with the Merced River, the river reemerges again near the historic site of Hill's Ferry, where the earliest of transriver ferries was placed in service back in the early 1850s. However, even the addition of the legendary waters of Yosemite's Merced River does little to improve the water quality.

The revived, reviled river flows on. Now it is a river of sweeping oxbow turns; mile after mile it serpentines its way northward. Farm after farm, it struggles past the original Crow's Landing. Near Patterson it slides up to the apricot capital of the nation, now succumbing to the growth slopping over from the Bay Area. One veteran farmer here frets about using river water to irrigate his orchards, knowing he is gradually killing the very land that is his trust and treasure. But the alternate supply from the nearby irrigation canals suffers from salinity, the "salt cycle from the bay," he explains.

Back in the channel the river struggles on to Graysons, its murky molecules hiding a once proud past. Along the river, stands of mature willows have reemerged, providing some measure of the riparian forest that once covered this primeval landscape. Over a century ago, during the height of the riverboat era, the willows were nearly eliminated to fuel the boilers of the river steamers. But today the willows are back; only the riverboats and the real river are gone.

At the confluence with the Tuolumne River, the San Joaquin River reveals another facet of its troubled past. All of the main tributaries are dammed or diverted, their natural discharges denied. Not until augmented by the dubious discharge from the Modesto wastewater treatment plant does the replenished San Joaquin take on a significant flow. Recharged yet again, it moves northward, passing the shadows of its past—a wake of a river now silted and sullied by the hand of man.

Further downstream enters the once mighty Stanislaus River, whose flows share something of a similar fate. Years ago, a group of Mormon pioneers set the foundation of a new colony a short distance upstream. Somehow, New Hope flourished for a while but then disappeared; it is, perhaps, an epitaph for the river and its tributaries today.

There have been other entrances and exits as well. In the past, ephemeral streams from the canyons of the Diablo Range to the west once emptied their liquid wealth into the main river. Their names reflected their early California heritage: Los Banos, Garzas and Orestimba creeks, but now most of them are gone, too—dammed or diverted.

Below the confluence of the Stanislaus, the hamlet of Durham Ferry emerges. The last ferry departed years ago, but here the river of rivers begins responding to the surge of the not too distant seas and their tides. When viewed from the air, the channel appears as a serpentine—a series of linked turns—inching its way ever so slowly northward toward Stockton. But the river no longer touches its namesake. At some not so distant time, San Joaquin City, the historic riverfront landing, was circumvented, when the meandering river decided to go its own way; such was the way of real rivers.

Turning and twisting, the river eventually reaches the Mossdale Wye, now spanned by a maze of bridges and far removed from the transportation scene of yesteryears. Here at a county park the river takes a recreation bent, with a diverse fleet of boaters and fishermen taking to the fouled channel. Two miles downstream it divides again, the main fork striking out toward French Camp and Stockton. Another fork wanders off to form the middle and old forks of the river, part of the maze of sloughs or channels that constitute the larger San Joaquin Delta and the continuing evolution of the landscape.

At Stockton, the delta's gateway city and port of call, the river heritage returns. Stockton is the San Joaquin River; the great city's ties to the river run deep, sustaining the city's very existence. Here, through great persistence and price, the river emerges as the Stockton Deep Water Channel, a man-made channel plied by seagoing vessels from around the world. Throughout its reaches, an armada of recreation boaters resides, plying the vast network of waterways afforded by the delta, further underscoring the river's diversity and dimension.

At Stockton, also, the river meets its northernmost tributary, the Calaveras River, now lined by homes, streets and all the other hallmarks of a large and modern community. Long gone from its banks is the huge mound of human skulls—Las Calaveras—that once served as a territorial marker and warning to unfriendly tribes or potential conquerors. Today, a deepwater channel dominates the delta scene, pointing still downstream to that vast maze of sloughs and channels. Farther downstream, the San Joaquin River meets the Mokelumne River, Suisun Bay and Antioch, where it merges with the larger Sacramento River, its 400-mile journey and its 13,000-foot descent at an end.

Both in a historical and regional context, the San Joaquin River covers a wide swath of California's rich and colorful heritage. As it has flowed, it has generated unusual depth and diversity. From the early Indians to the most recent wave of immigrants, the river has touched the lives of millions of people. From the forestlands of its upper drainage to the farmlands of the valley, the river system has lent itself to much of California's dynamic growth and development. It has helped define stewardship, conservation and preservation. The river has also powered much of the state's hydraulically oriented society. But the costs have been high, perhaps too high. In less than a century, the San Joaquin River has been consumed and corrupted like few others. It has been used and abused. If the destiny of our rivers, particularly the San Joaquin, is the destiny of ourselves, then the future for many Californians is not particularly encouraging. Anyway one looks at it, the San Joaquin River is a troubled river.

CHAPTER ONE

The Genesis of the San Joaquin River

Sometime during World War I, when the farmers in the San Joaquin Valley began turning to electrical pumps for irrigation, Madera County farmer Bill Clark and his son were out drilling a well on their farm. Early on, when the drill was down less than twenty feet, it hit a foreign object and began to grind to a halt. Backing the drill out of the hole, they were amazed to find splinters of an ancient tree still clinging to the drill bit. The elder Clark soon realized that he had dug up some measure of the past, for here were the rust-colored splinters of a tree—wood fibers—as well as a page in the evolution of the San Joaquin Valley and the river itself. "It looked like it was a sequoia tree, but I couldn't be sure; it had been down there so long. But it was still organic material. It hadn't fossilized," the younger Lewis Clark related years later.[1]

When the first settlers came into the valley after the great Gold Rush of 1849, they also saw hundreds of tree trunks dotting the vast prairie, relocated by the forces of nature—wood that provided firewood and fencing to those initial settlers for several years.[2]

The creation of the San Joaquin Valley follows a well worn path—the river itself. For untold centuries, since long before there was a defined San Joaquin River, the waters of this ancient drainage have flowed down the slopes of the ancestral mountains, meandering here and there, moving the sands and sediments to the valley. Within the vast alluvial materials that make up the valley can be found the ridges and the ramparts of the famed Sierra Nevada—the sands of time—carried down by the

once mighty river. Here also, within some of the richest farmland in the nation, can be found the remnants of spent volcanoes, mountain meadows and forgotten forests, debris that has flowed through the canyon's inner sanctum for millions of years.

The real creators of the river and valley have been time and temperature. Long before the evolutionists came on the scene, the forces of nature were at work, pushing up the peaks and carving away at the canyons. It was an ageless process of persistence and power, where weather and water became the master sculptors, chiseling here and polishing there.

The precise process which created the San Joaquin River and valley is not known. While some scientists are still debating the specifics, others now have a pretty good picture of how the great river drainage and the valley below came into being.

Geologists, it seems, have a way of adding a million years here or there, or taking off another million or two someplace else. Eons ago, the San Joaquin Valley and the Sierra rested below the level of the sea. Then, in a distant time known as the Jurassic period, about 150 million years ago, the floor of the sea was gradually uplifted by pressures from within the bowels of the earth. Over the ensuing eons a well-relieved landscape that was to become California and the western edge of the continent emerged.[3]

A series of continuing events further molded this antediluvian land. Perhaps fifty million years ago, the landscape consisted of rolling hills and broad valleys, traversed by an emerging river system, the forerunner of the San Joaquin River. As the weather and erosion began molding this ancestral terrain, it acquired a slight westerly tilt, leading to the formation of a more defined or incised primordial landscape. As such, the embryonic river meandered over the land, weaving and winding its way over the relicted land and setting the stage for events to come.

Then some ten million years ago, a more dissected panorama emerged as the entire range was further uplifted and tilted westward. Much of the uplift occurred along the eastern edge of the block, creating the strongly asymmetrical profile of the range. In the more mountainous areas, this heightened declination further accelerated the flow of the ancestral river, hastening the process of erosion and cutting the mountain river canyon even more deeply .[4]

Dr. King N. Huber, a geologist with the United States Geological Survey who has studied the late Cenozoic Uplift of the Central Sierra, believes the drainage of this ancient river once embraced vast areas east of the Sierra, including that now occupied by the Mono Basin. In size, this upper drainage contained an area that was perhaps twice as large as it is today. Up until 3.2 million years ago, the ancestral San Joaquin River carried sufficient volume to maintain a westerly course through the original range until it was severed or diverted by volcanic activity near today's Deadman Pass, northeast of Mammoth Lakes.

Then beginning two million years ago, the evolutionary process seemed to accelerate. In a series of violent events, marked by upthrust and then down-faulting, the mounting landmass cracked. In a comparatively short time, the Sierra crest emerged while the ancient range rose only slightly. With the eruption, the ancient river—the eastern trans-Sierra stem—having been cut off near Deadman Summit, then turned southward along the eastern escarpment of the emerging Sierra, eventually evolving into the upper Owens River drainage. In the process, the headwaters of the main fork was pushed to the west between the dominant peaks of an ancient range, the Ritter Range, and the main crest of the Sierra near San Joaquin Mountain, utilizing the previously incised channel.

Then the glaciers of the Ice Age arrived, bringing mind-boggling forces to bear. Rocks and sediments hardened by time surrendered to the scouring and shearing of the rivers of ice, up to five hundred feet deep. The great fields of moving ice ground and quarried the landscape, further incising the channel. At about four thousand feet they melted into the landscape, with their handiwork still incomplete. Geologists believe there were, perhaps, three major glaciations marked by a series of advances and retreats. In between the thaw and freeze, volcanoes continued to spew their plumes of fire and ribbons of lava, bringing even more change to the still young region. Gradually, as the range crept ever higher, the slope or declination increased again, further accelerating the erosion process. Along the way the canyons were etched deeper; new streams and tributaries were born along the western slope of the range, and the San Joaquin River drainage assumed yet another form.

Other reminders of the canyon's baptism by fire and ice—that is, the fires of the vulcanism and gouging of the Ice Age—abound in the upper channel. The canyon's creation can be seen almost everywhere. Hot springs, red cinder cones, glacial polish, and hanging valleys all attest to some of the past events. Devils Postpile National Monument stands out as one climatic event. About six hundred fifty thousand years ago, during one of the more recent periods of volcanic activity, molten lava flowed down from the fiery crest. Collecting at the bottom of the canyon, the liquid rock cooled, then solidified as a 300-foot-high mound of basalt. As it contracted, it cracked to form the three-to-seven sided columns that formed the centerpiece of Devils Postpile. Centuries later, the glacier scraped the tops of these hundred-foot-high vertical columns, leaving their "skid marks" in the glacial polish that are evident today.[5]

In the early to mid-1900s when geologist Francois E. Matthes began looking at the geology of the main San Joaquin River canyon, he was staggered by the

Against the background of the mighty Sierra, Balloon Dome rises nearly 1,800 feet above the canyon floor, marking the junction of the south fork and main fork of the San Joaquin River.

dimension of the great gorge. It was rugged by any standards. The great canyon, he observed, "maintains its great depth and rugged grandeur for fifteen miles, a distance of more than twice that of Yosemite Valley." The geologist also noted that the early government surveyors, "although experienced in making their way up rough, bouldery beds of mountain torrents, were soon halted by the chasm and forced to detour around this section of the gorge."[6] Within the realm of 13,000-foot Mount Ritter, the centerpiece of the upper San Joaquin River drainage, Matthes saw the remains of the ancestral mountains that were formed a hundred million years before the present Sierra Nevada was uplifted.

Today, the heritage of the river's requiem unfolds as a rich and elusive tableau. For example, when geologists study the flanks of the "tabletop" mountains near Auberry, they see pebbles of pumice similar to those found around the pumice mountains south of Mono Lake, further reinforcing the trans-Sierra scenario. Other dimensions of the river's controversial heritage can be found in the place-names modern man has left along the way: Glacier Lake, Volcanic Peak, Granite Stairway, Pumice Butte and more.

Down the geologic ages, down into what was once a large inland sea, flowed tons and tons of scouring sands and sediments. As the declination increased, the fledgling but forceful river assumed a heavier hand. In time—and in one of the great land fills of all times—this sea was filled with alluvial debris, forming the delta and reducing the length of the inland sea to the size of San Francisco Bay. As the backfill created a primeval prairie, the river was forced to meander far and wide across the landscape. As such, it often carved large oxbow turns, sweeping out over the new landscape, changing its course innumerable times. At one time, the river flowed close to downtown Fresno, nearly ten miles south of its southernmost point, some geologists suggest.

In the early 1900s, before the San Joaquin River was dammed and diverted, the old Skaggs Bridge felt the fury and force of the unbridled river. Madera County Historical Society

As the dominant land features emerged, other changes came across what is now Central California; the climate underwent episodic changes affecting both animal and plant life. Warm, semitropical climates promoted lush plant growth, and a jungle-like ecosystem may have existed where eroding rivers formed lagoons to the delta. The dinosaurs appeared and then disappeared; other strange and wondrous species entered and exited the primeval scene equally unnoticed. About ten thousand years ago, at the departure of the last of the Ice Age from the high country, the valley underwent yet another change that set the stage for the evolution of a sprawling prairie or grassland.

Then and only then, as the climate moderated once again, the first humans made their way into the valley, setting their primitive camps near the river, seeking its life-sustaining embrace. In time, others followed, creating crude residences along its banks. All the time, the river of evolution ebbed and flowed, carving its way to the sea.

Dr. Joseph Medeiros of the Great Valley Museum of Modesto, an educator and recognized authority on the evolution of the valley, said no one knows exactly how the San Joaquin Valley and river appeared before humans arrived in the valley and decided to stay. However, his research has afforded a pretty clear picture of the vast river land, and it was vastly different from the one we know today.

It was a vast, sprawling plain of a great variety of vegetation and animal life. It was a mosaic of grasslands, marshlands and woodlands, topographically altered by wild rivers, shallow lakes and vernal pools.

It must have been an Eden for its fauna, everything from insects to mammals. It once supported large herds of deer, pronghorn and elk. There was even enough space for grizzly bears to roam.

The valley supported huge flocks of herons, egrets and similar large birds. Bald and golden

At Stockton, the remains of the beleaguered San Joaquin River meet the man-made, deepwater channel for the final run to the Delta.

eagles, hawks and falcons represented organisms higher on the food chain.[7]

From one end to the other the valley stood as an endless wilderness, lined by mountains to the east and west, but interspersed with vernal pools, riparian forests and prairie, rolling out to infinity. The land was abundant with food and game which attracted the original inhabitants who led something of a nomadic life. Even after the first Indians arrived, they made little impact on the landscape, forced as they were to live in some type of balance with the land. But in the late 1700s, the first Europeans appeared and the land and the river began to change, as the newcomers looked upon the wilderness as something to conquer.

One of the first recorded glimpses of the river's creative ways dates back to the first white settlement on the upper San Joaquin River at Millerton, the original county seat of Fresno County, where the Christmas flood of 1867 gave a microsecond measure of the forces of nature in the river's runway.

The fall rains came early and became more frequent by November, when the rains turned to snow in the Sierra. By December, record amounts of snow had been observed in the mountains. Then the temperature moderated and warm rains began sending the river surging, wrote L. A. Winchell in his history of Fresno County:

The San Joaquin at Millerton steadily grew in volume and height. Day after day the rains came. Anxiously the people awaited abatement of the storms. Each hour the angry stream reached higher and higher. The occupants of the building along the lower street began moving their most valued possessions, yet hoping for relief from the merciless encroachment.

Nightfall came—black under the overcast skies. It was Christmas Eve; but there were no devotional offerings. The harassed people were beyond joyous expression; though, from the women, there may have been silent prayers for mercy. There was universal vigilance and excited effort, and concern for community safety. Despairingly, as the black night measured the hours, they watched the unceasing advance of the surging torrent. Lanterns gleamed through the street; lights shone in all the upper houses; and the rain fell, and splashed in sheets in the frowning earth!

At eleven o'clock that night—Christmas Eve—the river was higher than the white men had ever seen it. Suddenly, crashing, roaring sounds came to the ears of the wakeful villagers. Rushing with appalling speed and force a high wall of water, bearing on its surface an overwhelming tangle of broken and twisted trees from the forests of the high mountains. The whole blossom of this avalanche flood was thickly covered with the smashing, grinding, tearing logs—trunks, tops, roots were whirled along with the destroying speed of a tornado. Greater than the combined blows of all the battering rams and catapults of old, the massed projectile struck the town. Nothing in its tracks resisted it. In a few moments the awful work was done.

Millerton was wrecked.[8]

The cause of that devastating flood, as well as untold floods before and after, originated in the early snowfall, which was then deluged by warm tropical rains sweeping in from the Pacific. Triggering mighty avalanches above, acres of forests were swept from the mountain side. Collecting in the narrow granite gorges below as debris dams, the material eventually gave way, sending a tidal wave of water and waste down the canyon.

At Millerton, Jones' transriver ferry was swept downstream to Sycamore Point near Hill's Ferry, where the ferry had been destroyed only a few years earlier during the "Great Flood" of 1861. Debris from the 1867 siege damaged paddle wheel steamers plying the river. The steamers that were not damaged chugged around the inland sea plucking those residents lucky enough to have a second story home to which they could escape. At Stockton, already established as a major gateway to the interior of the state, much of the port city was inundated. The flood forced out the rowboats, or the residents hoisted up their skirts and pants and slogged about—as usual; floods had long been part of the Stockton scene. Boats were torn from their moorings and left as derelicts below. Stumps and debris from the Christmas catastrophe were seen as far away as Suisun Bay.[9]

During the 1870s, the early settlers in the Dos Palos area found the landscape dotted with the remains of trees and trunks brought down from the Sierra by other storms. Many settlers cut the wood into fence posts and lumber; others burned the stumps for fuel or simply to clear the land.[10]

Even today, a few reminders of those cataclysmic events still show up in the dewatered channel. Frequently the sand and gravel operators north of Fresno dig up rotting tree stumps from the depths of the old river channel—ancient relics brought down from the Sierra by past events in but a second of geological time. Such are the ways of nature.[11]

CHAPTER TWO

The Indians and the River of Many Names

As recently as two hundred years ago the virgin San Joaquin River wound from a mountain wilderness to the Delta in a land the first Spanish explorers saw as a "gran terra incognita." Emerging from the Sierra foothills, the wild river rans its way through a vast riparian wilderness of undefined dimensions. Within the Delta, a labyrinth of tule-lined sloughs and channels bore witness to the wandering way of the river. Above today's Stockton the banks were lined with willows, vines and other vegetation. Away from the river, grasslands, marshes and prairies, interspersed with vernal pools, dominated the endless landscape. From the confluence of the Merced River to the foothills, sections of channel stood relatively bare—having been scoured by repeated floods, but dotted with an occasional grove of ash and willow trees. As the channel entered the foothills more vegetation lined the streams—sycamore, cottonwoods and oaks. In the upper reaches, alongside the cascades and cataracts, the river was lined with towering pine, fir and cedars. Throughout its course, the drainage stood as a wild and wondrous land, ruled, regulated and sustained by the river.[1]

At numerous locations along the river and its tributaries dwelt the descendants of the first Californians, the native Indians. The Indians occupied small villages along the banks, using crude shelters constructed of reeds and willows. The river provided their support system; it was their primary source of subsistence. A recorded history, at least a written history, of their thousand year odyssey in the valley does not exist; what remains are the

midden soils, obsidian flakes, shells and beads and other artifacts that the archaeologists have been able to dig up. It is a faint trail, often clouded by interpretation, myths or modern man's misconceptions. How and when the first Indians came to the valley is another void. Many anthropologists subscribe to the theory that the first vanguard came to North America from Asia about twenty-five thousand years ago, using the so-called Bering Sea land bridge. In a movement that spanned centuries, these aborigines then fanned out from Alaska, gradually moving down the continent into the Great Basin and beyond, becoming the first Americans.

Apparently the Indians of the valley belonged to the general family of Yokuts, but tended to live in small groups, sharing little of the tribal structure that identified the great Indian nations of the east. In most cases these original inhabitants lived in small encampments or rancherias with their own customs and dialect. Various units of the Miwoks and Monos occupied the foothill area east of the river. By some standards they led a life of hardship and privation, yet one of abundance compared to other tribes. When times were good and food plentiful, the Indians tended to have more contacts and exchanges with neighboring tribes, often sharing hunting or gathering territories. Although the valley Indians were somewhat nomadic, they appeared to have a fixed location for their rancherias.[2]

Perhaps as early as seven thousand years ago—well after the last Ice Age—the first Indians arrived in the valley. At a location near modern-day Stockton the

For the Yokut Indians of the San Joaquin Valley, the river ran as the artery of life, providing the natives with many fringe benefits, including a refreshing post-sweat house dip. Latta Collection, Yosemite Research Library

northern Yokuts became established. Wildlife was plentiful and the tribes thrived. In time they emerged as expert hunters and gatherers, subsisting primarily on fish and small game. The men became excellent hunters, having fashioned several kinds of bows and arrows. With small boats constructed of tule reeds they paddled around the rivers and sloughs. Down the ages, they became skilled at spearing salmon and sturgeon or snaring ducks, geese and rabbits. They also learned to use spears and javelins. If they were lucky, they might even claim a deer or antelope, which abounded in the valley. The women worked as gatherers, seeking out acorns, roots, berries and the seeds of edible plants. They too became skilled artisans, weaving ever more attractive and utilitarian baskets, in which they collected and prepared their food and carried water.

Gradually, as their numbers increased, the Yokuts fanned out across the valley and into the lower foothills,

but always staying within the life-sustaining embrace of the river or its tributaries. When explorer Stephen Powers made his epic hike across the country in 1877, he concluded that the natives "would eat anything that swims, flies or crawls—except skunks." During periods of good weather the natives would be out on the riverbank cooking, sewing or working at other tasks. The Yokuts were exceptional basket makers.[3]

The late Frank F. Latta, a recognized authority on the Yokuts, defined their ranges as extending across the valley from the San Joaquin River delta on the north to the Grapevine Canyon and Tejon Mountains on the south. He figured there were over sixty different tribes or rancherias of Yokuts, with about four hundred fifty residents for each village. Each tribe had its own leaders and spoke its own dialect.[4]

While life was not always easy, opportunities for relaxation and recreation did exist, with games for

Western Mono Indians, descendants of those Indians who migrated across the Sierra centuries earlier, occupied the foothills canyon near today's North Fork. A. W. Peters

children and gambling for the adults. The climate was not always to their liking. The cold, foggy winters and the devastating spring floods were followed by the oppressive heat of summer. Infant mortality and disease claimed an inordinate number of the aborigines; warring tribes also took their toll, effectively reducing life expectancy to about twenty-five years. The Great Flood of 1803 apparently drowned many Indians. When drought and famine stalked the land, the natives became more protective of their prime hunting, fishing and gathering grounds, which often led to conflicts.[5]

Dr. Michael J. Moratto, an anthropologist who has done extensive studies on the Indians of Central California, believes environmental stress, that is, droughts, floods, famine, and disease, triggered much of the alleged violence that has been attributed to these original pioneers. In good times, the Indians were more peaceful and willing to share the bounty of the land with their neighbors, but when the food became short, so too was their willingness to share.[6]

On the western edge of the San Joaquin Valley, the native populations were comparatively small but still larger than originally projected by early ethnographers. In the winter these Indians camped on the high spots along the tributary streams of the west side. They often traded with the coastal tribes for beads, shells and salt. In most cases the Indians occupied the lower canyons along the eastern slope of the Diablo Range, using the floor of the valley as the season or weather allowed.

To the east of the valley, within the foothill arch of the main river, between the Cosumnes and Chowchilla rivers, the land was the territory of the Miwok Indians, dotted by pockets of Yokuts. Around today's Coarsegold reigned the Chukchansi, another subtribe of the Yokuts. The fierce and often feared Chowchillas occupied the foothill area of Madera County, claiming a mixed heritage of both Yokut and Miwok. Comparatively later, in the fabled valley that would one day be known as Yosemite, dwelt the Ahwahneechee, whose standard of living often made them the envy of neighboring tribes.[7]

Along the main canyon, near modern day North Fork and Auberry, dwelt the Western or Sierra Monos, who along with the Yokuts constituted the principal Indian nations of the river. As late as the 1890s the Monos called the San Joaquin River the "Shin-Wog-a-nea,"[8] from which they netted or speared salmon and other fish. While the Monos were excellent hunters, they also relied on acorns as a dietary mainstay. Within the shadow of the Squaw Leap area the tribe worked and played, living in bark-covered wickiups. Squaw Leap itself represents something of an enigmatic or even pejorative place-name, where legends and tales abound; yet its significance remains obscured by time and the lack of a recorded history.[9]

Every summer, as their foothill camps became oppressively hot, the Monos would migrate to the mountains. Here they would gather and trade with the Paiutes of the eastern Sierra slope and Owens Valley, from whom their ancestors had splintered off ages earlier, perhaps as early as four thousand years ago. From their trail of midden soils, arrowheads and other artifacts, modern archaeologists have determined that their numbers as well as their camping sites were far more numerous than previously estimated. Obsidian and pine nuts from the eastern slope were traded for acorns and dried salmon from the west. For the Mono basket weavers, renowned for their beautiful baskets, the summer exchanges became prime opportunities to exchange basket materials and information. Among other items, shell beads from the coastal Indians were exchanged repeatedly among tribes, eventually making their way across the valley and the Sierra.

Despite their primitive lifestyle and occasional acts of violence toward one another, the Indians were able to maintain themselves. For untold centuries, and despite the repeated scourge of drought and flood, the river sustained the ancient ones. The Indians survived and thrived for succeeding generations. But at the onset of the 1800s, they began hearing stories of strange people who had come onto the land; they were men with white skin who wore strange clothes and armaments. Even more apparent, these newcomers carried long rods that shot lightning and thunder, killing anything in sight.

Indian expert Frank Latta captured a vanishing glimpse of Indian life with this early 1900s view of a Yokut village of the San Joaquin Valley.

Latta Collection, Yosemite Research Library

Unknown to the interior tribes, Spanish missionaries had arrived on the coast of California in the late 1760s, led by the legendary, and eventually controversial, missionary Father Junipero Serra.[10]

By 1772 Father Juan Crespi had discovered San Francisco Bay and a great river entering the northeastern arm of the bay which he named "El Rio de San Francisco"—later it was renamed the San Joaquin.[11]

At a time when the American Revolutionary War was unfurling on the East Coast, a series of probing forays were subsequently launched toward the wilderness interior of Serra's back yard. At that time a unit of the Spanish militia led by Captain Pedro Fages forced its way into the uncharted wilderness of the valley, where he found the river choked with "a dense growth of nettles, wormwood, grapevines, willows, cottonwoods, oak, ash, bay, laurel and the ever present tules, or 'Los Tulares.'" In some places, he reported, the tules extended twenty miles away from the river, making travel impossible. In time, other forays followed.

At first, little attention was paid to the uncharted interior valley; the padres were busy establishing a network of missions along the coastal El Camino Real. How the early Spanish explorers figured out the maze of sloughs and channels that make up the San Joaquin Delta is not known, although some early reconnaissance

was made from the summit of Mount Diablo, providing a prime viewpoint for the wilderness of the unknown and uncharted delta. In October 1776, Jose Joaquin Moraga, a Spanish soldier, led a group of dragoons into this interior wilderness. After reaching a broad river, his unit turned back, fearing it might become lost on the great plain of the valley. Little additional exploration was done until 1797, when Mission San Juan Bautista was founded. As the fifteenth mission in the chain, it was perceived as the logical staging area for the anticipated move into the interior, located as it was about thirty miles west of Pacheco Pass.

While religious conversion of the Indians motivated the padres, their prayers for a new and larger order were not always answered. Converted Indians began rebelling against what they regarded as the oppressive mission life. Often these deserting Indians took the mission's horses, for food rather than transportation, and fled into the interior valley, forcing the mission's garrison to follow. The full relationship between the church and the military in California has not been fully addressed by historians. On the surface the military appeared to be the handmaiden of the church, affording the necessary support and defense. However, the Spanish military had perhaps another agenda. Besides serving as the muscle of the missions, the soldiers, it appears, dreamed of finding an El Dorado, with gold and riches, that would further the Spanish monarchy's dreams of an even greater empire.

Among those assigned to mission garrison, Lieutenant Gabriel Moraga, a member of the Spanish dragoons, looms as a standard bearer. First assigned to Monterey and then to Mission San Juan Bautista, Moraga became a pathfinder. In December 1805, Moraga, accompanied by a few soldiers and baptized Indians, left the mission and proceeded east along an old Indian trail to Pacheco Pass. Atop the pass they paused. Looking east from the summit, they viewed a great valley, which was to be known as the San Joaquin Valley, with a line of trees marking a large river that traversed the vast panorama rolling out before them. In the distance, they observed the already snow-covered peaks of the Sierra Nevada, the obvious source of the river.[12]

Moraga's men moved eastward, groping their way through the uncharted land, pressed by the need for drinking water and feed for their animals. Arriving at the river they found a wide but nearly dry streambed. Moraga designated the river the San Joaquin, after Saint Joachim, the venerated father of the Virgin Mary, although some conflicting reports indicate the naming occurred the following year. A short distance away, at the confluence of another smaller river, Moraga identified willow and cottonwood trees. About fifteen miles southwest of modern-day Chowchilla, he came upon another familiar tree—one common to his native Spain—the swamp ash, a Fresno tree, a name which he applied to the nearby river.

Moraga's party continued upstream looking for a place to ford the main river. In one area they observed Indians along the banks of the river, subsisting mainly on fish. Finally, at a shallow spot north of what is now Kerman, his riders found a suitable crossing, near today's Gravelly Ford. Moraga then moved to the southeast, reaching another major river in January of 1806 which he christened "El Rio de los Santos Reyes"—the river of the Holy Kings, today's Kings River.

In September of the following year, Moraga's patrol rode into a large Indian village along the river near present-day Vernalis, causing the two hundred fifty terrified inhabitants to flee into the nearby willows. About three weeks later, after counting nearly two dozen Indian villages along the river, his unit observed one village near today's Herndon, nearly 170 miles upstream.

As Moraga's clerk recorded

The Indians live in caves; they climb and descend by a feeble pole held down by one of them, while he who is descending slides down. It is impossible for us to get them to come down to a flat spot besides the stream, where we have assembled near a pool formed by the river.[13]

Moraga made numerous trips into the interior valley. In subsequent expeditions the bold explorer bestowed a long list of place-names, including the Mariposa and Merced rivers. The padres also migrated over the Diablo Range from Mission San Juan Bautista, stopping along the way to bathe in the tributary streams.

Along one such stream Father Felipe del Arroyo bestowed the named Los Banos—The Baths—providing the name for the creek, and then for the town that eventually emerged.

The early Spanish explorers left a meager record of the customs and traditions of these original aborigines. At first, their initial visits did not alarm the Indians as the explorers did not remain. But as the new colonists exerted more control, the two forces become more estranged and warlike. In his 1807 tour of the valley, Moraga reported that the Indians were "everywhere" and were repeatedly "trying to steal our horses." At the same time, the Indians began raiding the mission ranches, looking for horses, while often freeing the native proselytes.

As the Spanish responded to the Indian challenge, the number and size of their expeditions into the valley increased. Relations gradually became more hostile and warlike.

After 1810, the level of conflict escalated. The Indians soon developed a taste for horse flesh; the

Spanish routinely burned any Indian camps containing the skeletons of horses or cattle. One Indian related that it was common practice for Spanish cavalry to raid the Indian villages in the San Joaquin Valley, shooting into the air, killing any Indians who resisted, charging them with horses, cutting them down with "espadas," or short sabers. Young Indian boys and girls were captured, roped together and led away to the missions. [14]

Such raids devastated the populations of the Yokut villages on the west side of the valley, giving rise to the valley's own "Trail of Tears." Repressive actions such as these only produced corresponding atrocities and counter measures by the Indians. A "horrible death" awaited any soldier unfortunate enough to be captured by the Indians, Moraga noted.

However history judges Moraga, his legacy remains. Of the human parade that pushed its way into the wilderness of the valley in the early 1800s, few names stand taller than his. Before Mexico vanquished the Spanish, Moraga recorded forty-six trips into the valley. The duration and size of these expeditions raise more questions and go beyond map-making or the quest for yet another mission site. Often supported by sixty soldiers and hundreds of animals, Moraga's expeditions would span three months, suggesting that he had found his own El Dorado, the elusive treasure and the ultimate reason for the Spanish king's interest in the New World.

When the Mexicans replaced the Spanish after 1820, the missions were secularized and began slipping into obscurity. Moraga and his men also faded from the scene. However, the hostility between the new Mexican conquerors and the Indians became even more pronounced. Each new exchange only added to the violence and brutality. By the end of the decade, the Indians, having obtained horses and firearms, were fighting the Mexican Californios to a standstill. For those Mexicans holding remote land grant ranches, the Indian raids made occupying those lands, and legitimizing their title, nearly impossible.

By 1830, other forces were also at work. A handful of Americans had arrived in the valley, led by the intrepid mountain man Jedediah Smith. A band of French Canadian trappers had also set up a hunting camp on a slough known today as French Camp, just a few miles south of Stockton, and were eradicating the beavers. Other newcomers were also headed to the new land known as Alta California. When Colonel J. J. Warner visited the valley in 1832 with the Ewing Young expedition, he observed more Indians subsisting on "natural products from the soils and waters" than anywhere else in the country. The Indians, he reported, had plentiful wild game, fish, nuts and seeds, and they were experts in catching fish and snaring game. When trailblazer Joseph R. Walker came into the valley in November of 1833, having made the first crossing of the High Sierra and discovering Yosemite Valley as well as the famed Sequoia big trees, his party found the Indians along the Merced River helpful and the San Joaquin River beautiful and restful. [15]

But times were changing. In the initial exploration of the Central Valley in 1829, the legendary Kit Carson saw the tribes flourishing. But when he returned in 1839,

...cholera or some other fearful scourge broke out among them and raged with such fearful fatality that they were unable either to bury or burn their dead, and the air was filled with the stench of their decaying bodies.[16]

Another early traveler observed that between 1827 and 1830, distemper, (fever and ague) must have exterminated 50,000 of the Sacramento and San Joaquin Indians. They made the disease worse by jumping into cold water while suffer paroxysm of the fever.

Apparently, the Indian population of the valley was devastated by white man's diseases, for which the natives had no natural resistance. The Indians also contributed to their own undoing, warring at times over fishing rights. When Dr. John Marsh, one of the first American settlers, ventured into the Delta in 1840, his party happened upon a field of skeletal remains near present day Stockton.

So startled was he that he exclaimed, *"Las Calaveras!"*

(the skulls). As a result, Marsh and his men referred to it as Las Calaveras. From that encounter, the river lost its original name, El Rio de la Pasion (the river of passion) and assumed the present-day place-name of Calaveras.

Suspecting some kind of plague or epidemic among the natives, Marsh soon learned that it was tribal fighting over fish that had triggered the massacre.

Throughout the valley the Indians were subjected to other scourges, including a smallpox epidemic in 1845; but none of these events had the devastating impact that followed the 1848 discovery of gold and the invasion of Indian lands by gold seekers. From that point on, everything was downhill for the native ones. By 1852, when the first census was made of San Joaquin County, the Indian population numbered only 390. By that time the Ahwahneechee of Yosemite had been scattered by the Mariposa Indian War. In the foothills, the Chukchansi and Monos struggled on, clinging to a culture that could not hide from the onslaught of new aliens. In his 1864

exploration of the upper San Joaquin River basin, geologist William Brewer saw the Indian's signal fires and soon realized that the Indians were in their last hiding, trying to survive the invasion that was sweeping over the land. A few years later, one early settler in the Dos Palos area recalled uncovering a mass Indian burial grave, with tiers of skeletal remains marking their tragic disappearance, victims of some unknown epidemic.

Gradually, the Indian presence was all but obscured. The curtain rang down on their great trans-Sierra migrations in World War I. In 1919, the late Dr. Earl Coleman of Fresno observed what is believed to be the last summer encampments of Indians, who had come over Senger Pass to Mono Hot Springs, one of the prime gathering areas of the South Fork of the San Joaquin.[17]

For the Indians of the valley and the San Joaquin River drainage, the tragic "Trail of Tears" ran everywhere.

CHAPTER THREE

Stockton to Millerton—Port to Fort

"Gold!" Almost twenty years before the electrifying cry of "Gold" rang out from Sutter's mill on the American River, a ragtag band of adventurers had apparently discovered the magic metal on the San Joaquin River—one of the still unresolved mysteries that dogs California's rich and colorful history.

This earlier—yet questionable—claim stretches back to the times when the first American trappers and mountain men made an initial probe toward the interior of California. In 1826, a party of twenty-six men led by pathfinder Jedediah Smith made its way into Mexican-controlled California. It was a strange combination of forces that brought Smith's group to the West. Smith said it was "to explore," prompted in no small way by the concept of manifest destiny, power, politics, pelts and perhaps even gold. Short of supplies and seeking some outpost, his group made their way to Mission San Gabriel, only to be ordered out of the country by the Mexican authorities. While detained there, Smith apparently learned of the San Joaquin Valley and its natural wealth. Upon his release, Smith gave every indication of returning to Salt Lake, but instead turned and made his way over the Tehachapi Mountains into the wilds of the unmapped San Joaquin Valley.[1]

Some historians believe the young explorer was looking for the legendary Buenaventura River, a fabled river that flowed out of the Great Basin and bisected the Sierra, a river that could open the West to trade and transit. Pushing northward, Smith's band eventually reached the valley, living off the land as they went. After some extensive exploration and successful trapping, he began looking for the Buenaventura's great gash in the Sierra so that he might get his load of furs to his original base camp at Bear Lake, Utah. Unable, however, to locate the elusive Buenaventura, Smith, in May of 1827, tried to cross the still snowbound Sierra—at a location historians are still arguing about. After being caught up in lingering storms and nearly freezing to death, the spent unit retreated to their valley camp on the "Appelaminy River"—Smith's name for the Stanislaus River. Here they rested, recovered and reorganized.[2]

About a month later, with some of his men remaining behind, the tough young trapper made his way over the mountains to deliver the pelts and began preparations for his return to the valley camp. In late summer, Smith, with an enlarged party, headed back to the valley only to be attacked by Indians in the Mojave Desert and confronted by Mexican authorities again. Eventually his party rendezvoused with the men of the 1826 expeditions and began trapping in earnest.

Smith's men ranged far and wide throughout the valley that summer. Eventually reports of his presence reached the Mexican authorities at San Jose, who saw the Americans as a threat. Both the mission padres and the military authorities became alarmed. They feared Smith was responsible for some of the uprisings they were encountering with the natives, both at the mission and in the field. Smith had his own problems with the natives, but they were minor compared to those of the Mexicans. As a result, a detachment of Mexican troops was dispatched to his Stanislaus camp. Smith was away at the time, trapping in the Sierra foothills, but he was ordered to appear at San Jose and explain his presence.[3]

While the Indian uprising was subsequently traced to an embittered Indian convert from the mission, the Mexicans felt it was time to be tough with Smith and took him and twenty of his men into custody when they arrived in San Jose in December. After being ordered out of the country, Smith headed back to the San Joaquin River, camping January 1, 1828, on the old branch of the river.

Throughout January, Smith's men trapped the lower sections of the Calaveras, Mokelumne and Cosumnes rivers. One day, they encountered a band of Americans led by George C. Yount, another mountain man who had made his way west from his native South Carolina. Brought together in the vast wilderness, the two parties decided to team up to hunt and trap along the river. After several unproductive forays, all but three members of Yount's group became discouraged and abandoned the hunt, returning to their earlier camp near Napa. However, Yount and two others, David Jackson and William Sublette, remained, moving to Smith's Stanislaus River camp. Though they were hampered by the winter weather, their quest for beaver and other fur-bearing animals continued. Upon returning to camp one afternoon, the three men were electrified when Smith allegedly displayed several large gold nuggets.[4]

Despite the glowing reports, Smith's journals make no mention of the metal. In the spring of 1828, loaded with hundreds of pelts, Smith and his large band of nearly ninety men and three hundred horses began moving northward toward Oregon, intent upon reaching the Hudson Bay outpost at Fort Vancouver located on the Columbia River. On July 13, they camped alongside the Umpqua River in southern Oregon.

Smith and two others left the encampment the next morning to scout ahead, but not before warning their companions of the local Kelawatset Indians. Either his instructions were ignored or forgotten and the Indians soon filtered into the camp, and then, unexpectedly,

attacked. Caught by surprise and outnumbered, all but one of the fifteen trappers were killed. Arthur Black, the sole survivor, managed to fight his way free and flee to the fort, where he arrived two days before Smith's small group, bearing the tragic news of the disastrous "Umpqua Massacre."[5]

Smith was devastated upon hearing of the attack. Assistance came from unexpected quarters. The Hudson Bay Company offered its assistance and hospitality, despite British apprehension of the Americans born of two recent wars. Even before hearing of Smith's misfortune, the company had considered sending a trading and trapping expedition into the area where the Americans had been massacred. Only a few months earlier, the company launched a series of explorative thrusts into the Oregon Territory and California. The first, led by the company trapper Alexander McLeod, had apparently ranged as far south as Stockton. After taking a large number of beavers, McLeod's party ran into bad weather and hostile Indians on the way back and was forced to cache its large load of pelt. By the time the trappers managed to get through the rugged Siskiyou Mountains, they were discouraged and despondent, with not one pelt to show for their labors.

Upon learning of the fifteen hundred pelts Smith had lost in the Umpqua Massacre, the company took a new look toward the land called California. In the following year, 1829, Hudson Bay trapper Peter Skene Ogden left Fort Vancouver and headed south. Forcing his way into the uncharted wilderness of Nevada, Ogden skirted around the Sierra, coming into the San Joaquin Valley from the south.[6] Besides looking for beavers, the Canadian apparently sought to determine the Mexican and American presence in the interior of California. Moving northward, Ogden made his way through the valley, trapping as he went. By the time he returned to Fort Vancouver, Smith had also related his experiences to the company officials, further whetting their interest. When Ogden added his glowing accounts of the San Joaquin scene, the Hudson Bay Company knew it had to move.

In 1832, a two-pronged force of trappers under the direction of the intrepid trapper and mountain man John Work began their move toward the interior of Alta California. An advance party, led by veteran trapper and pathfinder Michael LaFramboise, was sent out. LaFramboise's unit managed to make its way through the Siskiyou Mountains and move south to the San Joaquin River, where they established a good campsite about four miles south of today's Stockton. The location afforded rewarding trapping, prompting the Canadians to build some reed shelters, not unlike those used by the Indians. Over time, other trappers made their way into the area. Eventually the Canadian's camp became known as "El Campo de les Franceses," or French Camp.[7]

Meanwhile, the main group under Work had managed to reach northeastern California, where they began trapping on the Pit River. From there they made their way to the confluence with the Sacramento River, and, eventually, into the Delta where some of his scouts finally linked up with members of LaFramboise's party. From there they were guided into the San Joaquin camp. For nearly a year Work's men roamed over the waterways of the San Joaquin Valley, reaching, perhaps, as far as the Merced River.

In many respects, the quest for pelts was also cloaked as much in politics as in fashion. While Mexico claimed the land, the trappers represented—perhaps only by their presence—the growing territorial interests in the new lands. At Fort Vancouver, for example, the British, with the memory of two wars still fresh in their minds, eyed suspiciously the movements of the Americans. Anxious to prevent the loss of any potential trapping territory, or having Oregon become another American colony, the Hudson Bay Company collected more than furs, relaying information of the American movements to the Crown. The British also questioned the motives of the Russians who held forth on their northern flanks at Alaska, and now, at Fort Ross on the California coast. And the Mexicans, having displaced the Spanish, and having inherited the enmity of the inland Indians, were paranoid, suspicious of all. It was against this background that the role of the enigmatic beaver hunters came to represent a more significant force than anyone could have foreseen.

When Ewing Young, another American trapper, made his 1829 trip into the valley and encountered Ogden's trappers along the San Joaquin, he was amazed to find the camp a "huge family affair." Besides sixty men, the encampment had a large number of women and children; he was staggered by the size of the competing Canadian camp. Some of Work's subsequent groups often numbered two hundred people.[8]

Other American trappers were also coming into the land. During Work's 1833 trip he ran into Jonathan Warmer and Moses Carson in the Sacramento Valley. In the rivalry that followed, the company sent a dozen different "brigades" into California, carrying such names as "California, Buenaventura or Southern" brigades. Some of these units reached as far south as Tulare. Composed largely of French Canadians, the brigades left their mark as they moved south to establish the Siskiyou Trail. But the price of the pelts was inordinately high, as the wilderness trip extracted its own price. Life in the open with all of its privations and hardships was tough enough, even for the hardy trappers. Hostile Indians and sickness, compounded by the great plague of 1833—perhaps malaria—further took its toll. After returning to Fort Vancouver later that year, Work noted:

> **The people were so weak that I was apprehensive the greater part of them would die on the way before reaching the fort.**
>
> **We had a great deal of trouble and some skirmishes with the natives on account of their stealing and killing some of our horses and attempting to kill some of the men...Our hunt only amounts to 1,023 beaver and otter skins. Indeed, the country is now so exhausted that little can be done.[9]**

Jedediah Smith never returned to California. After spending the winter of 1828-29 at Fort Vancouver, mourning the loss of his men, the despondent mountain man made his way to Montana and then Wyoming. After wintering there, Smith continued east, coming down the Platte to Franklin, Missouri. But the call of California was too strong. By the spring of 1831, the thirty-year old veteran had formed another group and headed out on the Santa Fe Trail. Again Indians hounded his trail. On May 31, 1831, a Comanche raiding party caught up with Smith's group in the Cimarron River country. Vastly outnumbered, the men fell one by one, with Smith being the last to die.

In 1834, a year after Walker had crossed the Sierra and the San Joaquin Valley, La Framboise and his French trappers fanned out over the valley looking for beavers. But gradually the beaver began disappearing—about the same time the beavers' pelts began to lose their fashion appeal. Other events were sweeping over the valley. The fading trail of Smith, La Framboise, Walker and the other mountain men forms a rich and colorful chapter in the history of the early San Joaquin Valley. In many ways, they represented a little-recognized force in opening up California—more so than anything preceding the great Gold Rush. Routinely, these early adventurers entered an uncharted wilderness under the most trying of conditions. Smith personified the rugged individualists and remains at the summit of California explorers. Some historians have speculated that Smith first discovered gold during his earlier trip when he was exploring and trapping along the Stanislaus River. They believe Smith realized that his group was not equipped to develop a mine, and that they would have to go the East to procure the necessary mining equipment. This group of historians believe Jedediah Smith should be credited with the original discovery of gold—and the San Joaquin River as the place of discovery.

Certain it is that, nearly a score of years before Marshall's find at Coloma was flashed to the world, which soon went crazy with the lust for gold, Jedediah Smith and his band of trappers had discovered and reclaimed large quantities of the precious metal.

There can hardly be a doubt however that he was on a secret expedition to dig gold in California—certain it is that in a previous year he had discovered the gold in abundance; and that only Smith and Black knew that spot gold had been discovered, and that Smith alone knew the spot where it could be obtained. [10]

Those few who subscribe to Smith's role in the discovery of gold believe the location was near the confluence of the Stanislaus and San Joaquin rivers—although the geology of that area does not support a known gold-bearing lode. Yet the claim and mystery linger, another of the unsolved legends surrounding the Golden State's controversial and often conflicting past.

By that time other forces were waiting in the wings to pursue the golden equation.

In 1837, Dr. John Marsh, the first American-born settler, arrived in the lower Delta, establishing Ranchos Los Meganos on the slopes of Mount Diablo, near present day Martinez. He was followed two years later by the daring Captain John Sutter, who, while fleeing his clouded past, sought to establish a settlement, New Helvetia, in the unmapped wilderness near today's Sacramento. Sutter got off to a difficult start, spending two or three days rowing up the San Joaquin River before his group could find the desired Sacramento River channel. Until Marsh and Sutter appeared on the scene, few of the trappers or explorers had expressed any interest in settling in the vast sprawling interior valley.[11]

In 1838, the Hudson Bay Company sent a Captain Edward Belcher of the Royal Navy with two small sailing ships into San Francisco Bay to resume the charting the Delta that the British had begun a decade earlier. Perhaps in anticipation of beaver but undoubtedly in fear of Russian or American incursions, the British had sent the mapping unit into San Francisco Bay as a precautionary move. Even then, the Delta remained a maze of sloughs and waterways, although some early entrepreneurs, such as Sutter, had figured out the main Sacramento and San Joaquin channels. Belcher was similarly challenged. After reaching Suisun Bay, he utilized the smaller H.M.S. *Starling*. "Confused and disappointed" over the labyrinth of waterways, Belcher hired a local Indian as a guide, only to discover that the man knew only where "to find Indians." Belcher pressed on. After considerable exploration, he succeeded in finding the river outlets and made his way up the two rivers. On the Sacramento River he eventually reached the confluence with the American River, near Sutter's Fort. What he perceived to be the San Joaquin River he dismissed as "unnavigable," when compared to the broader and deeper Sacramento.

Then in 1841, Charles M. Weber, a German immigrant, arrived in California after traveling overland with the John Bidwell party from Saint Joseph, Missouri. After a short stay at Sutter's established garrison, Weber moved on to San Jose where he met William Gulnac, a naturalized Mexican citizen. The two men soon formed a business partnership, concentrating their efforts on cattle ranching and mercantilism.[12]

Recalling the sloughs and waterways he had seen along the upper delta, Weber eventually prevailed upon Gulnac to apply for a Mexican land grant on a site along the San Joaquin, believing it would make a suitable cattle ranch. On January 13, 1844, Mexican Governor Micheltorena granted Gulnac eleven square leagues, or 48,747 acres. Located on the main river between the Calaveras River and French Camp Creek, the grant, known as El Campo de los Franceses, had ties to the early French trapper who had set up a hunting camp a decade earlier seeking beaver pelts. However, Gulnac's efforts to operate a cattle ranch were even less successful. Frustrated by repeated Indian raids, he sold out to Weber fourteen months later, for the staggeringly low sum of $200. Not long thereafter, Weber built a small home and a trading post on the promontory overlooking the river, which soon became known as Tuleberg or Weber's.

By then a growing number of newcomers had descended on Mexican controlled Alta California. The most formidable arrived in the person of John Charles Fremont, one of the most adventurous and expedient of individuals. In 1841, while on army duty in Washington D.C., the ambitious Fremont had managed to meet the sixteen-year-old daughter of influential Senator Thomas Hart Benton. Despite her parents' objections, Fremont married the teenager. Accepting the reality of his daughter's decision, Benton then began furthering the career of new his son-in-law, obtaining for Fremont some coveted military expeditions in the West. In January 1844 the daring or foolish Fremont managed to lead a party of adventurers over the snowbound Sierra and into Sutter's Fort. It was a harrowing crossing that nearly cost the bold adventurer his life. Turning south, Fremont and his men explored the San Joaquin River above its confluence with the Merced River.

Fremont observed:

> We ferried the river without any difficulty and continued up the San Joaquin. Elk were running in bands over the prairie and in the skirts of the timber. We reached the river at the mouth of a large slough, which we were unable to ford, and made a circuit of several miles around…The river is about a hundred yards in breadth, branching into the slough and interspersed with islands. At this time it appeared sufficiently deep for a small steamer, but its navigation would be broken by shallows at low water.[13]

On the following day, April 6, Fremont's group followed the river to a point where it entered the foothills of the Sierra.

> After having traveled fifteen miles along the river we made an early halt under the shade of sycamore trees; here we found the San Joaquin coming down from the Sierra with a westerly course, and checking our way as all its tributaries had previously done. We had expected to raft the river, but found a good ford and encamped on the opposite bank, where droves of wild horses were

Captain Charles Weber was the "father" of modern-day Stockton.

raising clouds of dust on the prairie. Columns of smoke were visible in the direction of the Tule lakes to the southward, probably kindled in the tulares by Indians as a signal that strangers were in the valley."[14]

Fremont's description of the river represents the first known account of the riparian area now defined by Madera and Fresno counties. Gradually, the wilderness cloak that had covered the interior of California had been peeled away. Fremont's entry onto the California scene would bring dramatic changes, culminating in his reckless orchestration of the Bear Flag Revolt and California independence in 1846.

While Weber was still struggling to establish his business at Tuleberg, a party of Mormon settlers fleeing religious persecution at Nauvoo, Illinois, forced their way up the river from the San Francisco Bay. Led by Sam Brannan, the Mormons made their way up the San Joaquin channel in a small sailing boat to the Stanislaus River. About a mile above the confluence, they went ashore. Putting hope and prayer before reason, they soon established a community, New Hope, in the wilds of the valley. A barn, sawmill and a collection of shelters were built. Others began tilling the virgin soil, planting wheat and other crops in preparation for the expected arrival of their spiritual leader, Brigham Young. Next, the settlers turned to the construction a small sailing craft, the *San Joaquin*—the first known boat to be built along the river.[15]

But somewhere along the line, something went wrong. The Saints' revered leader, Young, failed to arrive at New Hope. Puzzled by this incident, Brannan made his way to Salt Lake City, only to discover that Young had committed to the Utah location. Despite his personal appeals, Brannan was unable to sway the church's elder to the California site, and he returned to New Hope discouraged and dismayed. Gradually dissension set in and the members of the colony began drifting away. Today, New Hope remains only a fading enigma, its fate and precise location unknown.

Yet, few of these initial events gave any indication of the monumental changes that would inundate Weber's settlement—by now known as Stockton. The discovery of gold hit California like a tidal wave. Even before the discovery of gold, a certain glitter had developed to the Western frontier, drawing a handful of early pioneers. Manifest Destiny was sounding its inviting call. The Gold Rush became a metaphor for California. The nation, if not the world, became delirious with gold fever, setting off one of the greatest migration the world had ever known. From the far corners of the earth, a polyglot of cultures and creeds descended on the streams of the Mother Lode. In short order, Sacramento and Stockton emerged as the jumping off spots or staging areas for the "Forty Niners" headed to the mining camps of the Mother Lode, with the rivers serving as the preferred route. For the southern mining district, Stockton emerged as departure point for the mining camps of Mariposa and Columbia. By 1850 Weber's original trading post had grown into a canvas community of a

Early day Stockton served as hub for those venturing into the interior of state. San Joaquin County Historical Museum

thousand inhabitants, with dozens of ships crammed together around Weber's store.

Downstream at the mouth of the river, at what would become Antioch, J. H. Smith and his twin brother, W. W., had established Smith's Landing in 1849. Besides selling supplies, the two brothers often found themselves providing directions to the diverse armada of boats and vessels that came groping by, seeking their way up the uncharted Delta. Most of those bound for the gold camps had little idea where they were going. For some miners-turned-mariners this would be their first and only trip to the Mother Lode gateways of Stockton and Sacramento.

From San Francisco the first challenge involved finding the right channel and avoiding the shoals and sandbars. At the height of the Gold Rush there were so many abandoned vessels in the Stockton channel that Weber had to organize a group of local men to go down the river and burn the abandoned vessels that were

clogging the channel. Even after arriving in Stockton, those bound for the gold fields found still other hurdles. The newcomers were often dismayed by the frenzy and crowds trying to find transportation to the gold camps. The town's population fluctuated every day as new ships brought yet another wave of argonauts. Businesses sprung up overnight, only to be sold and resold as one proprietor after another joined the exodus to the mining camps. Stockton, one visitor observed, had became a city of expediency and entrepreneurship, catering to the daily turnover of those headed to the southern mining district.

When John W. Audubon, the son of the famed bird illustrator and conservationist, came to town, he found it "a seedy place of tents and makeshift shelters," with out-of-this-world prices. When it was time to move on, Audubon was ready. "None of us regret leaving Stockton," he observed. From the onset, both the Sacramento and the San Joaquin rivers emerged as the

Early on, when Stockton was besieged by repeated flooding, the port city often had a hard time defining its true elevation—or waterline. San Joaquin Historical Museum

prime transportation arteries. As early as November 1847, a steamer had made its way from San Francisco to Sacramento. Eventually, river steamers began pushing their way up both the Sacramento and San Joaquin rivers and the navigable tributaries, gradually replacing the early armada of sailing and rowboats that carried the miners and their commerce to the interior.

By 1852, however, others saw the port city in a better light. General M. G. Vallejo, in his report to the newly constituted state senate, saw a bright future for the former community of Tuleberg:

Stockton (named in honor of Commodore Stockton) is a highly flourishing town, and the seat of justice in the county. It contains about 2,500 inhabitants. Pleasantly situated on a slough of the San Joaquin River, on a plain, thinly overspread with oak and shrubbery, and within a

day or two from some of the rich 'placer mines,' it is destined to become 'the' city of the San Joaquin, notwithstanding the absolute lack of poetry in its name.

By this time, mining camps had become established along the length of the Mother Lode. As early as the 1850s, the freight wagons and stagecoaches had responded to the need, beating a rough and rugged trail between Stockton and Sonora.

Few areas of the Mother Lode escaped the search for gold. In the upper reaches of the San Joaquin River it was nearly a year before the first argonauts began arriving with their picks and pans in the relentless pursuit of the metal of metals. At a spot some one hundred sixty-five-wagon miles from Stockton, a couple of miners had scoured some flecks of the magic metal out of the San Joaquin River where the river entered the foothills, near

Millerton, Fresno County's first county seat, emerged as an outpost of civilization when much of the San Joaquin Valley was still a vast wilderness. Frank Dusy photo/Fresno Bee

the site of today's Friant Dam. Here a mining camp known as Rootville became established, a "rowdy-dowdy" center forged by the hardships of frontier life. One of richest and earliest discoveries occurred in the spring of 1850, when the Jenny Lind claim was established. A few miles upstream another early prospector, David Bice James, who claimed to be the second miner in the area, found gold in 1851 at a mining camp that was to be known as Finegold, which soon claimed a population of "500 mining people," the *Fresno Daily Evening Expositor* reported. Over the hill, at another promising spot known as Coarsegold, other miners were busily at work, seeking the magic golden metal.

The quest for gold was the final undoing of the Indians. Within the larger San Joaquin drainage, the forty-niners moved into the traditional territories of the southern Yokuts and Miwoks. Having occupied the land for eons, the Indians soon came to resent the newcomers. The miners not only took the Indians' lands but also shot

their deer and game, and then gave them diseases for which the natives had no natural immunity. Some of Indians began fighting back, trying to defend their ancestral lands. They began raiding the miners' camps, much as other tribes had done with the Mexican rancheros, often taking the miners' livestock for a meal. Small groups of miners were often attacked; several were killed. Miners venturing away from their camps came to fear for their lives. Other pioneers seeking timber in the hills above the camps frequently encountered hostile Indians. As the situation continued to deteriorate, the miners and settlers began petitioning the federal government at the Benicia arsenal for protection.

One of those who became involved was James D. Savage, formerly of Ohio, who had come to California in 1846 and joined the Bear Flag Revolt, serving under the adventurous John C. Fremont. For a time Savage worked for Sutter, helping Marshall build his soon-to-be-famous Coloma sawmill. Somewhere along the line, Savage had learned how to survive. Fremont may have been a good teacher; anecdotal reports suggest that Savage may have rustled cattle while serving under Fremont. As the Gold Rush took on added fervor, Savage joined the quest, moving to the southern mines near Jamestown. After striking it rich there, he migrated south to the Merced River, where he established another claim and a makeshift canvas store. An entrepreneur by any measure, Savage represented the quintessence of the Mother Lode man. Expedient, self-assured and perhaps somewhat enigmatic, he possessed something of a split personality. At his new trading post, Savage cultivated the Indians' goodwill, unlike many miners who felt "the only good Indian is a dead Indian." He learned to speak their language, and he tried to protect them. But he also used them, paying them a few pennies or scraps of cloth to work his gold claims. Apparently Savage also had a penchant for Indian women, allegedly collecting, at one time or another, a dozen wives or more. All the time his fortunes continued to soar, prompting him to open other stores.[16]

In the fall of 1850, Savage moved farther south to the San Joaquin River below Rootville, where along with another miner, Wiley (J. M.) Cassady (Cassity), he established a mining claim. The two men hired other miners, including several Indians, and began working the claim. Not long after, Cassady set up a trading post ten miles down stream with one C. D. Gibbes, and together the two launched a transriver ferry business. Continuing problems with the Indians led the pair to erect a crude barricade, which would eventually become known as Fort Washington or Camp Washington. Meanwhile, Savage had opened yet another trading post on the Fresno River, some thirty miles to the northwest, adding to his wealth.

Across the area, the Indian situation continued to deteriorate as some rancherias or tribes came together to resist. At that time, the native population probably outnumbered those of the newcomers by four to one. In December 1850, Savage was notified of an Indian raid on his Fresno River trading post in which three of his clerks had been murdered. Fearing the worst, he raced to his Aqua Fria store near Mariposa only to discover it too had been raided and six of his wives taken captive.

Casting about for assistance, Savage turned to newly appointed sheriff, James Burney. Convinced of Savage's story, the sheriff began organizing a defense force that soon swelled to seventy-four volunteers. By this time California had become the thirty-first state, composed of twenty-seven counties, including the vast and centrally located Mariposa County. A few days later, with Burney selected as captain and Savage as scout, the unit located and attacked a large band of Indians encamped near the Chowchilla River. A confused, indecisive battle followed. The volunteers managed to kill about forty Indians before they were forced to retreat, losing a half dozen of their own. Savage, known to many of the Indians, apparently drew much of the return fire; some believe he should have been the only target, having needlessly exacerbated the situation. Savage next appealed to state officials for help. Responding to the apparent crisis, Governor John McDougal ordered the volunteers to organize as the Mariposa Battalion, which was then enlarged by a hundred additional men. Somehow, Savage was selected to head up the outfit, assuming the title of major.

For a while, the federal government considered getting involved in the conflict, but eventually shied away after learning of the dubious genesis of the hostilities. For their part, the Indians maintained they were only trying to defend their lands. Nevertheless, the battle gradually spread across the mining district between Mariposa and Millerton. A dozen skirmishes followed. Around January 18, 1851, Savage led an assault on an Indian stronghold near Fresno Dome. About twenty Indians were killed in the fight known as Battle Mountain. In retaliation, a group of teamsters were killed near the mining camp of Finegold. Savage's mining partner Cassady was also killed by Indians in late February while hunting near Fort Washington, located on the river northeast of modern day Fresno. On March 7, the battalion received news that "Cassidy's [sic] body had been found three miles from his ranch, shot thro' with several arrows, one of his legs cut off and his tongue cut out."[17] But after a

The West would never had been won without the Herculean labor of Chinese coolies, seen here sandbagging levees in the San Joaquin Delta. San Joaquin Historical Museum

March 16 battle in which another ten Indians were killed, some of the natives realized the futility of the situation and began giving up. Others fled up the San Joaquin River canyon, taking refuge in remote areas unknown to the miners.

It was against this background that some of the peaceful Indian chiefs began talking to their warring brethren. Federal Indian commissioners managed to work an agreement whereby the hostile Indians would turn themselves in. When some of the Indians failed to appear at the peace conference, Savage and two companies of the battalion were dispatched to bring them in by force. One unit pursued the main band up the west side of the upper San Joaquin River canyon. Another went toward the south fork of the Merced River. After

encountering a small band of Indians near Wawona, Savage managed to make contact with Chief Tenaya of the Ahwahneechees. Despite Tenaya's protests that his people had not been involved in the warfare, along with his rejection of offers of federal protection on a Fresno River reservation, the battalion forced its way into Yosemite Valley on March 27, 1851, becoming the first white men to visit the remote valley. In the tragic sequence of events that followed, Tenaya's son was killed and the Ahwahneechees scattered.[18]

Thus, the Mariposa Indian War was short-lived. Within five months the war was over. Eventually, two peace treaties were drafted, one at Camp Fremont near Mariposa on March 19, 1851; the other about forty days later at a spot known as Camp Barbour, about one mile east of the mining camp at Rootville. With the Indian situation still tense in late May 1851, Camp Barbour was established as a U.S. Army military garrison on the San Joaquin River, named after Major Herbert S. Miller, the commanding officer at Benicia. A group of adobe and wood buildings was erected, set around a presidio-style parade ground. Cavalry, infantry and artillery units soon assembled there. Meanwhile, ten miles down stream, a smaller garrison was placed at Fort Washington, near the site Cassady and Gibbes had established earlier. Fort Washington had a troubled life, however, falling victim to the flood of 1852. Ironically, none of the peace treaties that came from the Mariposa Indian War were ever approved by Congress.

As the threat of Indian warfare subsided, the gold seekers returned to the river near Fort Miller. In time, a transriver crossing, or ferry service, was also organized, and "Millerton" became a spot on the emerging and crude maps of the day, a fleck on the frontier of the valley. Even the military was not beyond the magnetism of the metal, with members of the cavalry deserting to join in the quest. One of the military miners included Captain Thomas Jordan, who went to great effort to tunnel under Table Mountain, the backdrop of today's Millerton Lake, in the futile quest for the fortune below. Today his abandoned glory holes remain as a monument to man's relentless quest for gold.

At the peak of the mining era, dozens of camps lined the river and its tributaries above Millerton. Many of the rich and colorful names remain today, harkening back to those lustrous days of yesteryear, when Coarsegold, Finegold, Grub Gulch and Kaiser Diggings stood as the centers of early day life. Some of the names were quite appropriate—or inappropriate. For instance, the town of Temperance Flat was far from liquor-free. The mining camp came onto the scene in 1857, when one James Urquhart opened a saloon and trading post not far from the river; he and most everyone else knew that any mining camp without the familiar saloon was no mining camp at all. His watering hole stayed in business as long as the mine operated, for some four years. The name of the mine

was taken from the town, as one observer noted, and not from the lack of booze. Both the town and mining activity dried up in the late 1880s.[19]

The San Joaquin River never experienced the big strikes that enriched the Mariposa and Columbia mines. Somehow the quest for gold went on, but life on the frontier was not easy. An October 21, 1855, journey by Bishop Kip of the San Francisco diocese provides some insight to life on the frontier. During his first pilgrimage into the wilderness, he followed a faint trail through the desertlike landscape.

Between 10 and 11 o'clock we reached the hills overlooking Fort Miller, and walked on, leaving the heavy wagon to plunge down the steep hillside as it best could. We passed through the infant town of Millerton, on the San Joaquin River, about half a mile from the fort. It consists of some 20 houses, most of them of canvas, two or three being shops, and the majority of the rest drinking saloons and billiard rooms. The population is Mexican, or the lowest class of whites, and on this day they seemed to be given up entirely to dissipation.

The fort is situated on a plateau overlooking the town and river. It is an artillery fort, and at this time had about 70 men stationed here. The service of our Church had never been performed here, nor had there been anything to mark the day when Sunday came. Arrangements were soon made after our arrival for the service in the evening, and a broad hall in one of the buildings devoted to the officers was cleared for that purpose. The officers attended and many of the soldiers, and after the second lesson, I baptized the child of one of the privates. A beginning having thus been made, before I left the fort I licensed Dr. ——, the surgeon and communicant of our Church, to act as lay-reader, and arrangements were made for having the service regularly every Sunday.

We remained at the post for ten days, resting from the fatigue of our journey and enjoying the open hospitality of the officers. Our arrangements were made to leave on Wednesday, leaving behind Major T., whose professional duties required him to remain for a few days, and one other of our party. Here we left our wagon for a small stage had recently penetrated as far as Fort Miller. It had only made two trips when we had occasion to employ it. It runs to Snelling's—about 70 miles—where we are in the region of the regular stage routes.

It came for us before daylight, and taking leave of our hospitable entertainers, we commenced our journey on the banks of the San Joaquin. About nine o'clock we stopped at a solitary house intended for teamsters, where for one dollar each we had a breakfast, but everything was so filthy that we could hardly eat, even after our long morning ride.

The drive for the whole day was over the same kind of country as during the preceding week—desolate plains varied with on occasional hill, and now and then a cattle ranch. We drove on through the whole route without stopping, except to change horses, until night, when we reached Snelling's Tavern, a central point from which stages go up through Mariposa County.

The next morning the stage started at four o'clock, fortunately bright moonlight, which lasted till daylight took its place. We had half a dozen passengers, including a Chinese. After fording the Stanislaus River we had another wretchedly filthy breakfast at a tavern on its banks. The country we passed through began now to show signs of cultivation. Oak trees are scattered park-like through it, and we passed rich farms, increasing as we approached Stockton. We reached there at 4 p.m., just in time for the boat…to San Francisco.

I can now speak understandingly to any clergy man who can go there, and I trust before next spring some such will be provided. Forts Tejon and Miller will have services…The remainder of the country we have passed through cannot evidently be settled for many years, and I shall probably therefore never again be obliged to travel the same route.[20]

Thus it was that another outpost of civilization had been established on the river. In time, a number of communities became established between Millerton and Stockton. In 1856 Fresno County was split off from Mariposa County, with Millerton selected as the county seat. Other outposts followed, including a host of river communities downstream.

Yet the dreams of riches did not fade away. Throughout the drainage, the quest for metallic riches continued to beckon other dreamers. While the mines of the San Joaquin River drainage never produced the staggering wealth that came out of the deep quartz mines of the northern Mother Lode, they still produced millions of dollars in gold. Within the larger drainage, the quartz mines of the Mariposa area offered up a king's fortune and the greatest rewards. By some quirk of fate, the enigmatic entrepreneur of the Mother Lode, John Fremont, became the most successful mine owner, when his supposedly worthless Mariposa ranch produced a fortune in gold. On the south fork of the Merced River, one John Hite triggered the second gold rush when he found his own bonanza.

But comparatively few of those who toiled for gold even came close to Fremont's good fortune. Hydraulic miners operated in the northern tributaries until 1884, when the courts finally ruled that no new hydraulic mining could occur unless the tailings or debris could be contained. The so-called "gold vs. grain" controversy emerged, but never on the scale that it did to the north, where siltation from hydraulic mining triggered massive problems.

In the uppermost section of the drainage the search went on for years, with repeated claims of big "strikes" echoing throughout the land. The construction of the French Trail in the late 1870s rekindled interest for a while. Running from Fresno Flats (Oakhurst) the trail led up along the western rim of the great canyon, crossing over the river and range to the Mammoth Lakes mining district on the east side of the Sierra.[21]

The quest for riches was not always focused on gold. For a few years the trail spurred interest in silver, tungsten and iron and then lost its luster. In 1892, a story in the May 20 *Fresno Daily Evening Expositor* told of promoters behind the Minaret Mines calling for the construction of a railroad up the river canyon as a way of transporting the ore to the valley. Another proposal centered on a cable conveyor, an endless line of ore buckets. Still others talked about the rich copper ores that were available around Millerton.

The speculation continued for years. In all probability, more money was mined from the pockets of British investors than was ever taken from glory holes. All the time, the prospectors and the promoters failed to see that the real wealth was the "white gold" of the Sierra, that flowed as the waters of the San Joaquin and its sister rivers.

CHAPTER FOUR

The San Joaquin Beckons

The 1860s served as a major turning point in the teenage life of California. Change defined the Golden State. Though well removed from the tragic thunder of the Civil War, old loyalties ran deep, forcing the federal government to keep a close eye on Southern sympathizers. As the mines played out—and as gold lost some of its luster—many of the disillusioned miners began looking for more practical means of sustaining themselves, with many turning to the valley for relief. Here, at least, by turning a shovel or herding a steer, they could find something to eat. Other settlers, lured by the promise of good land and unlimited opportunities, also came into the interior valley, further encouraged by the 1862 Homestead Act and a host of other land grants.

The San Joaquin Valley of the post Gold Rush era presented a far different scene than it would a century later. Few roads or ranches marked this otherwise sprawling prairie; most of the valley remained a vast wilderness. For most purposes, travel through the valley came by the way of riverboats or back-breaking stagecoaches which fanned out from Stockton toward the mines in the foothills. In the winter months, fog shrouded this land of tules and swamps. Then came the spring floods, when the valley often took on the appearance of a great inland sea. With the coming of summer, the vast landscape changed again; the once raging river slowed to a trickle. The drought-stressed vegetation withered and died. It was a desertlike setting, an endless landscape stretching out until the distant horizon line was lost in the haze.

But the landscape was not without life. Although a few elk and antelope still roamed the prairie, the valley had become cattle country. Long-horned cattle brought to the missions and the Mexican land grants decades earlier had replaced the native animals. Their numbers had been swollen by the introduction of American-bred animals, Durhams, Hereford and other shorthorns. The herds roamed the valley free and wild—a serious threat to any travelers unfortunate enough to be afoot in the land, as one 1863 traveler related:

> When I arrived in Stockton I found that no steamer would leave for the San Joaquin River for two weeks, and as there was no stage line or team coming this way, I concluded to come across the country afoot. There were no houses on the plain at that time, and wild cattle roamed over them at freedom in vast numbers. When traveling between the Stanislaus and the Tuolumne rivers, I saw a band of wild cattle coming to me, shaking their heads. I immediately fell to the ground and crawled on my hands and knees for a long distance until they had lost sight of me. I afterwards learned that they were infuriated by being caught and branded, and would have killed me had they caught me.[1]

At the onset of cattle raising in California, hides and tallow were the dominant products. Meat was only an incidental byproduct, particularly in a era before refrigeration. For most of the years up through the 1870s, the San Joaquin Valley was open cattle country, with farming limited to a few isolated areas of the newly founded state. As more and more settlers arrived, the livestock industry boomed. Sheep and pigs soon entered the scene; then a few orchards and farms appeared. Gradually, the cattlemen found themselves defending what they thought was free: the open range.

But the major problem centered around the weather. In December 1861, a massive flood swept over the land, leaving the entire Central Valley as a large lake, drowning an estimated two hundred thousand cattle.[2] The "Great Flood" of 1861-62 was followed by the "Great Drought" of 1863-64. Once again, thousands of animals perished. Reportedly, the San Joaquin River ran dry late that year, underscoring the river's fickle ways. When the members of the California Geological Survey rode down into the valley on June 5, 1864, after exploring and mapping sections of the Sierra, they encountered a devastated landscape at the San Luis Rancho. William Brewer, the head of the field survey, wrote:

> **All around the house it looks desolate. Where there were green pastures when we camped here two years ago, now all is dry, dusty, bare ground. Three hundred cattle have died by the miserable water hole back of the house, where we get water to drink, and their stench pollutes the air.**
>
> **This ranch contains eleven square leagues, or over seventy-six square miles. In its better day, it had ten thousand head of cattle, besides the horses needed to manage them. Later it became a sheep ranch, and two years ago, when we camped here, it fed 16,000 sheep besides some few thousand cattle. Now, owing to the drought, there is no feed for the cattle, and over one thousand sheep, if that, can be kept through the summer. The last of the cattle, about one thousand head, were lately sold for $1,500, or only $1.50 each. Such is the effect of the drought on one ranch.[3]**

Jedediah Smith, premier explorer and entrepreneur of the primitive San Joaquin Valley.
Reproduction of Frederick Remington painting, courtesy of Bancroft Library, University of California

It was against this somber background that a handful of livestock operators began driving the animals to the mountains, where the grassy meadows provided some feed—and hope. The first recorded grazing within the upper San Joaquin River drainage apparently occurred during the summer of 1864. Early Dos Palos settler Dave Wood, remembering the mountain meadows he had seen in his emigrant travels, took his sheep to the Sierra near Yosemite.[4] Two other herders, identified only as McCrea and Darby, drove their sheep above today's Shaver Lake.[5] Later that same summer, three unidentified cattlemen brought in their herds, setting the stage for what was to become annual migrations to the lush mountain meadows.

In 1877 the scourge of drought returned, impacting more settlers and triggering yet another surge to the Sierra. Allegedly, a person could walk across the valley on the carcasses of the drought-killed livestock. A lasting reminder of the 1877 drought still remains along the upper river in such place names as Seventy-Seven Corral, Sheep's Crossing and Miller's Crossing. At the latter site on the river, famed cattle baron Henry Miller of Santa Rita Rancho built a bridge across the upper San Joaquin

From the slopes of the Sierra, the early loggers found the logs and lumber that enabled the Golden State to grow. Author's collection.

River so he could get his livestock to the grass of Cassidy Meadow. So cutthroat was the competition for the high meadows, that Miller put an iron gate and padlock on the bridge—as well as an armed guard—so he could control the use of the high mountain meadow.

"The drought of 1877 was the reason the cattlemen started going to the mountains," explained Morgan Blasingame of Millerton, the grandson of pioneer stockman Jesse Augustus Blasingame. "A few sheep and cattlemen had been going earlier, but in 1877 conditions were so desperate that you either moved your cattle to the mountains or they died. It was the only way the cattlemen could survive. There was no supplemental feed then—no permanent pastures."[6]

By that time, the need for building lumber had become critical. The first known sawmill in the southern Sierra appeared somewhere near Mariposa in 1852. Two years later, James Hultz left his Millerton mining claim and moved up the San Joaquin River canyon, where he founded a crude up-and-down sawmill near today's

Meadow Lakes. Through the years, the forest lands of the upper San Joaquin River drainage felt the giant saws of dozens of sawmills. Most of the mills were small, short-lived operations, cutting for a season or two and then moving on. Others, however, emerged as giant affairs, such as the Madera Sugar Pine Lumber Company or the Fresno Flume and Lumber Company, which boasted their own self-contained empires, complete with stores, hospitals, housing, railroads and flume systems.[7]

Besides the Homestead Act; the Morrill; Swamp and Overflow; Stone and Timber; and Mining acts opened even more land to settlement or development. For years, until 1880, uncontrolled "free cutting" and "cut-and-run" logging marked the Sierra forests; the natural resources were there for the taking. About the same time, the courts began invalidating many of the Mexican land grants, making available still more land to the newcomers. In 1861, for example, the U.S. District Court reversed a lower circuit court decision, thereby denying title to a Mexican land grant which Governor Pio Pico

The flooded San Joaquin River often barred the California State Geological Survey from reaching its appointed rounds. The field unit included, left to right, James Gardiner, Richard Cotter, William Brewer and Clarence King. Bancroft Library

had apparently granted to Lieutenant Colonel Don Jose Castro of the Mexican cavalry during the last days of the Bear Flag Revolt in April 1846. Under that grant, El Rancho de San Joaquin was to consist of eleven leagues of land along the San Joaquin River, "whose measure is to be commenced from the edge of the Snowy Mountains following downstream." The court found that Castro had failed to file a judicial survey and had not taken actual possession of the land within the prescribed period, even allowing for Indian raids—an argument which had validated some grants.

In addition to floods, droughts and basic privation, the early settlers and pioneers lacked accurate maps and surveys, including those that would define the mineral and timber resources. While government mapping crews were afield laying out the section lines, much of their work was either piecemeal or inaccurate. In the interior of the state, the rivers became a defining force. Even into the early 1900s, much of the upper San Joaquin River basin and the greater High Sierra had not been accurately surveyed or mapped, owing to the hostile terrain and climate of the area. In most respects it remained a terra incognita, an unchartered wilderness, known only to a few sheep herders, prospectors and professional hunters.

In response to a larger statewide problem, a number of state leaders began urging the creation of a state survey which would allow California to identify and develop its natural resources in an orderly fashion. For that purpose, the legislature had in 1860 appointed the acclaimed geologist Josiah Dwight Whitney, a recognized Yale scholar, as state geologist. As his aide, Whitney named a man he had never met, William H. Brewer, whose credentials were so respected that his appointment was not even questioned. A field crew was soon organized and a course of action chartered. However, the survey was plagued with problems from the start; funding and communications were continuing difficulties. The field unit often found itself out of touch, out of funds and stranded in remote areas. In its first year, the survey ranged over much of Southern California and the central coast, inventorying resources. During an October 1861 journey over Livermore Pass, Brewer was exposed to the realities of the wildness of the San Joaquin Valley and wrote:

The San Joaquin (pronounced San Waugh-keen) plain lies between the Mount Diablo Range and the Sierra Nevada—a great plain here, as much as forty to fifty miles broad, desolate, without trees save along the river, without water during nine or ten months of the year, and practically a desert. The soil is fertile enough, but destitute of water, save the marshes near the river and near the Tulare Lake. The marshy regions are unhealthy and infested with mosquitoes in incredible numbers and of unparalleled ferocity.

A day later and wiser, or at least more observant, Brewer made a more thorough description.

I find what I wrote about the San Joaquin plain may be misunderstood. There is water in the river that runs through it, but from the river to the hills on each side, a distance of four to fifteen miles, there is not water—fifty or sixty miles might be passed on the plain between the river and the hills without crossing a stream of water, for those figured on the map are all dry now.

In mid January of 1862, Brewer's party experienced another capricious and recurring dimension of the San Joaquin Valley: the Great Flood. On Feburary 9, 1862 he wrote:

The great Central Valley of the state is under water—the Sacramento and San Joaquin Valleys—a region 250 to 300 miles long and average of at least twenty miles wide, a district of 5,000 or 6,000 square miles, or probably three to three and a half million acres! Although much of it is not cultivated, yet a part of it is the garden of the state. Thousands of farms are entirely under water—cattle starving and drowning.

Nearly every house and farm over this immense region is gone. There was such a body of water... ice cold and muddy—that the winds made high waves which beat the farm homes to pieces. America has never before seen such desolation by flood as this...[8]

Four months later when his party returned, they discovered "all the ferries across the San Joaquin were still impassable, up to Firebaugh's, 80 miles up the river, and that to get to Stockton was practically impossible." A few days later, while camping along Orestimba Creek, Brewer witnessed Mexican *vaqueros* rounding up three thousand head of cattle for a great *rodeo*, which he observed as a "great event" at valley ranches and a

measure of the early dominance of cattle ranching. After nearly two weeks of probing for a crossing place, Brewer concluded that there was no way to get across the swollen river and abandoned his plans to reach the Sierra.

In April of 1863, the survey was back in the valley once more, spending the difficult night of April 12 next to Hill's Ferry, where they witnessed an outstanding display of horsemanship by the vaqueros in getting wild Spanish cattle onto the transriver ferry. Forcing their way south to Firebaugh, Brewer's party narrowly averted a band of desperadoes.

Firebaugh's was even a harder place than Hill's. I ought to have mentioned that near our Sunday's stopping place a murderer had just been arrested, and that at Hills's four horses had just been stolen. When we got to Firebaugh's we found more excitement. A band of desperadoes were just below; we had passed them in the morning, but luckily did not see them. Only a few days before they had attempted to rob some men, and in the scrimmage one man was shot dead and one of the desperadoes was so badly cut that he died on Monday. Another had just been caught. Some men took him into the bushes, some pistol shots were heard, they came back and said he had escaped. A newly made grave on the bank suggested another disposal of him, but all were content not to inquire further.

Moving onward through more desolate surroundings, the survey headed toward a stage stop known as "Frezno City"—some twenty miles west of today's Fresno. The developers and speculators were already at work. "Frezno City consists of one large house, very dilapidated, one small ditto, one bar, one small dilapidated and empty warehouse and a corral. It is surrounded by swamps, now covered with rushes," Brewer noted.[9]

A year later, after having finally reached the Sierra, where they explored the Yosemite and Mono Lake area,

The meadows and tributaries of the upper San Joaquin River basin helped the early ranchers maintain their herd during the desperate drought years of the late 1800s. Ray Coate collection

Brewer's group was back in the valley again, now besieged by drought and dust—dotted with the carcasses of dead cattle—and defined as the drought year of 1864. At Firebaugh's ferry, he noted, "not a vestige of herbage of any kind covered the ground." Under less than ideal conditions, his party made camp nearby, "where we got hay for our animals and took a grateful bath in the cold San Joaquin." Frezno City took on an even grimmer dimension.

> **I cannot conceive of a much worse place to live, unless it be the next place we stopped. Yet here a city was laid out in early speculative times—streets and public squares figure on paper and on the map—imaginary bridges cross the stinking sloughs, and pure water gushes from artesian wells that have never been sunk.**

Discouraged, the survey pushed on, arriving at Visalia about June 6. A few days later, Brewer's party undertook what has become one of the great steps in American mountaineering, entering the Sierra at Big Meadow. From there they moved eastward toward the still snowcapped crest of the Sierra. For the next month the group explored the high country of the vast Alpine wilderness, naming the peaks and rivers along the way, including 14,495-foot Mount Whitney. The main group consisted of Clarence King, Richard Cotter and Gardiner, with topographer Charles Hoffmann, and Brewer, plus a half dozen assistants. Together they rambled over much of the Kings Kern Divide, leaving an unrivaled legacy of mountaineering adventures, eventually emerging in the Owens Valley on July 28, when another commitment forced King's departure from the group.

Making their way northward along the eastern slope of the range, the party reentered the Sierra by way of Rock Creek and Mono Pass, crossing the crest and reaching a tributary of the south fork of the San Joaquin on August 3.

There, along Mono Creek, they observed Indians who announced the intruders to their tribesmen with blazing signals. They camped in Vermillion Valley, now inundated by man-made Lake Thomas Edison. Brewer wrote:

> In places the canyon widens into a broad valley. There are many beautiful spots, but they have been rarely seen by white men before. It is the stronghold of Indians; they are seldom molested here, and here they come when hunted out of the valleys.[10]

For the next two weeks the field unit roamed the upper San Joaquin drainage, mapping the area and inventorying its resource. With their supplies running low, Brewer dispatched four accompanying soldiers to Fort Miller. Then leading three other members of the survey, Brewer began exploring the basin, turning first to the distant form of 13,555-foot Mount Goddard, the dominant peak of the region. For hours they hiked over a maze of mountains and ridges, seeking the source of the south fork. They pressed on, finally dividing into two groups. Dusk found them far from their goal—and even farther from their base camp—compelling them to spend a sorry and frigid night in the open. At daybreak, Brewer and Hoffmann reconnoitered their situation and began a weary retreat, reuniting with their companions who had also spent the night in the open. The four then returned to the main camp and rendezvoused later that day with the soldiers, who had managed to obtain provisions in the valley. After a two-day rest, the crew dropped down into the main canyon, seeking the north fork. On August 15, they descended into a great canyon, "but soon found that we were 'in a fix'—great granite precipices descended ahead…" Here within the heart of the upper canyon, Brewer observed "a most remarkable dome, more perfect in form than any before seen in the state"—one resembling a "gigantic balloon struggling to get up through the rock." This he named Balloon Dome, marking the confluence of the main and south fork of the rivers.

But trouble also dogged their trail. Hoffmann became seriously ill with a sore on his leg and was unable to walk. One of the accompanying soldiers had become separated from the main group. While searching for him, the group stumbled upon some grazing cattle and two herders who had brought their animals up from the drought-stricken valley. After finally locating the missing soldier, the Brewer party beat a hasty route to Wawona, pushed by Hoffman's deteriorating condition. Here the party remained for nearly three weeks, hoping for some improvement in their ailing companion. Taking a brief respite, Brewer journeyed separately to Yosemite Valley, only to return several days later to find Hoffman still unimproved. Realizing the gravity of his condition, the group fashioned a stretcher and carried Hoffman all the way to Mariposa. Here they managed to secure transportation to Stockton and San Francisco, where Hoffman finally received medical attention.[11]

Thus ended the first exploration of the upper San Joaquin River canyon by the California State Geological Survey. Despite their extraordinary efforts, the survey was never regarded as a great success. While they had drafted many maps and reports, they had not uncovered any new lodes of gold. Critics complained that they were too busy climbing mountains and exploring little known canyons rather than locating new sources of mineral wealth. Yet the survey stands as one of the more memorable epics in California's rich history. When Brewer eventually got around to counting up his travels, he found he had ranged over 15,000 miles within the state, with some of the most exciting and memorable times being along the crest of the Sierra or along the banks of the San Joaquin River.

For the next decade, the upper San Joaquin River canyon remained practically unknown. The herders, a handful of Indians and miners still forced their way along its shoulders, but the rugged chasm had a way of discouraging all but the most adventurous—or desperate. Up until the time the United States Forest Service took over in the late 1890s, the mountain meadows were frequently the scene of some bitter struggles, the so-called range or forage or "grass wars"—not only between competing cattle and sheep men, but also within their own ranks. "They were simply fighting over grass, that is, some of them were stealing grass," reflected one veteran Sierra rancher.[12]

During the 1870s, W. F. Blayney, a sheep rancher from the Millerton area, claimed a large meadow on the south fork that would one day bear his name. Blayney eventually sold the meadow to John Shipp, another sheepman who in July of 1891 killed two Portuguese or Basque sheep herders who were trying to move their flocks onto a higher meadow that he had used for years. While Shipp was eventually arrested and tried for murder, he was found not guilty. The conflict was only one of many that blazed away within the drainage. Graveyard Meadows, just a few miles north of Blayney Meadows, acquired its dubious name from a similar range war shooting.[13]

In 1894, Theodore S. Solomons, an early member of the Sierra Club, began exploring the still uncharted course of the upper San Joaquin, looking for a route for a hiking and horseback riding trail that would one day be known as the John Muir Trail.[14] By that time other changes had touched the upper basin. The cattlemen succeeded in gaining control of the mountain meadows, and the annual cattle drives became a traditional part of Sierra life. In the same decade, the U.S. cavalry took over the administration of the newly created Yosemite National Park, gradually chasing the sheepmen from the upper Tuolumne, Merced and San Joaquin drainages, mapping the mountains as they went. Through it all, the river continued to flow, sustaining an ever increasing number of newcomers along its lower flanks.

CHAPTER FIVE

Henry Miller—The Man, the Myth and the River

Of all those who followed the great Gold Rush, none did more to shape the destiny of the San Joaquin River—or California water politics—than a young German immigrant who arrived in San Francisco in 1850, alone and unaided. With roots reaching back to Brackenheim, Germany, young Heinrich Alfred Kreiser, born July 21, 1827, was the only son of five children of Christian Johann Kreiser and Christine Dorothy Fischer. For reasons unknown, he had left home at fourteen, arriving at New York in 1841. Relying on his apprenticeship as a meat cutter, the young immigrant soon found employment in a butcher shop. Within two years he had his own butcher shop and was prospering. Somewhere along the line he heard about the Gold Rush in California, sold his business and joined the exodus. Buying a secondhand, supposedly nontransferable steamship ticket issued to a friend, Henry Miller, who had decided to stay put, Keiser left New York, never to return, and headed for the promised land of California.[1]

While crossing the Isthmus of Panama, the young man became seriously ill and was forced to deplete his savings. By the time he arrived in San Francisco "the new Henry Miller" had but six dollars in his pocket. Miller immediately began looking for employment, and there his trail is lost in a maze of stories. Unlike many others, the twenty-three-year-old adventurer had not come to dig gold. Miller saw the future and recognized that it would be easier line to "mine" the pockets of the miners by supplying them with food and supplies rather than digging for the gold. One account has Miller working as a sheep skinner. Another has him peddling hot dogs on the waterfront. Whatever, Miller had a knack for the butcher business. Within six months he had his own shop again and was prospering. Three years later, he had emerged as the second largest meat dealer in San Francisco. As such, his reputation soon gained the attention of Charles Lux, the city's largest meat packer, who subsequently suggested that the two join forces. While Miller lacked the money to effect the partnership, Lux realized the young German had the brains; in 1858 the two became partners.[2]

At this time San Francisco was thriving, and their partnership made money from the start. Lux served as the "moneyman"—the banker—while Miller became the "doer"—the producer, the buyer of land and cattle, and the "major domo." Anticipating further growth, the two began looking about for a place where they could raise enough meat to meet the burgeoning demand. Miller took the lead, inspecting several sites that could accommodate the huge herds and facilities they would need. After learning about a distant valley in the center of the state, Miller traveled south of San Francisco, crossing the historic trail over Pacheco Pass, and had his first view of the San Joaquin Valley.

There opened before him one of the most extensive panoramas in the world, a valley 50 miles wide and 200 miles long. Through the middle, the San Joaquin River, the second largest river in the state, wound its way to the Bay of San

Charles Lux, San Francisco's largest meat packer in 1857, was the figurehead half of the partnership of Miller and Lux. Fresno Bee files

Land and cattle baron Henry Miller knew the imperative of water and importance of riparian lands.

Francisco, and beyond rose the ranges of the Sierra Nevada with their snow clad tops and saw-like pinnacles. Along the course of the river could be seen green foliage, but the balance of the valley was one great plain; dry, parched, hot, without any growth but short grass, without habitation except the jack rabbit and coyote, but it was the land of his dreams.[3]

He knew that yonder mountains held the snow and ice which fed the river, but he little realized then that before he died he would even take a prominent part in regulating and determining the time that the snow and ice would flow as water down upon the parched plain. He knew that the rich valley land was fertile beyond words, and he knew that there was room enough

for the herds that must supply the wants of man in the fast growing metropolis.[4]

Moving swiftly, the two merchants soon acquired the sprawling 8,800-acre Rancho Sanjon de Santa Rita from Henry Hildreth, one of the first ranchers in the valley. Located near present day Dos Palos, the ranch had its roots in a 1841 Mexican land grant. The sale included 7,500 head of beef cattle and Hildreth's double H brand—HH—a brand that would one day identify more cattle than any other in the West.

Many stories have been told about Miller, including those he apparently embellished as he went through life. According to one early anecdote, when Lux and Miller decided to formalize the name of their partnership, Miller refused to accept the accepted alphabetical order, that is,

Lux and Miller. In his broken English, marked by the strong accent of his native tongue, he insisted it should be "Miller and Lux." Miller pointed out that he did all the work and made the money, while Lux just sat there. The discussion came down to a "take-it-or-leave" proposition. Miller and Lux it was; the date: 1858. [5]

On one issue there was no disagreement. Henry Miller was a driven man. Frugal and hardworking, he reflected every dimension of his Teutonic heritage. He was thrifty and industrious; idleness and waste were cardinal sins. By some measure he embodied the quintessence of the Pan-Germanic vanguard that would immigrate to the Americas. Most of all, Miller was smart, and under his watchful eye the new ranch soon began to prosper. As Miller and Lux's wealth soared, so did their acquisitions. Miller bought more land and more livestock. Sheep and pigs became part of their animal farm. Then they began growing grain. Soon Miller found it increasingly difficult to manage their vast collection of ranches, often located several days' ride apart. More and more workers and foremen were added, as the Miller and Lux empire spread across the valley.

With the coming of Henry Miller a new driving force entered the San Joaquin Valley. Hardly had Miller succeeded in buying out the various owners of the Santa Rita grant than he began buying up the surrounding government land—not merely by the acre but by the township.[6]

From the onset, Miller recognized the importance of water to the Miller and Lux operations. He knew that even with the rich soil, the land was worthless without the magic elixir of water, particularly with the feast-or-famine flows of the San Joaquin River. To ranch or farm successfully, it was imperative to have adequate supplies of water. Having become familiar with California water law—the so-called riparian doctrine—Miller made a point of acquiring land on both sides of the river. As such, he could claim the vital water rights. Seldom during his lifetime was an acre of Miller and Lux land sold, unless it

was to exchange the parcel for a better one. Nor was Miller reluctant to go to court and defend his water rights, which generated some of the contempt and criticism he engendered.[7]

When the first attempts at irrigation came along in the San Joaquin Valley, Miller was not far behind. In the late 1860s, a group of San Francisco speculators led by W. S. Chapman organized the San Joaquin and Kings River Canal Company and proposed building a huge barge canal along the west side of the valley. Their "Great Canal" would run from Tulare Lake to the confluence of the Merced and San Joaquin Rivers—an ambitious, freight-carrying waterway that would irrigate thousands of acres along the way. But the irrigation company had to deal with the methodical Miller. He owned the water rights and the site for the proposed diversion point near Mendota. In addition, the canal company wanted the use of Miller's name and reputation. Eventually a contract was hammered out in which the canal company agreed to provide Miller with all the water he could use, at a price below that which the company planned to sell other users. Of course, there was the fine print.[8]

As the work proceeded northward, it soon became apparent that the project was poorly engineered; much of the work had to be redone. In short order, the canal company found itself in over its financial and legal head.

Other difficulties arose. There were prior claims to Tulare Lake, which provided some of the water for the project by way of Fresno Slough. As assessments were made to cover these added costs, the disgruntled shareholders became agitated. When the developers read the fine print of their contract with Miller, they discovered he had the rights to any uncommitted water. At that point the company threw in the towel and sold out to Miller and Lux for a fraction of the original investment. Miller and Lux then organized their own canal company and with their own crews gradually completed the Main Canal, the first large scale irrigation company in the valley.[9]

Down the years, Miller and Lux built even more canals, eventually developing the San Joaquin Valley's largest privately owned irrigation system. It was Miller's

Simon Newman, founder of the city of Newman, spurred development of the valley economy.
Newman Museum

eccentricities. By any measure, he was shrewd and
ambitious, and always controversial. Those who had lost
water battles with Miller considered him a "thief or a
crook." Others revered and respected him, particularly
his employees; while there were no "soft jobs" on Miller
and Lux ranches, he paid his workers well and expected
work in return. In some respects, Miller probably
expected his employees to work as he would—as a
workaholic.

Countless stories exist of Miller's diligence. For
example, at lambing time, when it was necessary to guard
the sheep from marauding coyotes and other predators,
Miller once found several of the guards sitting around
doing nothing but watching the sheep and talking. The
next day, they found themselves busy clearing the fields of
weeds and rocks or fixing harnesses—while still watching
the flocks. "I pay for what I get, and I want to get what I
pay for. I pay $20 a month—and a month is both days and
nights," he reportedly told his workers.

As the Miller and Lux empire spread across the
valley, enveloping much of the land between the Merced
and Kern Rivers, Miller became a prolific writer, detailing
to his foremen how best to run their operations. For
instance, he suggested, salt for preserving the hides was
cheap, and a little extra rubbed into the hide will keep it
from shriveling or cracking. Grease was another
inexpensive commodity, which would keep the wheels of
Miller and Lux running smoothly.

Miller was a gambler, but he gambled only on sure
things: his faith in the land, cattle and water of the valley.
It seemed to Lux that Miller was always buying land.
Swamp and overflow lands were especially prized since
they could be obtained for less than a dollar an acre. In
1874, when Lux warned that their finances were
dangerously low, Miller insisted upon buying yet another
ranch. When Lux further cautioned that there was only
$100,000 in the bank, Miller responded that he would
have bought even more land had he known there were
still funds available.

As his empire grew, Miller created the new
communities of Los Banos and Gustine, named after his

obsession with water, along with his willingness to go to
court, that brought him scorn. In the 1880s, Miller
profoundly influenced the course of California water law
in the landmark case *Lux v. Haggin*. This suit was
brought over proposed water diversions on the Kern
River, upstream from Miller's riparian landholdings in
Kern County. In the longest court proceedings of the
time, the state supreme court finally ruled that the state
would operate under a dual system of water law. When
Miller couldn't win in court, he would turn to the state
legislature, where he had cultivated powerful friends who
could go so far as to write new laws.[10]

As his power and influence continued to grow,
Miller developed some real—or rumored—habits and

In the late 1800s, the Wild West community of Newman displayed much of the enthusiasm that accompanied the development of the San Joaquin Valley. Newman Museum

beloved daughter. He had his own shops and stores, hotel and lumber yard. He launched his own fleet of barges and scows, which he used to move his wares by way of Salt and Temple sloughs into the San Joaquin River for shipment to Stockton and on to the Bay Area. By any measure, Miller was a driven man.

Miller's personal life stands out as a much different story. His first wife, Sarah W. Sheldon, died in 1859 after a few years of marriage. Gustine, one of two daughters, died as a young child in a horse accident. His son, Henry Jr., was born crippled and died in his early forties, under allegations of having contracted syphilis. A grandson, the only one who bore the name of Miller, perished in an Oregon blizzard. [11]

Lux died in 1888, leaving his share of the partnership to his widow and a score of lesser heirs. While he and Miller had gotten along well for most of their partnership, Miller balked at the prospect of dealing with a dozen different Lux heirs and began buying out their shares. The buyout cost him millions and took years, but by 1905, Miller reigned as the sole owner of the giant land and cattle company. [12]

As the center of many lawsuits, Miller became something of a legend. Bitterly denounced on one side, yet loyally defended on the other, Miller represented something of a split personality. He could be patient and reflective or sharp and decisive. From the ranks of his workers, he was perceived as fair but firm. He would often get up at four o'clock in the morning so he could eat with his workers. But at times he would yell and shout at his foremen, throwing his hat to the ground and flinging tools about. It was even worse with his superintendents; from them he expected even more—and nothing less than he could do himself.

While revered by the communities he served, Miller was often reviled by his competitors, who found him cruel or ruthless. Much of the early rivalry that existed between the communities of Gustine and Newman can be traced to the contempt Miller exhibited toward Simon Newman, another German immigrant and the founder of the town of Newman. As in most of his business dealings, Miller exhibited little sympathy. With Newman it was also racism; Miller disparaged Newman as a "damn Jew."[13] Yet, during hard times, drought or depression, Miller could be quite generous. Often he forgave debts and notes he held against some of his hard-hit neighbors or employees. By any accounts, Miller was a man of many moods and temperaments. By some measures, the tales of this enigmatic man are as turbulent as the San Joaquin River he conquered.

If a man were hungry, he could kill a Miller cow for its meat—as long as he skinned it and left the hide on the nearest fence. All tramps were fed, and the Miller ranches were noted in song and fable as the 'dirty plate route.' Miller held that his cooks should not have to work for hoboes, so his instructions were that they should be fed—after the employees had eaten—and on the same plate. In that way, the dishes had to be washed only once.[14]

Miller founded the popular Los Banos' May Day celebration. For nearly twenty-five years he sponsored the annual event at the Canal Farm. Historian Ralph Milliken's early interviews suggest Miller based the festival on a similar holiday in his native Germany. Miller's celebration was something between the Fourth of July holiday and a company picnic. Typically, he would provide all the food and essentials, including up to twenty-five head of beef for the traditional barbecue. Reportedly, Miller would greet each guest—in most cases his own employees and their families—shake hands with all participants and ask if they were enjoying themselves and getting enough to eat.

The hardworking Miller persisted. He lived to be ninety-one years of age. When he died October 14, 1916, he had outlived two wives and three children. By then, the once penniless immigrant had amassed a fortune estimated at approximately $40 million dollars; his land holdings totaled 1.4 million acres, with about 900,000 of those acres situated in the San Joaquin Valley, making Miller the largest private landowner in the United States. As controversial as he was in life, Miller's estate was even more so after his death. It was more than forty years before his estate was settled.[15] His water rights holdings on the San Joaquin River would figure prominently in the subsequent construction of Friant Dam.

For many years after his death, Miller's persona took on legendary proportions. Tom Mott of Fresno, whose father served as irrigation superintendent for Miller and Lux in the early 1900s, described Miller "as shrewd a business man that ever lived who was also a visionary," one who could see the need for irrigation and the efficient use of water in the valley. Edward F. Treadwell served as Miller's attorney and authored his biography, *The Cattle King*, in 1931. Treadwell wrote of Miller as the "Cattle King," but "he was really the land, cattle and water king, and the great man of the West Side," Mott said. "Miller realized you couldn't do anything with the land unless you had the water to go with it. Perhaps more than any other person, Miller had more of a lasting impact on the San Joaquin River than any other individual," Mott observed shortly before he passed away in 1988.

CHAPTER SIX

Water and Irrigation—Power and Politics

In the West, the great humorist Mark Twain once suggested, "whiskey was for drinking, but water was for fighting." Today, long after Twain downed his last drink, controversy and conflict continue to swirl over the murky waters of the West, underscored by the reality that water is life itself. As such, the vital elixir may be made to defy the law of gravity by flowing uphill, or, at least, to the source of political power and money. Nowhere in the West is the unholy alliance of water and power politics more entrenched than in the Golden State. Along the same course, few of the state's rivers reflect the reality of water politics more than does the beleaguered San Joaquin River.

Conservationists claim the river's natural hydrology has been destroyed by greed and ignorance. Furthermore, they contend the once proud river has been strangled by the "Hydraulic Brotherhood, a combination of industrial agriculture, state and federal dam-building agencies and friendly politicians"—with a worse case scenario that foresees the demise of valley agriculture. On the other hand, water users and dam builders defend the great water projects with their distant diversions. They point to the flood protection and economic benefits that irrigation has brought to the valley affording an unrivaled bounty of food and fiber which benefit the entire nation.

Against this background, it is not surprising that the river has also generated some of the most bitter and longest running lawsuits ever to clog the courts. Arguably, it is the most litigated river in America. Over the past 120 years the river has been awash in lawsuits. In 1942, while justifying the then-staggering $23 million cost of Friant Dam, the southern "arch" of the Central Valley Project, officials of the U.S. Bureau of Reclamation claimed that the cost of seventy-five years of litigation over the river's waters had exceeded that figure alone.[1] But even after the dam was built, the lawsuits did not go away. The epic, sixteen-year-long, legal marathon known as *Rank v. Krug* involved a suit in which the landowners below the dam sought relief in 1947 from the dewatering of the river caused by diversions from the dam. This case further underscores the litigious nature of water in general and the San Joaquin River in particular.[2]

Then there was the land. Another major force in the development of California centers around the system of Mexican land grants. These great grants set the foundation for something akin to feudal baronies in early day California, leading ultimately to the concentration of large tracts of land with comparatively few owners. Many of the grants remain in place today, serving as county lines, city limits or other boundary markers. Of the nearly twenty grants within the San Joaquin River drainage, the foremost centered around the El Campo de los Franceses, a 48,747-acre grant that gave rise to the gateway and port city of Stockton. The other, the 48,824-acre Sanjon de Santa Rita grant, became the centerpiece of Henry Miller's vast empire, located in Merced County east of Los Banos.

Many other lands within the basin were also affected. But the grants left a trail of troubled titles and ownerships. Under the Treaty of Hildago, following the

Mexican-American War of 1846, the United States guaranteed these grants, along with other rights. Unfortunately many of the boundaries were inaccurate or inconsistent with the maps of the day. Legal titles were often incomplete or even fraudulent. Of the total 813 grants claimed, more than half were not made until after 1841 and of that number 42 percent were filed by non-Mexicans.[3]

There was also an earlier system of Spanish rancho grants, but these were little more than grazing permits because title remained with the crown. Most of these grants embraced lands around the coastal missions, although some were validated or patented after Mexico replaced the Spanish in California. To settle the larger problem of grant claims that arose after California statehood, the Land Act of 1851 was established. The empowered commission eventually approved 553 claims of 8.8 million acres, while 197 were rejected for fraud or failure to comply with the terms of the original grant.[4]

The river's troubles have been enduring, exacerbated by the feast-or-famine dimensions of the river's annual runoff, creating waterflow variances of more than tenfold, as reflected in a century of measurements. "Major drought and floods have been recorded features of California weather since the days of the Spanish Dons," one early newspaper observed, recognizing the fickle ways of nature.[5]

During a so-called average year, the San Joaquin River produces a runoff of 1.7 million acre feet of liquid "white gold," measured at Millerton. But the flows can go to extremes. At the depth of the 1977 drought, only 361,000 acre feet came down the channel—as opposed to the record 4.6 million acre feet that surged through the canyon in 1983.[6]

The first recognition of the capricious water supplies emerged not long after statehood. Caught in the midst of the 1851 drought, the first state legislature passed a bill requiring the newly appointed state surveyor to prepare plans for improving navigation, irrigation and drainage on all the major rivers. At about the same time, in a decision that would have far greater implications, the

lawmakers adopted the English common law doctrine of riparian water rights. Riparian law allows the landowner a portion of the water that flows through or immediately adjacent to that person's property, limited to the amount that can be used reasonably and beneficially.

Opposition to the riparian doctrine surfaced immediately, led by small farmers and hydraulic mining interests. Opponents argued that a rain-soaked tenet from foggy England had little in common with the water problems of the arid West. In many cases, Californians supported the opposing doctrine of appropriated rights, that is, the "pro-irrigation" approach that several other Western states had or would soon adopt. Appropriation water law permits water users not adjacent to the river to divert water away from the initial source, using a canal or irrigation facility. This doctrine granted to the first person who used the water for beneficial purposes the exclusive use of the water—with no distinction as to whether that use was adjacent or removed from the river.

For years the appropriators fought to overturn the riparian doctrine, citing the flexibility and advantages of appropriative water law. They argued that the riparian doctrine was a mistake, benefiting only the wealthy, land speculators and absentee landowners. On the other side of the water issue, the proponents of the riparian doctrine were equally defensive. They pointed to the large federal land holding upstream and warned that any change would expose the appropriator to endless lawsuits because the source of such water was usually federal lands.

For the first two decades after statehood, the adopted riparian water doctrine posed no major problem because of the comparatively low populations and the continued emphasis on cattle or sheep ranching. But even then there was a water supply problem. In the drought years of the 1860s, a few ranchers began taking their animals to the Sierra where feed and water could be found. After the great drought of 1860s, almost all the ranchers were forced to do so or see their animals die. For the few grain growers, the droughts spelled disaster. But in the wet years, the rivers overwhelmed the land, often leaving the

Near today's Lost Lake at Friant, the San Joaquin River was diverted into Upper San Joaquin Canal; however, the leaky "Big Sandy" canal could not convey the waters to promised sites. Fresno County Historical Society

valley as a great inland sea, dotted by inundated barns and the carcasses of drowned animals. The flood of the winter of 1861-62 reigns as just one such catastrophe. The misery and destruction that followed floods and droughts were legendary and costly, both in human and monetary ways. It was the unreliable nature of the flow that made living so difficult, the old-timers reported.[7]

The initial efforts to augment California's capricious climate with irrigation are clouded in time. A handful of historians have suggested that native Indians may have developed small canals to meet their needs. However, their known way of life, based on hunting, gathering and gleaning, lends little support for such claims. Others point to the mission padres whose early but often crude irrigation produced more results than their prayers. In all probability, it was the forty-niners-turned-farmers who paved the way for irrigation, recognizing their earlier diversions in moving water around the diggings. As early as 1854, Silas Wilcox, the

first surveyor for Stanislaus County, suggested that "the plains of this county are so situated they could be irrigated by taking water from the river water at the foot of the mountains and distributing it as needed through some system of canals."[8]

However, irrigation came comparatively late to the San Joaquin Valley. Throughout much of the 1860s, most California farmers still believed they could rely on adequate rainfall, as they had known in the East and Midwest. Ultimately, the extended dry periods convinced them otherwise.

The arrival of new settlers—many in the form of frustrated miners—along with a gradual shift from livestock ranching to farming brought more calls for irrigation projects. The need for flood protection and improved navigation arose as well. Initially, the first major attempts at agriculture focused on dryland grain farming, particularly on the West Side, that is, west of the river. But these pioneer farmers remained at the mercy of

A series of barriers, such as this timber diversion dam at Mendota, were only the forerunner of others that diverted the San Joaquin River. Central California Irrigation District

the elements. Drought years meant failed crops and severe hardships. Water, they knew, germinated seed and grew crops. Early on, those few ranchers with artesian wells soon realized that the virgin soil of the valley would produce bounteous harvests if only irrigation water were available.

No one really knows who diverted the first irrigation water in the San Joaquin Valley. The first-known irrigation canal in Central California was built in 1851 on the Tejon Ranch in Kern County by Edward F. Beale. However, much of the credit for the initial large scale irrigation canal goes to two Fresno County pioneers, A. Y. Easterby and Moses J. Church, who arrived in the area during the drought years of the late 1860s.[9] A native of New York, Church had come west in 1852 to work as a blacksmith at Stockton. A year later, he helped build a canal along the Cosumnes River, which was apparently used both for gold mining and for agriculture. Church then turned to sheep ranching, relocating in 1868 to the plains south of Millerton.

Easterby, another sheepman, came by way of Napa County, using a more circuitous route, having traveled to Egypt and other foreign lands, where he had apparently inspected large irrigation projects. After acquiring 5,000 acres along the Kings River near Centerville, Easterby chanced to meet Church and gave him permission to pasture his sheep on Easterby's land. In the following spring, Easterby hired Church to plant wheat in the area, but the meager rainfall, coupled with the recurring problem of free-ranging cattle, caused the crop to fail. Nevertheless, the two remained convinced that it was possible to grow grain in the area if they could bring water to the fields. Casting about, Easterby soon located a ditch that an early gristmill operator, J. B. Sweem, had constructed nearby. He then hired Church to divert the water to those more distant lands, using his own laterals, or distribution, system. A second planting of wheat was successful. Thus reinforced, Easterby then hired another farmer, who successfully grew and harvested some two thousand acres of wheat the following year.[10]

Church and Easterby organized a canal company and expanded their irrigation system by twelve hundred miles of canals and ditches. One success encouraged another, prompting the pair to form a land cooperative known as the Scandinavian Colony, which assured potential buyers a firm supply of irrigation water. With such a promise, their development sold out rapidly, giving rise to the popular colony concept of the day. In short order the "sand desert" of the valley had been conquered, pushed aside by the miracle of irrigation.

Other newcomers were also watching the unfolding wonders of irrigation. When the surveyors of the Central Pacific Railroad came into the area, they couldn't help but see the glowing grain fields which had come onto the scene. The railroad soon concluded that it would be more profitable to haul tons of grain—as opposed to a few ounces of gold. As a result, the railroad bypassed the mining camps at Millerton for the grain fields of Fresno, in a decision that signaled the end of the riverfront county seat.

While Church and Easterby were nurturing their irrigation dreams, other visionaries were pursuing theirs. As early as 1869, the water problems of the West were known across the nation, prompting newly inaugurated President Ulysses S. Grant to visit the valley. His tour led to a 1874 federal report which outlined "hypothetical irrigation canals" for utilizing the water resources of the Sierra streams; it also recommended that "the government, both state and national, encourage irrigation… particularly in the San Joaquin and Tulare Valleys."[11] While no major construction was undertaken, the executive order and resulting studies spurred further interest in irrigation. It also spawned the idea of a national reclamation agency, which led some thirty years later to the formation of the U.S. Bureau of Reclamation, an agency that would one day lay its heavy hand on the San Joaquin River.

As the miracle of irrigation spread across the West, it took on quasi-religious or missionary proportions. "Irrigation is as essential to our lands as the air of Heaven. With a thorough system, no section in the world can equal it in an agricultural point of view," one early Fresno newspaper editorialized.[12]

Throughout the valley other projects soon sprang up along the other tributaries. On the Tuolumne River, for example, a farmer by the name of Michael Kelly unveiled plans in 1870 to build a small dam and then divert water for irrigation, mining or any other water-powered use near LaGrange. His plans caught the imagination of Charles Elliot, J. M. Thompson and M. A. Wheaton, who subsequently purchased his land and then formed the Tuolumne Water Company, whose goal was to build a network of irrigation canals in the area.[13]

But all of these initial efforts were overshadowed by one that would take shape on the West Side of the valley. Onto the parched prairie came a visionary by the name of John Bensley, who began investigating the feasibility of constructing the largest canal system in the state. With the backing of a group of San Francisco "capitalists," including William Chapman and Isaac Friedlander, he spearheaded the formation of the San Joaquin and Kings River Canal Company. Their "Great Canal" would divert water at the junction of the San Joaquin River and Fresno Slough and run northward, irrigating farmlands along the way. During the first year the canal was extended thirty-eight miles; however, shoddy engineering and construction led to even bigger problems, paving the way for Miller and Lux to gain control of the company. Reorganized as the San Joaquin Canal Company, Miller and Lux eventually finished and then extended the canal to Orestimba Creek, thereby supplying the water to thousands of acres in Merced, Stanislaus and northwestern Fresno counties.

Another of the bold irrigation schemes emerged as the so-called Grand Valley Canal of 1875. The brainchild of a civil engineer, T. P. Wilson, a 160-mile-long canal was envisioned that would divert water near Millerton and channel it to Summit Lake, a marshy slough some twenty miles west of Fresno. From there, the canal would run northward to Antioch, irrigating farms and fields. For several reasons, not the least of which was the estimated $2.5 million construction costs, the project never got off the drawing board.[14]

The Hill's Ferry bridge, one of the early crossings on the San Joaquin River, often found itself under the spring runoff, known as the "June Rise." Newman Museum

Still another project, the Upper San Joaquin River Canal, did get off the drawing board only to experience an even worse fate. The brainchild of R. Robert Perrin and his brother, Dr. E. B. Perrin, their sixteen-mile-long canal was intended to irrigate up to seventy thousand acres northwest of Fresno. After raising $50,000, they began construction by hiring workers, but paying them in script which was redeemable only in lands to be irrigated by the canal. The project was plagued with problems. A diversion structure built across the river below Friant was repeatedly damaged by floods. When water was turned into the canal, it seeped through the sandy soils or gopher holes, eroding the canal banks, triggering numerous breaks. While repairs were made, they were to no avail; a concrete liner could have saved the project, but the bankers concluded that it would have been throwing good money after bad. The "Big Sandy" and its waters went down the natural drain. By 1887 the canal was abandoned.[15]

By the late 1800s irrigation had become a way of life in the valley, allowing farming to overtake cattle and sheep ranching. Across the once vast prairie, hundreds and thousands of canals and ditches fanned out. Initially the canals were built by hand. With the completion of the railroad down the valley, many of the farmers had turned to the Chinese laborers who had helped build the railroad to dig their canals. Using simple hand tools and baskets, the canal builders eventually progressed to horse drawn plows and scrapers, further speeding the irrigation effort.

As the demand for irrigation water increased, the festering controversy surrounding the riparian water doctrine resurfaced, spurred in no small way by the adoption of the appropriative water law doctrine by several other Western states and the federal government. But the issue came center stage in the landmark suit *Lux v. Haggin*, decided in 1882. This was perhaps the most decisive of all the lawsuits brought by Miller and Lux as the major riparian holders on both the San Joaquin and Kern rivers. In this controversy, two Kern County farmers, James Haggin and Lloyd Tevis, sought to appropriate water from the upper Kern River to irrigate lands lying some distance from the river.

Public sentiment was against Miller and Lux. After a bitter and lengthy trial, the court ruled in favor of Haggin. Outraged at the decision, Henry Miller appealed to the California Supreme Court. From that appeal came one of the longest opinions in the court's history, upholding the riparian doctrine. Angered by the turn of events, however, the irrigationists turned to the state capital for relief, forcing a special session of the legislature in the summer of 1886. The political fallout became intense. The Haggin forces preyed on the fears of the irrigationists, whipping them into a antiriparian rage. Water politics ran at full flow. Bribery was reportedly "commonplace." Haggin controlled the Assembly, while Miller and Lux had the Senate "in their hip pocket." The session produced not only a stalemate, but also underscored the need for some type of reform.[16]

More than a decade earlier, in 1875, about fifty valley members of the state Grange had gathered alongside the San Joaquin River at Grayson to discuss ways of irrigating the parched lands to the west, which led to the formation of the West Side Irrigation District. However, their plans to build a canal from Tulare Lake to Antioch were thwarted after the courts ruled that the district was illegal; among the reasons cited was the proposed condemnation of some Miller and Lux land.[17] In the next session of the legislature, a compromise was worked out that divided the water; henceforth, California would operate under a dual system of water rights, one constitutional and the other legislative. The courts ruled that beneficial riparian use takes precedence over appropriative use, based on the standard of "first in line first in time." However, beyond that, water law often becomes a murky issue, defined more by litigation than legislation. Today, as the litigation flows on unabated, critics have concluded that the dual system of water law lends itself more to litigation and big money than to the best needs of its citizens.

In 1887, prodded by a young Modesto attorney, state Assemblyman C. C. Wright, the legislature approved the Wright Irrigation Act, a landmark measure which defined the use of water for irrigation of land away from a river as a "public use." As such, the act allowed for the creation of public irrigation districts with the power to condemn private irrigation companies and establish public districts with taxing authority. The measure also linked water rights with the land to be irrigated. Finally, the act also signaled the beginning of the end for many of the private irrigation companies, many of which had been less than fair to their farming customers.[18]

While widely acclaimed, the Wright Act did not calm the troubled waters. The water wars did not go away. Some small farmers saw the act as one that would shift an inordinate share of the costs to them, as opposed to the large landowners. For many farmers, irrigation meant litigation. Notwithstanding the difficulties, the farmers between the Tuolumne and Merced rivers voted to establish the Turlock Irrigation District, embracing nearly 180,000 acres, less than three months after the passage of the Wright Act. A short time later it was joined by the Modesto Irrigation District with about 80,000 acres to the north and on the Stanislaus River. Formation of the two districts generated tremendous enthusiasm and excitement in the farming areas.

The euphoria was short-lived as new problems surfaced. In 1890, the two districts came together to build the LaGrange Dam on the Tuolumne River, a project that was plagued by lawsuits and the inability to sell the required revenue bonds. Construction of a twenty-three-mile-long canal also proved to be more difficult than anticipated, and the project floundered for a while. Irrigation was experiencing its first growing pains.

The promise of irrigation grew even larger. In 1890, Miller and Lux ordered the construction of another canal, the Outside Canal, further expanding their irrigation system to serve another 148,000 acres. By that time, the canal company controlled a massive network of canals radiating out from the Mendota Pool, where an unreliable and troublesome brush diversion dam had been established. The barrier was susceptible to repeated floods. In 1890, after years of having the dam washed away, the company constructed a wooden dam at the

dammed and diverted, the virgin San Joaquin flowed as a wild, often wicked, waterway. Before the coming of the railroad, the river was at the center of valley life, yielding not only its liquid treasure, but also serving as a major transportation thoroughfare to upstream communities such as San Joaquin City, Hill's Ferry and Firebaugh. For those riverbank residents, a dry year meant dead crops and livestock. A flood brought another disaster, marked by drowned livestock. In 1877, the *Sonora Daily Union Democrat* reported:

> **During the winter of 1806-07 the San Joaquin Valley suffered a devastating flood, which reportedly drowned many Indians, and on the opposite side of the ledger, a drought in the late 1820s was so severe that the water in portions of the main Tuolumne River ceased to flow and the Indians had to go to the large, deep holes in order to get water and catch the fish that had been forced to concentrate there.**

Another disaster was the winter of 1861-62, when twice the normal amount of precipitation fell in the valley. Reportedly, the loss of life and property was the greatest ever suffered in this region in recorded history. Every bridge and nearly all the ferry boats on the San Joaquin and Sacramento Rivers were washed away. Thousands of cattle, horses and sheep were drowned as the Central Valley was turned into a great inland sea.

During its first one hundred years, Stockton came to recognize floods as a almost regular fact of life, prompting one early resident to joke that the city was underwater as often as it was above. "Great floods" and Stockton often went together. Stockton had a flood almost every year, but some years were worse than others. "A flood was nothing to get excited about," suggested yet another resident. Many of the flood-weary old-timers used to joke about the difference between the rich and poor during times of flood. It was a matter of perspective and position: the rich, more affluent, had second story homes to which they

Assemblyman C. C. Wright of Modesto spurred irrigation development by drafting early legislation. Modesto Irrigation District

headworks. It consisted of regulating the dam on one side of River Island with a movable dam or sluiceway on the west, which would permit the passage of steamers or barges. As the canal company grew, so did the resentment against the mighty Miller, who was perceived not only as a land and cattle baron but also as a "greedy water monopolist."[19]

The die had been cast. Eventually dozens of irrigation districts came into being on both sides of the valley—only to add to the insatiable thirst for even more water. Other problems remained, as well, particularly the recurring cycle of drought and flood. Before the river was

could escape during periods of high water. On the other hand, the poor or ground level residents had to take to the rooftops or rowboats.

The big flood years had a way of etching themselves into people's memories. In the valley, the river at flood stage was a sight to behold—from a distance. Upstream, the situation was only slightly improved. As a young man in the early 1900s, Glenn Burns of Millerton remembered seeing the rampaging river exploding with flood waters:

There were dry years when you could walk from one side of the river without getting more than your toes wet, but there were other years when you didn't want to get anywhere near that floodswollen river.

In 1937, the year of the last big flood, Lane's Bridge was washed out. The old bridge at Friant was often awash. I remember seeing a barn go by

one day with chickens on the roof...and then seeing it a couple days later several miles downstream on somebody else's property. At Herndon, the railroad loaded some of the coal cars with rock and moved them out onto their bridges to keep them from being washed away. [20]

As a young girl who grew up next to the river north of Fresno, Evelyn Rank remembered the silt and mud that marked the arrival and departure of the big floods:

Before the Friant Dam went in, it seemed as though we were always worrying about floods. And if it wasn't the floods, it was the dry years. The floods brought us mud and silt, and it was terrible when it got into the houses. I can remember all the work we had trying to clean up after the floodwater had gone down. But it was those floods that made this land so fertile.[21]

CHAPTER SEVEN

Steamboats on the San Joaquin

Undisturbed, the age-old San Joaquin River flowed from glacier to sea, winding its wonted way, awaiting the die of destiny. No craft of man had rippled its waters save the crude tule rafts of the Indians, till one day in 1846 the bow of a little schooner worked its way up the crooked channel of the Suisun Bay to the mouth of the Stanislaus. This Mormon boat was the first-known craft to which the San Joaquin submitted but when the gold seekers invaded the hills and valleys of California, the river yielded to an armada of strange crafts with which man burdened it. Odd vessels thronged its waters— whaleboats, sailboats, steamboats—plowed its smooth bosom, and dashed its unaccustomed tide to foam and wave. And thus again the river gave its riches to the newcomers.[1]

Over a century later, in 1952, a couple of latter-day Tom Sawyers exploring the river banks near Firebaugh stumbled upon the remains of a rotting river barge in the underbrush. After a cursory examination, the two raced home to tell their families of the discovery. Their find generated a little excitement and some limited newspaper coverage. For a moment, at least, the two had recalled the days when the San Joaquin River flowed as a "real river," plied by steamboats and grain barges and traversed at a dozen locations by cross-river ferries.[2]

While the heartland river never carried the traffic of its sister river to the north, the larger Sacramento River, the San Joaquin played a major role in spurring the settlement of the valley. Long before a network of modern roads and highways traversed the valley, before the railroads arrived in the early 1870s, the San Joaquin River served as a vital avenue of transportation and commerce. Even before Modesto, Merced or Madera emerged as leading valley cities, following the rails of the iron horse, the river flowed as a major artery of commerce, with its own towns and communities. As one early pioneer suggested, "the river was the best way to go," whether it was taking the miners to the "diggin's" or hauling hides to market. Not every traveler held the San Joaquin River in such high regard. Upon seeing the San Joaquin River for the first time, one early traveler observed that it "was very ugly; it only required alligators to make it perfect in this respect."[3]

At the onset of the Gold Rush—after the pathfinders and mapmakers had figured out the maze of sloughs and channels of the Delta—Stockton and Sacramento emerged as gateways to the mining camps of the Mother Lode. About two years after the first steamer had reached Sacramento, the river boat *John A. Sutter* became the first known paddlewheeler to arrive at Stockton, making its debut November 15, 1849, less than a year after the site, Tuleberg or Weber's settlement, had become known as Stockton.[4]

Driven by the ageless quest for gold, Stockton soon became the departure point for those headed to the gold fields of the southern mining district, such as Sonora, Mariposa or Millerton. By the late 1850s, three boats a week were making their way between San Francisco and Stockton, serving a growing number of customers. As the inland port, the new maritime center served as a transportation hub, complementing the early stagecoach service that enabled the anxious miners to reach the gold fields days ahead of those who were forced to walk the wilderness way. There were other obstacles. One 1850 gold seeker complained:

> **On my arrival in Stockton, I found a sea of mud so vast that a man needs stilts or a boat to cross the street. Every way I looked, I could see a black sticky mud—dogs mired in the streets and teams that forsook the usual route of travel. The only way out of town was by water.[5]**

As the inland maritime scene unfolded, other entrepreneurs began pushing their crafts and service further upstream—and into the Stanislaus and Tuolumne rivers. On May 1, 1850, the little steamer *Georgiana* forced its way upstream to the confluence of the Tuolumne River. At nightfall, the captain tied up to a tree overhanging the river bank, not far above San Joaquin City. On deck, the passengers rolled their blankets and spent the night in the open, fending off mosquitoes and surviving conditions that would be unthinkable today.[6]

From the onset, low water was a recurring problem for the riverboats. Unlike the Sacramento River, the San Joaquin River never enjoyed the flows which enabled its sister river to sustain year round service. At Hill's Ferry, about a hundred miles above Stockton, near the confluence of the Merced River, the navigation season averaged about six months, capped by the peak runoff in late May and early June—the so-called "June Rise."

While many accounts of those early river trips have been lost to time, a few survivors provide some interesting turns to early river navigation. In the spring of 1852, the U.S. Army found itself short of supplies at Fort Miller and chartered a small steamer at San Francisco to supply the isolated outpost, located nearly four hundred watery miles upstream. The captain of this vessel was ordered to "wait for high water and get up the river as far as you can." What followed became a military mission as well as a journey of discovery. In anticipation of the steamer's

Andrew Firebaugh, pioneer militiaman, ferryman and community founder. Milliken Museum

arrival, along with the expected difficulties of getting upstream, the fort commander had ordered the construction of a road along the south side of the river to Sycamore Point some thirty miles downstream, along the route of the old Indian trail. In addition, several loading docks were built at selected points along the way. Then the soldiers waited. Eventually the steamer chugged into view near Sycamore Point to the cheers of the waiting militia, whereupon it tied up and began discharging its precious cargo.[7]

As the fickle nature of the channel became known, other inland mariners pushed to discover the uppermost point of navigation. On March 31, 1857, the little steamer *Gipsey* left Stockton, bent upon finding that elusive point. After skirting numerous sandbars, the steamer finally reached Firebaugh's landing several days later, whereupon the captain inquired of conditions upstream. After some reassurance, he decided to "go as far as wood and

Before irrigation diversion dewatered the San Joaquin River, a fleet of barges and steamers moved hides, grain and other goods from riverside landings, such as Grayson, to more distant ports. McHenry Museum

water would carry us," apparently leaving Firebaugh April 16. One passenger recalled:

> From the ferry to this place, the river is quite wide, but generally narrower and deeper than for a few miles below. From this place up for the balance of the afternoon's run, the river grows somewhat more narrow, and presents less obstructions from bars. No difficulty was encountered, only from the scarcity of wood. We tied up pretty early this day, some 30 miles from Firebaugh's…Wood was the great trouble, and it seemed to take longer to chop wood than it did to burn it—and apparently consumed more time than we made running.[8]

Above Firebaugh, they found only the less desirable willow; it was not until they pushed on some forty miles above, where the high riverbanks offered better trees for fuel. Above Sycamore Bend, the *Gipsey* encountered stronger currents, but continued to push upstream. In the channel above, the way was lined by the gradually unfolding higher banks or bluffs. At one point, the wayfarers came upon a pioneer woman working in a field— one of the earlier settlers—and asked the distance to Millerton. "Twelve miles by land and twenty-five by water," she responded, providing the first welcomed information since leaving Firebaugh's.

The *Gipsey* continued onwards, reaching the high banks of the north wall of the river. Eventually, the little steamer could go no further. At a location near today's Rank Island, about three and a half miles downstream from Millerton, the steamer tied up. After a brief visit to the fledgling settlement, the crew managed to turn the

A sternwheel riverboat prepares to accept cargo from grain storage facilities near Hill's Ferry. Author's collection

steamer around and head back down the channel. Unfortunately, the current was so strong that they could not control the vessel, and it was swept under some overhanging trees, knocking off the upper portions of the deck, bridge and railing. Eventually the *Gipsey* made its way back to Stockton, soon passing into the obscurity of time.

Fluctuating river flows caused numerous problems while navigating the river. While low water was a problem that often left the boats and barges high and dry, the spring runoff produced the opposite problem. In big snowmelt years, the "June Rise" sent the San Joaquin River surging out of its banks, spilling out over the valley. On such occasions, it caused the helmsman to lose the main channel, often leaving the steamer stranded on a sandbar. One early traveler complained that going

upstream against the current, the top speed was only three miles an hour—and the reason it took four days to get between Stockton and Hill's Ferry.[9]

Steamers from Stockton came up the river to Hill's Ferry routinely, hauling barge loads of lumber, groceries and farm implements. On their return, they carried wood, grain, hides and sometimes livestock. With the exception of the Stockton-San Francisco service, most of the river boat ventures were short-lived. Some even proved disastrous when their crude boilers blew up. But the steamers struggled on, providing a valuable service for many years. Out of necessity, most of the riverboats on the San Joaquin were small, with a length of one hundred feet or less. The *Georgiana*, for instance, was a side-wheeler, but measured only sixty feet and displaced only thirty tons. The largest, the *A.C. Freese*, measured 119 feet

In the early days of river navigation, sailing boats and scows carried much of the traffic between Stockton and the Bay Area. San Francisco Maritime National Historic Park

and displaced 205 tons. One of the most visible, the *J.R. McDonald* appeared up and down the river until 1911. Some of the other familiar traders included the 86-ton *Erasmus Corning*, the 135-ton *Viciously*, the 166-ton *Tulare*, the 102-ton *Empire City*, and the 93-ton *Harriet*. Other less frequent steamers included the *Gaily, Caroline* and steamers whose names and profiles have long been forgotten. The names for many of the steamers were changed to reflect new owners or their family members— or in an attempt to distance themselves from less capable operators.

In May 1859, James Hutchings, one of the early travel writers who touted the wonders of California with his *Hutchings' California Magazine*, utilized the steamer *Helen Hensley* of the California Steam Navigation Company to reach Stockton, thereby avoiding the more arduous three-day stagecoach ride by way of Livermore. His journal provides a historic perspective:

Perhaps it would be well here to remark that the San Joaquin River is divided into three branches, known respectively as the west, middle and east channels; the later named being not only the main stream but the one used by steamboats and sailing vessels bound to and from Stockton— or at least to within four miles of that city, from which point the Stockton Slough is used. The east, or main channel, is navigable for small, stern-wheel steamboats as high as Frezno City [*sic*].

An apparently interminable sea of tules extends nearly 150 miles south, up the Valley of the San Joaquin; and when these are on fire, as

In a lastgasp effort to restore river transportation, the steamer J.R. McDonald fought its way to Skaggs Bridge in 1911. Lowering water in the river made its return to Stockton difficult. San Francisco Maritime National Historic Park

they not infrequently are, during the fall and early winter months, the broad sheet of licking and leaping flame, and the vast volumes of smoke that rise, and eddy and sury, hither and thither, present a scene of fearful grandeur....[10]

From the onset, the need and the importance of the river as an avenue of transportation—as well as a barrier—had not gone unnoticed. In the fall of 1849, Judge D. D. Dickerson of Stockton ordered a small boat and crew up the river for the sole purpose of establishing a crossing point for those headed to the goldfields of the southern Sierra.[11] Such was the .origin of Hill's Ferry, some one hundred eleven twisting and turning miles above Stockton. Within a couple of years, similar trans-river crossing services had become established at San

Joaquin City, Grayson, Crow's Landing, and Firebaugh's Ferry. At the peak, a dozen ferries spanned the river between Stockton and Millerton, providing another interesting chapter in the river's colorful history. Above Mormon Slough, their names included Durham's Ferry, Doak's, Hunter's, Grayson's, Crow's, Clark's, Hill's, Firebaugh's and Whitesbridge. Above Sycamore Point, their kind embraced Landrum's, Lane's, and Cassady's near Fort Washington; upstream plied Jones' or Converse ferry, serving the transriver trade at Millerton.[12]

These early ferries were little more than converted whaling boats or large rafts that had been brought up from the bay to meet the needs of those headed to the Mother Lode. In most cases, the ferries were crude floating platforms, capable of carrying a wagon and team of animals, that went from one side of the river to the

Before the deep water channel became a reality, Stockton served as the home port to a fleet of riverboats and barges. San Francisco Maritime National Historic Park

other. As the ferries and ferry service evolved, larger and better built craft came onto the scene. The more developed ferries made their way across the river on a cable anchored to the opposite bank. By using a block and tackle to angle the ferry into the current, the desired effect of moving the craft across the river was produced.

Until the first bridges were constructed in the late 1800s, the transriver ferries were the only way to cross the river. While some of the ferry operators made handsome profits, others encountered nothing but problems. Frequent floods often swept their crude crafts from their cables, casting them adrift to be destroyed downstream. Then in the drought years, the ferries were left high and dry on the mud flats while their customers drove their buggies and wagons across the shallow streambeds.

Andrew D. Firebaugh emerged as one such ferryman. A native of Virginia, he was a veteran of the Mexican War of 1848. He came to California to try his hand at gold mining at Millerton, only to be caught up in the Mariposa Indian War. After being mustered out of the militia at the fort, Firebaugh migrated downstream

looking for something better than mining or soldiering. About sixty miles downstream, past a dozen large "ox bows" in the river, he spotted a location that seemed to be an ideal crossing spot, and here in 1854 he established Firebaugh's Ferry. A trading post and hotel followed. When business failed to materialize, Firebaugh concluded that too much of the foot and horse traffic was using the northern approach to the gold fields. He then turned to building a toll road over Pacheco Pass, hoping to entice more travelers this way. When the Butterfield Stage decided to come that way a few years later, Firebaugh found himself in an ideal location. Not only did he prosper, but he also left his legacy and the community that now bears his name.[13]

The riverboats routinely stopped at all the major "landings" or ferry crossings, where small stores and settlements soon became established. Transportation of grain was the prime commodity—and an immense undertaking. Hides from the valley's vast cattle herds and wool from spring clipping trailed right behind. Vintage photographs of the early steamers often show their decks stacked with bags of grain. What most fail to show, however, are the barges that followed the steamers. Going upstream they were loaded with lumber and ranch supplies. On their downstream return, they were stacked with hides, sacks of grain and other farm products.

For a brief period, the tributary Tuolumne and Stanislaus rivers enjoyed steamer service. Those going up the Tuolumne went to Tuolumne and Empire cities. On the Stanislaus, a solitary steamer went upstream to Burneyville, now known as Riverbank. Above Firebaugh, considerable traffic went into Fresno Slough where several wharfs were located and which served as a terminal for Tulare Lake. Besides the steamboats and transriver ferries, the San Joaquin supported a fleet of grain barges. Some of the old-timers, like the late Billy Stockton of Los Banos, figured there were about forty to fifty barges on the river at the peak of the river traffic. Henry Miller's "fleet" consisted of five barges and five scows. Some of the larger ones were long, narrow, flat-bottomed craft, twenty-two feet wide and one hundred feet long and capable of carrying 10,000 sacks of grain. The scows were fifteen feet wide and fifty feet long. The barges were brought upstream by the steamers and dropped at the various river landings. At Salt Slough, where Miller had a large warehouse, a pair of horses often pulled the barges along the canal to the loading area.[14]

The grain was stored in the warehouse until high water would permit the steamboat and barges to proceed up the river. Salt Slough often carried as much or more water than the main channel of the San Joaquin, and the steamer could easily make the trip through the slough in time of high water. The loaded barges tended to draft three and a half feet, and, as a result, often became stuck. Occasionally, a barge or scow would run out of water, only to become landlocked until the following season. In drought years, such as 1877, many of the transportation contracts were canceled before the river runs got underway. Such was the fickle nature of the flows.

Many of the steamers were coal burners, using coal from the Antioch pits; however, when supplies were short, the owners of the steamers were often forced to use ash or willow from the riverbanks to keep the steam up, leading to the deforestation of streamside vegetation. Toward the end of the steamboating era, the steamers were converted to oil burners. Some of them even carried electric lights, and the early settlers viewed with amazement their nighttime passage, an illuminated apparition moving through the dark channel, Stockton recalled.[15]

The construction of the San Joaquin and Kings River Canal in 1871 and the arrival of the Central Pacific Railroad on the east side of the valley a year later signaled the beginning of the end for river navigation. The proliferation of irrigation canals took the river's water, the faster railroad its customers. Besides lowering the flows, the early brush dams that were used to divert water into the headgates created a barrier to passage. Such weirs were also a problem unto themselves, often being swept away by floods or high water. When a permanent wood diversion dam was proposed at Mendota in the late 1890s, it had to be designed to allow passage of river navigation; federal law prohibited the construction of a dam or weir across a navigable river. To address that concern, a falling-gate or collapsible weir was built. This falling-gate dam could be lowered by a cable and winch so that it would rest on the bottom of the stream, thereby allowing passage through a "steamboat chute."[16] When the wooden dam was replaced after World War I with a concrete dam, a turntable gate permitted boats and barges to proceed upstream through an adjacent sluiceway. When conditions were favorable on the main river, the steamers forced their way into Fresno Slough, also known as the Kings and Tulare sloughs. At one point, the steamer *Alta* attempted to get into Tulare Lake but got stranded by low water in Fresno Slough; it remained there until the early 1950s when it was consumed by a tule fire.[17]

The arrival of the Central Pacific Railroad on the east side of the valley did more than sound the death knell to riverboats. The iron horse brought people in even greater numbers than had been lured earlier by the Gold Rush. More farms sprang up across the valley landscape.

As the rails were set in place, the riverfront cities moved back away from the river to relocate alongside the railroad. Landmarks changed; Grayson became Westley, as a handful of settlers jacked up their buildings and went westward, carried along by wagons. Crows Landing emerged as another Crows Landing, only removed from the river; and Hill's Ferry found a new life three or four miles to the west as the grain city of Newman.

Each of the relocated communities had its own heritage. Originally known as Graysonville, Grayson was founded by Colonel Andrew Jackson Grayson in 1849, three years after his family had crossed the Sierra. At that time, the town was a rowdy riverfront approach to the southern mines. Eventually it prospered as a dryland grain farming center and a major shipping port for that grain.

Crows Landing took a slightly different course, providing its own heritage. Forty-niner Walter Crow of Kentucky apparently liked what he saw in golden California and returned home, where the older Crows had become an institution for making fine whiskey. He returned with four sons and livestock, only to die en route. His descendants hung on, however, settling in Stanislaus County. In 1867, John Bradford Crow purchased 4,000 acres of land near Orestimba Creek. Then in 1870, he teamed up with O. C. Eastin and went into the ferry business near the present Crows Landing Bridge. Business boomed; eventually a brother and a brother-in-law joined, and the foursome expanded into river transportation, concentrating on the grain business.[18]

As they prospered, the Crows built their own steamers, the *J.R. McDonald* and the *Harriet*—which appears to have been renamed the *Clara Crow* and served as a grain barge. Later more barges were added to the fleet and a second landing was established. On January 6, 1868, Crow wrote Henry Miller:

Mr. Louis Haas and I have just completed a steamer which we expect to run regular once a week to Fresno... We call her *Harriet*, and any freight you have to go up the river we would be

happy to carry for you...we propose to work for fair prices and will run as long as we can get patronage. Our boat is about as large as the *Tulare*—ours is neatly fitted for passengers. Give us a trial.[19]

Their first landing along the river became known as John Bradford Crow's Wharf and then "Crow's Landing." Later, when the post office was built, a second landing was constructed just south of the junction of Orestimba Creek, known as Crow's Upper Landing. Eventually it became a spot on the map—another dot of California's golden past—but without the obligatory apostrophe. Descendants of the family still farm the area, and the original family home still stands.

Upstream at Hill's Ferry a slightly different scenario had emerged, trailing back to the founding of the first ferry in 1850, although namesake Jessie Hill didn't come onto the scene until 1853. As late as 1870, the riverfront community remained a major crossing point on the San Joaquin River for those latecomers headed for the gold fields. The town counted about two hundred fifty residents with the usual assortment of shops: blacksmith, livery stables, wagon maker and general stores. Over time, two large riverside warehouses and the ferry landing emerged.[20]

Hill's Ferry was surrounded by approximately fifty farms of about two thousand acres each. Grain, of course, was the principal commodity, augmented by livestock and farming. During the years of the big floods, Hill's Ferry was frequently awash. Some of the old-timers recall when the steamers could pull up to the second story of the hotel to rescue those who had taken refuge from the floodwater. Hill's Ferry had other high moments. By some measure the rivertown was the original sin city, with many of the trappings of a frontier river community. The town boasted a thirty-room hotel, seven saloons and a large, well-staffed house of ill repute. It acquired a reputation as a wild and wicked place, with an inordinate number of fights, robberies and murders.[21] The *San*

Francisco Morning Call reported the sordid details with an October 21, 1883, dateline:

> **The place became noted for its tough characters, its stories of robberies, ruffianism, and crime. Mexican horse thieves and white outlaws finding the most convenient crossing place to their rendezvous in the mountains, always used it after their raids among the settlers of the Valley and always tarried long enough in the place to clean out Mr. Hill's barroom at the point of their pistols and clean out his bottles and jugs with their mouths.**

Despite those adverse reports, the newcomers kept coming, using the river for their principal transportation and supply system. A German immigrant, Simon Newman was only twenty-six years old when he arrived at Hill's Ferry in 1869. Like Henry Miller, he had left home at fifteen, arriving in America in 1863. He subsequently enlisted in the Union Army and fought in the Civil War. At Hill's Ferry he entered the mercantile business.[22] With a superb work ethic, he began to prosper. Over time, he expanded into dry goods, groceries, hardware and agricultural implements. Newman then became involved in farming and acquired vast acreage of land in the area, encouraged by early reports that Henry Miller's big canal was headed that way.

As Newman continued to prosper, he became involved in the transportation of grain, eventually acquiring a partial interest in the steamer *Centennial*, which ran between Stockton and the Bay. But when Newman heard that the West Side railroad would bypass the river front community of Hill's Ferry, he promptly donated some of his land to hasten its arrival. In the process he spurred the development of the town of Newman, four miles to the west, thereby hastening the demise of Hill's Ferry in the process.[23]

Throughout the length of the valley, other forces continued to turn the wheel of progress. As farm and fields began dotting the horizon, a maze of horse and buggy trails fanned out across the landscape. For years, the stagecoach had been the major mover, linking Stockton to foothill communities and riverfront communities. While Sacramento had long served as the Overland stage capital, Stockton, with its ties to the southern mines and Millerton-Visalia Road, was not far behind. In 1859, the Butterfield stages began moving up from Saint Louis and the southwest, touching Visalia and then Firebaugh, before turning west toward Pacheco Pass and beyond.[24] But with the arrival of the iron horse, the venerable carriers were gradually relegated to the role of feeder lines, linking Hill's Ferry to Modesto.

Other changes had also occurred in the valley as the number of horse and buggies reflected another measure of progress. In 1887, the Crow's Landing Bridge was built across the San Joaquin River for $35,196; it was a classic "turn-table" conveyance that would pivot to allow the passage of river steamers. The bridge experienced much of the trauma that went with travel of the day. In 1890, a river steamer crashed into the bridge, closing the span for several weeks until extensive repairs could be made. On June 21, 1893, the spring runoff put the span completely under water as the river experienced its highest flows in twenty-five years, again closing the span for several days. The life of a San Joaquin River bridge was anything but tranquil.

In 1887, the San Pablo and Tulare Extension Railroad began pushing down the West Side from Tracy, hoping to capture freight from the grain fields. Once again the West Side, the frontier, changed. The dramatic improvement in transportation ushered in yet another wave of settlers. One early Los Banos resident recalled seeing the early settlers arrive by railroad boxcar, one family to a car, which they shared with the family's cows and horses—all their worldly possessions. The lure of cheap land, promised by real estate companies and known as "colonies," beckoned many to the valley[25]

The iron horse was cheered at first, but as the freight and ticket rates skyrocketed, it soon became evident that the railroads were more interested in profit than popularity. Even the arrival of the competing West Side

In 1902, Lane's Bridge spanned the San Joaquin River north of Fresno, enabling the horseless carriage set to motor to new frontiers. Author's collection

railroad did little to ease the ironclad grip which the main Southern Pacific Railroad held on the valley. It was perceived as a cold-blooded octopus, bent upon extracting ever higher rates from the struggling farmers and settlers. Against that background, several affected communities began looking at the river for relief from what they considered the railroad's confiscatory freight rates.[26]

Those who spoke out also knew that the river was unpredictable in its flow—and that uncertainty only worked to the advantage of the railroad. Many remembered the summer of 1877—the great drought year—when the river traffic hit rock bottom. However, a railroad strike in 1894 provided an unusual opportunity. For weeks the only freight that moved in the valley arrived or departed by mule-drawn freight wagons. Even the

mails were stopped until a band of bold bicycle riders began carrying the mail in relays between Fresno and San Francisco. Gradually, public support for an alternative form of transportation grew and galvanized.[27]

Looking to the vast canal projects that were underway in the area, a group of valley farmers and merchants joined together. Pointing to the continued success of river transportation between Hill's Ferry and Stockton, along with the growth of Stockton as a port city, the group called for the return of upstream riverboat service. Generally they proposed dredging the river between Stockton and Henry Miller's diversion dam near Mendota. From that location, a more direct barge canal could be built to either Herndon or Fresno. By utilizing a system of small dams and canals, the proponents argued, the flow of the river could be evened out, thereby sustaining river transportation much of the year. Some even bolder dreamers envisioned an extended canal system that would link Visalia and Bakersfield—canals which would be supplied by the rivers feeding Tulare Lake.[28]

In time, their persuasive arguments were heard all the way to Washington, D.C., where they convinced lame-duck President Theodore Roosevelt to order the Corps of Engineers to make a feasibility study. Roosevelt's order was greeted with great interest in Fresno and Madera, where the need for relief from the exorbitant charges of the railroad seemed the greatest. To sustain public enthusiasm, the local leaders scheduled a promotional celebration centered around the appearance of a river steamer. To this end, a half dozen leaders went to Stockton and chartered the aging sternwheeler, the *J.R. McDonald*, now reaching the end of its serviceable career. Next, the promoters arranged for the construction of a small landing, or dock, at Skaggs Bridge, just below the spot where the first nonmovable bridge was being considered.

On June 9, 1911, the veteran river boat chugged out of Stockton, its single stack belching a telltale column of black smoke. Zigging and zagging and fighting sand bars and low hanging branches, the *J.R. McDonald* made its way past Crow's Landing and Hill's Ferry. Three days later it reached Firebaugh, where at 3:00 A.M. it was welcomed by a large crowd. After a brief stop the venerable steamer pushed upriver, passing the diversionary dam near Mendota. Nearly a week after leaving Stockton, and after losing the main channel in the runoff swollen river, the *J.R. McDonald* pulled into the hastily constructed dock near Sycamore Point, with a brass band and a large crowd cheering its arrival.

A brief welcoming ceremony followed. As the usual assortment of politicians pontificated, the river barge *East Side* was rechristened the *Fresno*—using a container of San Joaquin River water. Fresno Mayor Chester Milo Rowell got to the heart of the matter by emphasizing the need to improve the river for "permanent navigation."

The skipper of the boat, Captain C. P. McMurtry also extolled the possibilities, contending the river should be navigable all the way to Herndon for six months of the year, subject to some channel clearing and straightening. "Some straightening would be desirable, but with boats built for the purpose, I believe we could go right up as far as old Millerton if the immovable bridges were not in the way," sounded McMurtry. Then the bands played some more, refreshed by something other than riverwater, and the celebrates went home, convinced that their efforts had been successful.

The steamer's journey, the *Fresno Morning Republican* reported June 16, represented the first successful journey upstream past Miller and Lux's diversion dam at Mendota since 1869. However, the celebration was anticlimatic. After unloading her wares and taking on wheat and raisins, the *J.R. McDonald* turned around and began its retreat down the river. Unfortunately, the large scale diversion of waters into the irrigation canals had already begun. Somewhere near Firebaugh, the *McDonald* ran out of navigable water and became stranded. The story goes that it took several days of persuasion by the captain to convince the dam tender at Mendota to release enough water back into the river channel to refloat the vessel. Only then could the old steamer beat her way downstream—and that was about the end of steaming on the upper river.[29]

It was several years before the government report emerged. By that time the nation's attention had been distracted by World War I. "Historical Sketches of the Upper San Joaquin River Navigation," submitted to Congress in 1917, suggested a series of dams and locks that would improve navigation between Stockton and Herndon. However, the thrust of the report was not what the advocates of river transportation wanted to hear. It stated quite bluntly that irrigation, not navigation, was to be the future of the river. In the words of the report:

> **Navigation cannot now, nor can it for many years in the future, if ever, be extended to a point on the San Joaquin River at or near Herndon.**[30]

From the onset, the issue of navigability was a prime concern and controversy. Many of the early settlers pushed the issue because it would require the state to maintain a clear channel for both navigation and flood control. Shortly after statehood, the state declared the channel navigable from its mouth to Tulare Lake, by way of Fresno Slough. In practice, the designation was far more political than practical, with the state unable to fund channel work. "The San Joaquin River is navigable for ordinary steamers to Grayson, Hill's Ferry, and Firebaugh, and in the spring to the mouth of Tulare Slough—about *150* miles," one 1870 report indicated. In April 1870, the legislature extended navigability to a ill-defined location known as "Jones' Store"—perhaps the one at Millerton. However on March 21, 1885, the point of uppermost navigability was redefined as Sycamore Point—about four miles west of Highway 99 near Fresno—where it has remained since. Most recently, the State Land Commission has asserted the Sycamore Point designation marked a retreat from a higher point. They suggest that the change was politically influenced to allow the railroad to build a less costly and nonmovable trestle, or bridge, over the San Joaquin River, where Highway 99 eventually crossed the river.

Ironically, the goods and grains the steamboats delivered only led to the river's own demise. As the thirst for irrigation water became unquenchable, the diversions increased and the river level decreased. Gradually, the steamers and barges ran out of water and then disappeared from the scene. While river transportation sustained itself below Hill's Ferry until the early 1920s, it was already history above the Mendota Dam. In their day, the riverboats contributed much to the life and lore of the San Joaquin Valley. Now they are gone; only fading photographs and newspaper clippings tell about the steamers and barges of yesteryear's river.

On January 18, 1968, the *Los Banos Enterprise* reflected:

> **Strange as it seems, the San Joaquin River was once the second largest river in California, and the third largest on the Pacific Coast. Now, robbed of its water by the Friant Dam, the river through Merced County is but a dry stream bed.**

Today, the only steamer traffic is down a man-made river below Stockton, via the Stockton Deepwater Channel. The ancestral river, the original river, no longer exists.

CHAPTER EIGHT

John Muir and the Headwaters of Conservation

In the spring of 1868 another page in the human history of the San Joaquin River unfolded when thirty-three-year-old John Muir made his way over Pacheco Pass. His trail followed close to that of Gabriel Moraga, Henry Miller, Andrew Firebaugh and a host of other newcomers. But unlike those earlier pathfinders who had come seeking to tame the wilderness, the wandering Scotsman came looking for wilderness—pristine, sublime wildness—anything, he noted, that was far removed from the artificial world of San Francisco's Barbary Coast.

As Muir walked across the San Joaquin Valley, he gazed upon a two-hundred-mile-long plain, fifty miles wide and carpeted with wildflowers. He likened the vast landscape to the Garden of Eden. Even then he saw the land already surrendering its wildness to the forces of growth and development. Beyond the valley, Muir beheld the still snow-capped Sierra standing as a shining distant sentinel, sustaining the river near which he walked:

Never were mortal eyes more thronged with beauty. When I walked, more than a hundred flowers touched my feet at every step closing above them, as if wading in water. Go where I would, east or west, north or south, I still splashed and rippled in flower gems. But all this beauty of life is fast fading year by year—floundering in the grossness of modern refinement.[1]

Muir strolled on, his route set for a place known as Yosemite. Two days later he crossed the San Joaquin River at Hill's Ferry, and then walked on toward Coulterville in the foothills west of Yosemite. It took the wandering Scotsman nearly six weeks to reach the fabled Sierra canyon. Yosemite had first been made known in 1851, when members of James Savage's Mariposa Battalion were pursuing fleeing Indians. Muir's entry into the Enchanted Valley produced no known reaction, but, for all purposes, he was home.

The son of a religious zealot, Muir was born in Scotland and grew up in Wisconsin. After leaving home and attending the University of Wisconsin, he developed a keen interest in botany, nature and mechanical devices. For a time Muir worked at an Indianapolis carriage firm, where he nearly lost his eyesight in an industrial accident. During his recovery, he began reexamining his priorities and launched a new course by making a thousand-mile walk to the Gulf of Mexico in 1867. A year later, his goal was a mysterious—almost mythical—place known as Yosemite.[2]

Muir's reaction to Yosemite Valley was something akin to love at first sight. At the initial juncture he could not have foreseen how his exposure to Yosemite would change the course of his life. Nor could he have anticipated how his presence and philosophies would one day assure him a place in history as the father of the American conservation or national park movements.

Even before Muir's time, Yosemite's profound grandeur had worked its magic on visitors. Among the first wave was James Hutchings, a British-born forty-

John Muir, America's foremost conservationist, was moved and sustained by the waters of the San Joaquin River. Yosemite Research Library

niner turned journalist and editor of *Hutchings' California Magazine,* who wanted to relate the wonders of "The Great Yo-Semite Valley." To that end, in 1855 Hutchings had brought in artist Thomas Ayers, whose sketches were to lend visual support for Hutchings' subsequent articles on the grandeur of Yosemite.[3]

How Muir first learned of Yosemite is not known. Some historians have speculated that a friend may have read one of Hutchings' articles to Muir while he was recovering his sight. Others suggest Muir may have learned about the fabled canyon only after arriving in California. Well before his arrival, stores and stables, resorts and ranches had been established in Yosemite Valley to accommodate the visitors. Hutchings, along with others, had even attempted to homestead the valley; he had also built something of a hotel to cater to the early visitors. These activities had not gone unnoticed,

prompting some concerned Californians to speak out in defense of Yosemite. In time, their concerns matured around a new concept—a state preserve—based on the protection and preservation of wildlands, in this case Yosemite Valley and the Mariposa Grove of big trees. In 1864, U.S. Senator John Conness introduced an act granting to the state "the cleft or gorge in the granite peak of the Sierra Nevada Mountains…known as the Yosemite Valley…for public use, resort and recreation."[4] To this grant was added the Mariposa Grove of big trees. At the height of the Civil War, Congress and President Lincoln approved the Yosemite Grant, marking a new era in the protection of the nation's most scenic lands.

It was against this background that Muir made his way to the valley and beheld the thundering waterfalls and towering peaks of Yosemite. In the spring of 1869 Muir made arrangements with Pat Delaney, a Snelling-area rancher, to oversee two herders who were taking two thousand of Delaney's sheep to Tuolumne Meadows for the summer, in the wake of another dry year. Muir accepted the job only after he was assured there would be ample time to roam and write about the mountain landscape rimming Yosemite Valley.

As Delaney's flocks moved eastward, Muir began a summer of exploration and wandering, always seeking the high country. His baptism to the Yosemite high country served as his confirmation on high—his cathedral—the genesis of his sermon on the mount. Amid the towering peaks and mountain meadows, Muir came to identify nature as the ultimate manifestation of God. By any tenet, it was a church from which the oracle would never stray; Muir had fallen under the spell of the mountains.

In the fall of 1869, the maturing mountaineer made his way back to Yosemite Valley, where he found work in a small sawmill which Hutchings had erected. After building a small cabin near lower Yosemite Falls, Muir settled down to spend the winter months in the great valley, coming to know and enjoy the awe and wonder of the other seasons. But in the summer he was back in the high country, ranging ever farther afield, coming to know the mountains and meadows as long-lost friends.

As his explorations widened, Muir began contemplating the very origin of the tumultuous landscape that unfolded before him. While the prevailing wisdom suggested a singular cataclysmic event, where the great canyon had been created when the interior of the mountain collapsed—the so-called "dropout theory"—Muir came to postulate an alternate theory of glacial scouring. He believed glaciers, that is, ice, water, and, most of all, time, had created the great canyon. His radical approach stood in direct opposition to several eminent scientists, including Josiah Whitney, head of the California State Geological Survey and one of the foremost geologists of the period. Time would eventually show that while Muir had overestimated the extent of the glaciation, his observations were far more accurate than Whitney's.[5]

But Muir was not marking past events alone. Appalled by the grazing and destruction that was occurring in both the valley and high country, he began writing about Yosemite. In the course of his travels, he had become an inveterate mountaineer, ranging farther and farther along the crest of the Sierra, existing for days on end with nothing more than a few bread crumbs and hot tea. In October 1872, alone and unaided, Muir made the first ascent of 13,156 foot Mount Ritter, the headwaters peak of the main fork of the San Joaquin River, in what has become an epic story of man against mountain. Muir wrote:

> How glorious a greeting the sun gives the mountains! The highest peaks burned like islands in a sea of liquid shade. The lower peaks and spires caught the glow, and long lances of light, streaming through many a notch and pass, fell thick on the frozen meadow. The majestic form of Ritter was full in my sight, and I pushed rapidly on over rock-bosses and pavements, my iron-shod boots making a clanking sound.[6]

Muir soon found himself starting upwards, intending only to make a reconnaissance of the lower flanks of the great peak, which forms the mountain massif separating the main and north forks of the San Joaquin River. In his epic, *The Mountains of California,* Muir wrote:

> I began to scale it, picking my holds with intense caution. After gaining a point about half way to the top, I was suddenly brought to a dead stop, with arms outspread, clinging close to the face of the rock, unable to move hand or foot either up or down. My doom appeared fixed. I must fall. There would be a moment of bewilderment, and then a lifeless rumble down the one general precipice to the glacier below.
>
> When the danger flashed upon me, I became nerve-shaken for the first time since setting foot on the mountains and my mind seemed to fill with a stifling smoke. But this terrible eclipse lasted only a moment, when life blazed forth again with preternatural clearness. I seemed suddenly to become possessed of a new sense. The other self—bygone experience—Instinct or Guardian Angel—call it what you will—came forward and assumed control. Then my trembling muscles became firm again, every rift and flaw in the rock was seen as through a microscope, and my limbs moved with a positiveness and precision with which I seemed to have nothing at all to do. Had I been borne aloft upon winds, my deliverance could not have been more complete. But the strange influx of strength I had received seemed inexhaustible. I found a way with effort, and soon stood upon the topmost crag in the blessed light. How truly glorious the landscape circle around this noble summit!—giant mountains, valley, innumerable glaciers and meadows, rivers and lakes with wide blue sky bent tenderly over them all.

In mid-August of the following year, having the San Joaquin River drainage etched onto his mind earlier,

Muir began making some of his most ambitious explorations. Crossing the Merced Crest in the Yosemite high country, he ventured into the north fork of the "Joaquin Yosemite." He headed for Mount Ritter and the Minarets, exploring the vast upper reaches of the river. Once again the towering spires and summits of the ancestral Ritter Range caught his attention.

> **When I first came in sight of various glacial fountains of this region, I said there must be a very deep and slanty-walled canyon at their meeting place—a kind of slate Yosemite—and I feared it might be difficult to cross in going to the Minarets. I was right, for certainly this Joaquin Canyon is the most remarkable in many ways of all I have entered. An astonishing number of separate meadows, rich gardens, and groves are contained in the canyon, and it is a composite-scale Yosemite Valley with huge black slate rocks that overlean, and views reaching to the snowy summits.[7]**

Muir made repeated forays or crossing of the upper San Joaquin basin. On one such trip, he found himself hiding from remnant bands of Indians still occupying the Sierra. After an extended stay in the headwaters, Muir went back to Yosemite only to return a month later, intent upon exploring the Kings River country. This time he approached the San Joaquin watershed again, having reentered the high country through Wawona and Chiquito Creek with three friends. On September 26, 1877, he observed that the terrain within the river gorge was very rough.

> **One is constantly compelled to ascend knobs and buttresses that rise sheer or steeply inclined from the water's edge. The scenery from the first main fork is very grand. The walls are steep and close, fold on fold, rising to a height of 3,000 to 4,000 feet.**

As Muir's exploration of the Sierra continued, he came to know the terrain by the river systems. Each of the major Sierra rivers had carved its own chasm—another "Yosemite." Besides the "San Joaquin Yosemite," the Kings, Kaweah and Kern rivers have their own "Yosemites." Throughout the balance of the decade the venerable mountaineer moved up and down the crests of still other mountains. In time, Mount Whitney, Mount Shasta, the Cascades and mountains of Alaska provided other peaks for Muir's continuing explorations.

In the fall of 1877, after his second thrust into the Kings Canyon, Muir headed back to his Martinez ranch by way of the little community of Hopeton on the Merced River. Somewhere along the river Muir managed to salvage enough lumber to construct a small rowboat, which he subsequently launched into the tributary. Proceeding downstream, he entered the main channel of the San Joaquin River four days later, November 15. With the great drought of 1877 at its worst, Muir found the river low, marked by numerous exposed sandbars and obstructions, all of which slowed his progress. "The amount of water now in the river—a dry year—is a current about 10 feet wide and two feet deep, flowing three miles per hour."[8]

The next day Muir camped along the river about five miles below Hill's Ferry, where he burned a big oak tree to combat the nighttime chill. Down the channel he rowed, covering eighteen miles the following day. Despite the drought, he saw a river alive with fish and wildlife. "Salmon in great numbers are making their way up the river for the first time this season, low water having prevented their earlier appearance," he observed. Near the confluence of the Tuolumne River, he found the tributary choked with silt and muck from hydraulic mining. Downstream, dead cattle were floating in the river, fouling the water and providing growing evidence of the transformation sweeping over the waterway and the once wild valley.

For a week the mountaineer-turned-mariner pursued his course down the great waterway. One day he complained that up-channel winds and whitecaps had

The early 1900s battle over Hetch Hetchy in Yosemite National Park became the first major dispute between water users and conservationists. Yosemite Research Library

made rowing difficult, slowing his progress. Yet he pushed on. Finally on November 27, Muir arrived at his Martinez ranch, his river travel completed.

Over the following years, Muir's reputation as a mountaineer and conservationist began to spread. Lectures, newspaper articles and other writings only added to his stature, though he was quiet and unassuming. Yet Muir remained a troubled man; his travels through the West had opened his eyes to the continuing damage being wrought upon his beloved Sierra from indiscriminate mining, logging and grazing. Even the tiny state preserve of Yosemite was not beyond the threat, as a continuing wave of new entrepreneurs and extractors invaded the sanctum sanctorum, Yosemite Valley.

In 1889, after two of his Yosemite articles appeared in *Century* magazine, the public began rallying against the continued abuses at Yosemite, calling for the creation

of a national park. Under federal administration it would be similar to the protection afforded Yellowstone in 1872, when it became the first national park, in what was still Wyoming Territory. In 1890, a bill was introduced in Congress containing many of Muir's recommendations for a Yosemite National Park. While bitterly contested, the measure eventually became law, serving as a benchmark decision in federal land protection. The defined boundary embraced approximately seventeen hundred square miles, including much of the upper San Joaquin River headwaters, embracing the Minarets and Ritter Range, Devils Postpile and Rainbow Falls. Excluded, however, were the lands set aside in the original state grant.

By this time, livestock grazing in the Sierra had become commonplace as well as competitive. In an era before irrigated pastures, the mountain meadows stood as the difference between life and death for the stockmen.

Sheepmen were battling not only cattlemen but other sheepmen for the life-sustaining grasses; their animals were everywhere, cropping the grass to dust. Even the recently designated park was not beyond their feet; herders routinely ignored the boundaries of the newly defined parkland. In an effort to protect the park, the U.S. Cavalry began chasing the herders and their flocks from the park. However, the wily herders did not give up readily. With a knowledge of the mountains acquired over the years, the herders were often able to evade the mounted patrols. But for those intercepted, the prevailing practice was to escort the offending herder to the boundary of the park and then drive his animals to the opposite side.

Meanwhile, the miners were continuing to chip away at other areas of the Mother Lode and greater Sierra, following their eternal quest for metallic riches. In 1877, another wave of gold fever hit the Sierra, sending the gold seekers off on another frenzied search for both silver and gold. Along the crest, traces of both metals were discovered at both the Tioga Pass and Mammoth Lakes area, triggering mining activities. To reach the "Lakes District" mining area, a rough trail, the French or Old Mammoth Trail, was built up the San Joaquin River canyon from Fresno Flats—today's Oakhurst—between 1878 and 1881.[9] Established as a toll road by John S. French, a San Francisco business man, the route was set on the western slope of the canyon, apparently following an early Indian trail established along the upper rim of the canyon.

In short order, stagecoach service was established between Fresno Flats and the Hogue Ranch—about one-third of the total fifty-four miles to Mammoth Lakes. The miners had to proceed from there on foot or horseback. For several years, French operated a pack train up the canyon, serving the half-dozen mines located around Mammoth Lakes.[10] The trans-Sierra trail was described as "a killing experience" by one early traveler. With elevations starting at 2,200 feet, the route went up and down, crossing a dozen tributaries before dropping down into the upper middle fork, only to start a more strenuous

Rainbow Falls, the highest waterfall on the San Joaquin River, became the center of a 1910 dispute between conservationists and those who sought to develop the area as a hydroelectric site. Author's photo

climb to Mammoth Pass at nearly ten thousand feet; it was no trail for a tenderfoot. In summer the route was often hot and dry, while winter brought snow and freezing temperatures.

At the height of the devastating 1877 drought, the trail saw heavy use as desperate cattlemen and sheepman vied for the lush meadows as never before. Along the way, they left their names and claims, including such landmarks as Miller's Crossing, Sheep's Crossing and '77 Corral. Miller's Crossing, for instance, came onto the early maps after Miller and Lux built the first bridge across the upper river in 1877. In the battle for the mountain meadows—the so-called "grass wars"—the company installed iron gates and locks on the bridge and controlled the access with armed guards, recalled Gene

Tully, one of the early rangers on the Sierra Forest Reserve.[11]

Then in the late 1880s, after nearly forty years of abuses and giveaway land grants, the public finally recognized what was happening on the slopes of the Sierra. Indiscriminate grazing and logging were destroying the watershed, upon which valley agriculture depended. The conservation cry went out, demanding the government act. In 1891, at the urging of the state legislature, Congress created a forest reserve system administered by the General Land Office within the Department of Interior. Two years later, on February 14, 1893, the Sierra Forest Reserve, the largest reserve in the nation at five million acres, was created by President Benjamin Harrison, embracing the western slope of the Sierra from the Tuolumne to the Kern rivers.

At that time few individuals perceived any difference between the new forest reserve and the national parks that had been designated at Yosemite, Grant Grove and Sequoia in 1890. Initially, even Yosemite had been designated a forest reserve, a designation that persisted for several years. Perhaps, most significantly, the creation of these two entities, national parks and forest reserves, signalled the end of the pioneering era. Over the next decade, the Sierra Forest Reserve was reorganized under the Department of Agriculture to become known as the Sierra National Forest. It also hired some of the first rangers, including Tully, to patrol the mountains, trying to prevent wildfires, illegal grazing and the theft of timber. But these early rangers also blazed trails, marked timber for sale, issued grazing permits and tried to address Indian land claims. In most cases they worked alone, patrolling the high country during the snow-free months, then returning to North Fork in the winter months. "It was hard, lonely and sometimes dangerous life. Sudden illness, a fall, weather, slides and the threatened vengeance of a restful stockman made early rangers always watchful," Tully noted.[12]

The quest of gold and silver in the Sierra persisted. By 1900, a half-dozen different mines were operating in the uppermost San Joaquin River drainage, particularly in the Minarets. The differences between the miners and the conservationists were always tenuous. No sooner had Yosemite National Park been established than the miners began making demands to remove the Minarets from the park. The pressure continued to build, and in 1905, over five hundred square miles of the land were deleted from the park and returned to the Forest Service so it could be used by the mining and timber interests—all of which came as a devastating blow to Muir and the conservationists. The affected land included the Minarets and the San Joaquin River's headwaters.

Then in 1910, a group of miners approached the Forest Service and asked permission to blast the Devils Postpile so a rock dam could be placed across the main fork of the San Joaquin River. The miners proposed to use the impounded waters to generate electricity for their mining operations along the main fork. However, the proposal caught the attention of Walter Huber, a Forest Service engineer, who sounded the alarm and began pressing for the preservation movement. Once more the forces of preservation rallied and succeeded in stopping the proposed project, eventually setting the area aside as a national monument.[13]

Meanwhile, the construction of the Big Creek hydroelectric facilities in the San Joaquin River canyon below was already underway. Work had begun down river at Big Creek on the largest hydroelectric system ever envisioned. North of Yosemite, the City of San Francisco began pushing the construction of a large municipal water and hydroelectric project in the Hetch Hetchy area on the Tuolumne River—once more inside Yosemite National Park. Despite suitable alternative sites outside the park, President Woodrow Wilson signed the Raker Act in 1913, permitting the construction of O'Shaugnessy Dam, ignoring the pleas of John Muir and the Sierra Club.[14]

Eventually the national parks and forest would go their separate ways. The forest reserve system matured into the Forest Service, whose mission embraced a utilitarian conservation approach, emphasizing sustained multiple use of its various resources. In some ways the National Park Service came on the scene as a result of the loss of Hetch Hetchy. As a result of that loss, its mandate was to preserve and protect the natural scene and leave it unimpaired for all times

In many ways, the upper San Joaquin River had served as the crucible for this ongoing unfolding experiment in resource management. At that time, every dam, power plant and highway was perceived as a measure of progress. Today, it seems somewhat ironic that the San Joaquin River and its upper watershed—a water basin that nourished much of the American conservation movement, as well as the concept of a national park service—now stands as one of the most exploited rivers in the nation. Today, few of the four million people who admire the grandeur of Yosemite National Park each year ever realize that only a few miles away, to both the north and south, lie two other adjacent canyons that rival the grandeur of Yosemite Valley. Yet for all purposes, these areas have been lost to public access and appreciation.

CHAPTER NINE

Tools Tempered in the River

The late 1880s brought pronounced changes to the San Joaquin Valley and river. Throughout the valley, hundreds of ranches and farms sprouted up as a tidal wave of immigration moved across the once vast wilderness. And again Henry Miller was up to his neck in land and water wars. Away from the river, cities like Modesto, Merced and Madera emerged in the wake of the railroad, ushering in yet more newcomers, lured to the valley by promises of cheap lands and unlimited opportunities.

Nearly two hundred miles upstream from Stockton, the arrival of the railroad at Fresno came as a mortal blow to the not-so-old town of Millerton. For nearly twenty years Millerton had served as the county seat and center of commerce—and the gateway to the southern Sierra and San Joaquin River Canyon. In a puff of railroad smoke it was gone, pushed aside by the iron horse of change. As in the case of other communities that had been bypassed by the railroad, Millerton began retreating into history.[1]

The railroad was not the only thing moving across the floor of the valley. At many locations, the virgin soils felt the first cutting bite of the plow. Then came an emerging network of canals and irrigation ditches, as more settlers began diverting water from the San Joaquin River and its tributaries.[2]

At first the farmers relied on small, hand-dug ditches similar to those the padres had used on the mission farms a century earlier—or even a few artesian wells. From the abandoned mining camps of the Mother Lode came wooden flumes that had been effectively used to divert water into the sluice boxes and long toms. As irrigation increased, the farmers began looking to more efficient ways to dig ditches and move earth than using simple hand tools. Along the way, necessity nurtured countless innovations and adaptations that would ease the farmer's task. Typical of such efforts was the simple metal blade that Henry Miller's blacksmith affixed to the leading edge of a V-shaped wooden spreader with which he had dug some of his canals.

However, the device that spurred the most interest and construction was a small, relatively inexpensive, earth-moving device known as the Fresno Scraper. Often identified as the single most important invention to shape the future of agriculture in the valley, the scraper arrived at the cutting edge of innovation by an unusual route. Look at the vintage photographs of early canal construction, and in many cases, the famed scraper will be in the center of things.[3]

The Fresno Scraper greatly reduced both the labor and time required to dig some of the first canals. With a team of horses or mules, a farmer could move large quantities of earth and dig his own irrigation ditch. Once the grade was established, a plow would be run along the proposed route to loosen the soil. The scraper would go to work, gathering the loosened material and then dumping it at a selected point to form the bank of the ditch. By any measure of the day, the scraper represented true progress.

Like many other inventions, the Fresno Scraper was born out of the collective talents of several pioneers, spearheaded by Frank Dusy and Abijah McCall, who got

Valley farmers pioneered the development of many agricultural implements in the late 1800s, including this mule-drawn grain harvester. Author's collection

together in the blacksmith shop of McCall's ranch near Selma trying to meet the new challenge. Dusy was something of a Renaissance man, a leading stockman and visionary with numerous talents. Historians believe McCall envisioned the scraper while he was building one of the first improved roads from the valley to the mountains, a road that would one day bear his name. When he next turned to the construction of the Kerby Canal near Selma, he met Dusy, who was involved in a similar task on the Fowler Switch Canal. Facing a common problem, they began discussing more efficient ways of moving the soil. Soon they began improvising a prototype scraper, never realizing they were about to change the face of the valley and many places around the world.

While an early scraper known as a "slip scraper" had been used in the Eastern states, it was ineffective in moving the large volume of earthen materials needed for canal construction in the West. Even before Dusy and

McCall completed their prototype model, one Henry Hawn had fashioned a "buck scraper" that claimed to be able to move a cubic yard of soil at each pass; however, the device came up short in several other ways.

Another lesser known pioneer, W. H. Shafer, often recognized as one of the giants of canal and irrigation construction, witnessed the development and contribution of the Fresno Scraper. In a 1944 newspaper interview, he gave the following account:

> **Dusy was given one-half interest in the scraper idea for money to secure the patent, which cost about $150. The first scraper was originally designed to be 8-feet-long, but this proved too large for six horses and two small for eight horses, it was later cut to 6 feet and still later cut to 5 feet, the size of the present scraper.[4]**

While some historians credit W. H. Dedrick of

The famed Fresno Scraper paved the way for thousands of irrigation canals—and the eventual demise of the river that nurtured its creation. *McHenry Museum*

Selma for the design of the first scraper, Shafer maintained that Dedrick only modified the device which Dusy had brought to his blacksmith shop because it was better equipped to make the changes Dusy and McCall wanted. Nevertheless Dedrick filed a subsequent claim upon the modifications, much to the dismay of Dusy and McCall.

In 1886, a year or two after the two had obtained their patent, McCall died, at which time Dusy sold his rights to James Porteous, an inventive Fresno blacksmith who was then making a similar earthmover. A man of many talents, Porteous made still further improvements to the scraper, and its popularity took off. In time, the scraper and the donkey steam engine became the backbone for Porteous' Fresno Agricultural Works.[5] Through the years, thousands of scrapers were built under license at locations around the country.

With an army of Fresno Scrapers working together, Henry Miller demonstrated what could be done in the way of digging ditches. In 1896, he built the Outside Canal from the Mendota Pool north, which led to the construction of the Outlet Canals. The building of the Parallel Canal in 1905 doubled the volume of the Main Canal. As his expertise in canal construction and operation increased, Miller organized canal companies, and in so doing, managed to control the water distribution for thousands of acres of farmlands around Los Banos.

As had the emerging number of irrigation districts, the Fresno Scraper served the early water users well.[6] Besides building canals and roads and grading farmlands in the valley, the scraper left its mark around the world. It helped dig the Panama Canal and carved rail beds in Syria, South Africa, India and the Far East.[7] When a railroad was needed to build the giant Big Creek hydroelectric project in the upper San Joaquin River canyon, once again the ubiquitous Fresno Scraper led the way. It saw service in digging the trenches and tank fortifications of World War I. It also played a leading role in the great reclamation projects of the Southwest. Ditches, dams and mountain roads appeared in its wake, aided in no small way by a lot of mule power.

Porteous would go on to develop forty-six other inventions, nearly all of which centered around farming equipment. All together he held over two hundred patents, including the vineyard weed cutter, a raisin stemmer, a five-gang plow, a raisin grader, a raisin and fig press, a cultivator and vineyard brush burner. His company's steam powered donkey engines also played a key role in logging the timberlands of the Sierra.

Ron Goble, former farm editor of the *Fresno Bee,* noted that it was ironic that the one implement Porteous didn't invent, the Fresno Scraper, was the one which brought him the most fame. Goble explained:

> **In the days when horsepower referred to the four-legged breed, the Fresno Scraper was considered to be on the "cutting edge" of agricultural technology. Even today it is difficult to find a single invention that has shaped agriculture in the world more than this small earth moving device.**[8]

For the power to pull the scraper, the plow and all the other animal-drawn implements of the day, much of the credit goes to a little-known Stanislaus muleskinner by the name of Irwin S. Wright.[9] As far back as 1868, Wright thought up the idea of controlling the big spans of work animals by the use of a "jerk line." His approach was to run a single rein down the left side of the team to a leader animal who was trained to move left or right with one or two jerks of the line, plus any necessary verbal commands—or expletives. In effect, Wright brought new meaning to the words "mule power."

In the forest lands of the upper drainage, mule power and jerk lines enabled the early loggers to get the lumber down to the valley, where it went into ranches, homes, grape stakes and fruit boxes. On the sharp hairpin turns, the mules were later trained to move sideways.

Stockton's Holt Manufacturing Company's Caterpillar ushered in a new era of earthmoving and mechanized agricultural expansion.

There were "leader, pointer and wheeler" mules, and experienced muleskinners had to know each one by name, getting them to move at the right moment to the commands of "gee" or "haw" with the added pull of the jerk line.

The mechanized revolution went well beyond the ubiquitous scraper. Across the fertile plain, huge horse- and mule-drawn ag implements, plows and combines, made their appearance, bringing more mechanized muscle to the farm scene. Their success and innovation, in turn, produced new farms and more ranches—and the demand for even more irrigation. The emergence of California agriculture produced benefits that transcended anything the great Gold Rush had known. It underscored the fact that the real wealth of California could be found in the grain fields, orchards, vineyards and the cattle range. From a regional perspective, much of the mechanized change that enveloped agriculture grew out of Stockton. As early as the 1870s, blacksmiths and boat builders at the port city had recognized the need for improved mechanical devices. Stockton responded and subsequently emerged as a major center of commerce and agriculture, surrounded by a growing number of farms and ranches that had been reclaimed from the deep peat soils of the Delta.[10]

Stockton became the cradle for mechanized farming around 1876, when David Young, heeding a growing call

During World War I, Caterpillar became Stockton's foremost industry and defense contractor. Caterpillar, Inc.

from grain farmers, developed the Centennial Harvester. Capable of harvesting up to fifty acres of grain a day, Young's harvester represented a giant leap forward in the mechanization of agriculture. But there were other movers and shakers waiting in the port city whose inventions would subsequently move mountains, valleys and rivers. In 1863, Charles Holt, a transplanted New Englander, arrived in San Francisco and began supplying wood to the family sawmill at Concord, New Hampshire. Not long after, three other brothers came west and joined the Holt Brothers firm. At that time lumber for the famed Concord stagecoaches was obtained principally from Ohio and then shipped to New England. There the

lumber were cured and shaped into carriage wheels and parts, and then sent around the Horn as completed carriages. Unfortunately, once in service, particularly in the dry climate of the valley, the wood shrank and the wheels fell apart.

Recognizing that the damp climate of San Francisco wasn't the solution to the problem, the Holt Brothers moved to Stockton in 1883 and established the Stockton Wheel Company.[11] The youngest brother, Benjamin, was selected as president. Under his guidance the firm gradually established a reputation for quality and inventiveness. At first, stagecoaches consumed their commercial efforts. But Holt was also a man of vision

When construction of Friant Dam began in 1939, the already familiar Caterpillar was hard at work, rearranging the landscape at the dumpsite. United States Bureau of Reclamation

who could see better ways of improving agriculture and Stockton's reputation as a manufacturing center. From carriages, the firm began making an improved combine to meet the area's grain-growing activities. By 1886, the brothers had assembled their first "link-belt combine harvester" which overcame the inherent problems in their competitor's combines, which were driven by cast iron gears.

Buoyed by this success, the Holts began looking at still other ways to improve mechanized agriculture. Their next success came with the "sidehill combine," whose adjustable mower was particularly useful on the steep hilly slopes of the West Side. Later on, and under special license, the firm also built Fresno Scrapers. But one problem that continued to stymie all of the area man-

ufacturers was the vexing difficulty of working the deep peat soils of the Delta. When wet, the land could become impassable, if not treacherous. Horses working the fields had to be fitted with fanlike "tule shoes" to keep from bogging down in the goo. Even when the first steam-driven tractors came along, they had to be equipped with extra-wide wheels; otherwise they became mired in the Delta's deep soils.

In the early 1900s, Benjamin Holt hit upon the idea of replacing the wheels with a movable track, even though other manufacturers had tried unsuccessfully to develop a similar track earlier. With financial resources to meet the necessary research and development, the Holt firm began experimenting with several models. In November 1904, the company tested its first crawler track on the soft soils outside of Stockton, using a steam-driver tractor. The *Stockton Newspaper* of April 1905 reported:

> **The Holt Company fitted up one traction engine with the new endless chain wheels and sent it down to Robert Island...plowing ground...that has not been burned deeply and where machines could not be operated owing to the soft character of the soil. In a tract where a man could not walk without sinking to his knees and where tule-shod horses could not be used... the new traction engine was operated without a perceptible impression in the ground...**

With this additional success, the company refined its advancement and moved ahead. A year later the Holt Company adopted the trademark "Caterpillar." By this time the Holts had begun to experiment with a new source of power, the internal combustion engine, which was to usher in another giant step for American industry and agricultural technology. In 1908, their Caterpillar tractors made irrigation history when they were put to work in the construction of the 230-mile-long Los Angeles aqueduct. Such an application not only heralded another epic chapter in the development of the "Cat" tractor, but also served as an example of vision and imagination in meeting California's insatiable quest for ever more water.[12]

In 1908, Holt also acquired the Best Company of San Leandro, another pioneer manufacturer of agricultural equipment. This company had developed around Daniel Best, a young Iowan who had come west in 1859 and had turned to farming after striking out in the gold fields. A year later, as the Holt Company fortunes improved, Holt also bought the East Peoria (Illinois) factory of a bankrupt Illinois steam traction company and opened a plant there. The Caterpillar tractor continued to move to the forefront of earthmoving equipment. It posted impressive gains, enabling the company to open additional sales outlets across the country. By the end of 1911, the Stockton plant was the largest employer in town, claiming 625 full-time employees—earning the handsome wage of seventy dollars a month.

The movable track from the Caterpillar tractor went to war in World War I, after the British adapted the Holt track to a moving metal fortress known as a tank. During that time, the level of production gradually moved to the Illinois plant. In 1925, Best's son, who had formed another successful tractor firm, C. L. Best Tractor Company, merged with Holt to form Caterpillar, the giant of the earthmoving business.

Other men and machines played a role in the development and advancement of California and San Joaquin Valley agriculture. Behind the inventors of the Fresno Scraper and the Caterpillar, there followed a long line of visionaries and inventors. For instance, Robert G. LeTourneau of Stockton moved the scraper along the road of progress, supplementing mule power with mechanized horse power, the internal combustion engine.[13] In the 1920s, he began building land leveling and earthmoving machinery, which eventually gained worldwide recognition similar to the Caterpillar. Today, either machine can do the work of a hundred or more field hands.

Through the years, Stockton's strategic location nurtured still other inventions and industry. By the late 1800s, it ranked behind San Francisco as the state's foremost industrialized city, led by agricultural implements and boat building. The huge "clamshells" of the Stockton Iron Works helped reclaim the swampland of the Delta, dredging the sloughs and raising the levees that form the delta and deep water channel.[14] But there was a downside to inventions that came out of the valley. Much like the soils the machines moved and the crops they cultivated, the new technology brought more farmlands into production—lands that required additional irrigation. So it was that the river gave of its liquid and life again and again. Despite their collective abilities at moving mountains and rivers, the likes of the Caterpillar and LeTorneau machines only spawned the need for still more water projects. It is somehow ironic that the machines and muscle nurtured by the river led to its own demise. In 1910, when the world's largest hydroelectric facility got underway at Big Creek, a Fresno Scraper was at the front of the scene. By 1937, when work was begun on Friant Dam on the San Joaquin River near Millerton—by this time the Fresno Scraper had been consigned to the scrap heap—the world famous Caterpillar tractors and LeTourneau scrapers were on the scene and hard at work.

CHAPTER TEN

San Joaquin Hydropower

Of all human forces that shaped the future of the upper San Joaquin River basin and modern-day California, few generated more power than did John W. Eastwood, the brilliant engineer who became the guiding light for hydroelectric development in California during the late 1890s. Perhaps more than any other individual, Eastwood pioneered hydroelectric development in the upper river and "turned on" the Golden State and the nation to the potential of hydroelectricity in ways never envisioned. Again, it was the San Joaquin River which met the need.

Born in Minnesota in 1857, Eastwood had a heritage of engineering and water science that went back to his Dutch ancestors. After attending Minnesota State Normal School at Mankato in 1878, he went to work for the Minneapolis and St. Louis Railroad. After five years at that location, Eastwood heeded the call west and moved to Fresno, accompanied by his bride of a few weeks, Ella Tabor. Here in the fledgling farm community of ten thousand persons, the young engineer set up a private practice.[1]

When Fresno became an incorporated city in 1885, Eastwood was hired to survey the new streets and canals. Eventually he became the city's first engineer—a short-term arrangement that allowed him to continue his private practice. Among his clients were the lumber mills in the Sierra, which were cutting some of the best timber stands in the west. For the giant Fresno Flume and Irrigation Company's mill on Stevenson Creek, Eastwood engineered sawmill equipment and laid out their small logging railroads.

When the first applications of commercial electricity flashed upon the country in the late 1800s, Eastwood became interested. At that time electrical power remained virtually unknown; everything was either man, mule, horse or steam powered. But for all practical purposes, electricity was light-years away—an unknown entity. As late as 1890, no major American city had a unified electric service. The first electrical consumers relied on small, gas-fired, steam generating plants that served a limited neighborhood. Otherwise, they cursed the darkness and relied on kerosene or gas lanterns. Years ahead of his time, Eastwood saw the potential of huge amounts of electricity and what it could do to improve the quality of life. In addition, he reasoned, electric motors could pump water to irrigate valley agriculture. At that time, pumping for irrigation was limited to some crude, "one-lung" diesel motors that were anything but reliable.

Remembering the deep canyons and cascading rivers that he had seen on his earlier trips into the San Joaquin River canyon, Eastwood began making preliminary surveys of elevations and river flows. He soon realized that here flowed one of the great rivers of America, with untold potential for hydroelectric generation. Few rivers provided the "vertical drop" and the volume of water that the San Joaquin afforded. Armed with this information Eastwood then approached several Fresno businessmen, seeking their involvement and financial support for his bold plan. One of those he approached was the president of the Fresno Water Company, John Seymour. After lengthy negotiations in

1893, the two formed the San Joaquin Electric Company; Seymour became president and Eastwood vice president and chief engineer.[2]

Eastwood began preparing detailed plans, while contacting a handful of manufacturers who were pioneering the fabrication of electric generating equipment—the fledgling Westinghouse and General Electric companies. On April 1, 1895, construction began on the powerhouse located on what was then known as the north fork of the San Joaquin River—today's Willow Creek. The thrust of Eastwood's plan was to capture the water where the creek began its rapid drop into the main canyon. This energy would spin the waterwheels in the powerhouse below. The power generated would then be sent to Fresno, about thirty-seven miles away. It was a bold and daring plan. As designed, the project stood on the leading edge of a new technology. By any measure, the young engineer was powering new ground, using pressures and forces that had never previously been considered.

Construction of San Joaquin No. 1 powerhouse moved along rapidly, although the project was not without its critics. Skeptics charged that Eastwood's efforts were too far-out. In particular, they said the "head," that is, the 1,400 vertical feet the water would drop, was too great. It would create pressures of 600 pounds per square inch—far greater than any other existing hydro plant. At that time, the only other hydro projects in the country utilized low-head dynamics of 50 to 200 feet. Others criticized his plan for transmitting the generated power thirty-seven miles to Fresno. Up to that time, the inherent problems of electrical resistance limited the maximum transmission to three or four miles. Eastwood was placing "hope before reason," his critics charged.[3]

As work progressed, several things did go wrong. A consulting engineer—an out-of-town expert—provided a near disastrous touch during the initial start-up tests.

When all was ready for the first test, the water was turned on, but instead of the expected

Hydroelectric pioneer John Eastwood captured the potential of the upper San Joaquin River's generating capacity. Author's collection

smooth operation of the waterwheels and generators, a roaring torrent flooded the powerhouse floor. The German engineer had forgotten to screw into place the nozzle tip inside the wheel housing. Excited and disturbed by the mishap, he touched off an automatic valve which closed the water gates at the forebay and abruptly stopped the fall of the massive column of water in the 20-inch penstock pipe. The resulting shock collapsed the pipe 500 feet above the powerhouse.[4]

Eastwood had not recognized the need for a surge chamber that would absorb the tremendous pressures involved. "In those days everything was experimental and everybody connected with the business was a novice," he acknowledged years later.[5] At the opening ceremonies at the Fresno substation, the delivery of power to the ventilation system sent a noisy cloud of dust and debris over the assembled guests. Thinking an explosion had occurred, the guests bolted for the doors—unconvinced of the promise of invisible hydroelectric power.[6]

Still, Eastwood charged ahead. Within a few months his plant began cranking out power and electrifying much of Fresno. The newly founded *Journal of Electricity* described the project in glowing terms, noting that the rates were "remarkably low." For *$6.45* a month, a customer could use the equivalent of eight twenty-five-watt bulbs—bright by standards of the day—twenty-four hours a day. The favorable rates encouraged several firms, such as Sperry Flour Mills, to locate in Fresno. At the same time, the city's water department converted its steam-powered pump to electricity.[7]

Notwithstanding this promising start, the San Joaquin Electric Company soon ran into unforeseen trouble. Two consecutive drought years started the difficulties; another break in the penstock, along with a lack of backup generating capabilities, created other problems. But the main trouble came from the firm's competitor, the Fresno Gas and Electric Company, which generated power with gas-fired, steam generators. As the competition between the two increased, the gas company made an "end run" on Eastwood's powerhouse by buying the land along his Willow Creek diversion, thereby gaining riparian control of the water his plant required. The gas company then diverted the water down the mountainside to irrigate the hillside brush, leaving Eastwood's plant without power. While Eastwood managed to build a diversion ditch to bring in replacement water, the additional costs and delays eventually forced the San Joaquin Electric Company to declare bankruptcy in 1899.[8]

Both Seymour and Eastwood lost heavily in the company's failure, with Eastwood's loss set at $797,000— a staggering sum in its day.[9] Although devastated, Eastwood remained committed to electrical energy. Within a few weeks he was back in the mountains, older

and wiser, realizing that any successful hydroelectric system would require vast amounts of stored water. For weeks he roamed the wilderness of the upper San Joaquin River, alone and unaided, calculating stream flows and plotting suitable dam sites. He was convinced as to the future of hydroelectricity—and consumed by the desire to build the largest hydroelectric system the world had ever known. Out of these travels emerged what was to become typically Eastwood: bigger and bolder by a quantum measure. His new vision involved a vast hydroelectric system comprised of a series of dams and reservoirs, connected by a network of tunnels and powerhouses where the water would be used again and again as it moved down the mountainside.

> **This was an exploration saga unique in the annals of early power development. With only a string of horses and pack mules to carry his equipment, the indomitable Eastwood alone explored the rocky gorges and watershed of the region.**[10]

As he began looking about for a developer who could implement his new plan, Eastwood turned to William G. Kerckhoff, a Southern California businessman who had become interested in the generation of electrical power. In 1902, Eastwood wrote:

> **It gives me great pleasure to inform you that I have completed the survey for a tunnel line to the junction of Pitman and Big Creek and I can place before you the most remarkable power project yet presented.**[11]

After viewing Eastwood's Big Creek proposal, Kerckhoff turned to two associates, Los Angeles trolley car magnate Henry Huntington and businessman Allan C. Balch—men of substance and "capitalists" of the day. The three had become aware of the growing need for additional power in the southland. Organizing as the Pacific Light and Power Company, they adopted East-

Workers cling to the walls of the San Joaquin River canyon during construction of the Big Creek project in the early 1900s. Southern California Edison Co.

---

wood's plan and placed him on the firm's payroll to prepare final designs. By the time Eastwood's final report was completed three years later, Huntington had emerged as the major PL & P shareholder and was the one who would make the ultimate decision. While the enormity of the project would have dissuaded others, Huntington apparently saw the huge project as a challenge—something that could test his unbridled energies and ego.

The Big Creek project was everything its name suggested, perhaps even more. By the standards of the day it was mind boggling, equaled only by the construction of

the Panama Canal. Mountains would have to be moved. Construction of the interconnected system of dams, tunnels and powerhouses would take years, cost millions and involve countless difficulties. At the onset, hundreds of horses and mules were needed to move the supplies and equipment up the mountainside. For the first two years, a twelve-horse team moved out of the Clovis supply depot every five minutes to meet the initial needs. After taking a second look at their transportation needs, the company called for the construction of a railroad up the canyon, and in 1912 the San Joaquin and Eastern Railroad was born. From a spot north of Clovis, known as

Snow surveyors began ranging over the upper San Joaquin River basin in the early 1920s, trying to determine the potential snowmelt that would be available for power generation. Ed Steen photo

El Prado, a fifty-six-mile standard gauge line was pushed up the river canyon in a record 157 days. Climbing nearly four thousand feet, the railbed had some eleven hundred turns, with some trestles anchored to the sheer cliff of the gorge. Before it was completed, the railroad had earned a dubious reputation as the "SJ&E—Slow, Jerky and Expensive," but it's reputation improved later to "The Railroad that Lighted Southern California."[12]

Before work could be started on the project, however, Huntington and his army of attorneys had to work out an agreement with the inscrutable Henry Miller and others who held the San Joaquin River water rights. Early on, Eastwood had reasoned that some of the staggering costs of the project could be offset by charging downstream water owners for storing the water in the proposed dams. He thought they would find it to their advantage to have evened-out flows as opposed to nature's feast-or-famine deliveries. But not Henry Miller. While the famed land and cattle baron had no major problem with storing the water, it was his by riparian law, and he saw no reason why he should pay for it. For all purposes, the discussion ended there. After going back to their attorneys and bankers, Huntington's forces regrouped. Finally persuaded that the reservoirs could be beneficial, Miller and Lux signed a series of secret contracts with Huntington; these contracts acknowledged Miller and Lux water rights and provided a minimum flow of water as well as late season deliveries in exchange for the right to store water for generating purposes.[13] Only then did the Big Creek project move ahead.

While the Big Creek project was getting underway,

On the south fork in 1926, workers set the forms for the dam that created Florence Lake, the largest of John Eastwood's multiple arch dams. Southern California Edison Co.

Eastwood's former partner, Seymour, had been reorganizing the original San Joaquin Electric Company as the San Joaquin Power Company, which he then sold to Kerckhoff and Balch. They, in turn, hired A. G. Wishon, a Missouri-born real estate agent, who had also recognized the potential of hydro power, as manager. He not only put Eastwood's original plant into good operating condition, but set the groundwork for additional power facilities. Eventually the men entered into a long-term partnership that would make them hydroelectrical pioneers in their own right. In 1910, Wishon reorganized the firm as the San Joaquin Light and Power Corporation, which gradually extended its service area as far south as Bakersfield. Twenty years later the company was acquired as the San Joaquin division of the giant Pacific Gas and Electric Company, which had grown out of five hundred earlier predecessor companies, reaching back to 1905.

As for the Big Creek project itself, Eastwood encountered yet other disappointments. When work was finally begun in 1910, Pacific Light and Power hired the giant engineering firm Stone and Webster Engineering Corporation to guide the project; Huntington felt the project was too big for one man—even an Eastwood. Nor did Eastwood fare any better in his business dealings with the shrewd Huntington. For his plans and water rights, Eastwood received a large block of PL&P stock. But as the project proceeded, assessments were made against those securities. In time, Eastwood was forced to surrender shares to cover those assessments. Eventually, he was left with nothing except the satisfaction that he had engineered the most ambitious hydroelectric project ever conceived by one man—a project that powered the growth and development of the great metropolis of Los Angeles. [14]

In 1917, PL&P merged with the other utility giant, Southern California Edison Company, taking the SCE name. Almost immediately, the enlarged company began expanding the Big Creek system, raising the height of Huntington Lake dams and adding the Florence and Shaver Lake dams to the project. The sprawling Big Creek project was not even finished when SCE engineers began looking at even larger sources of the electrical elixir. During World War I, power demands had so strained the generating capacity that the utility envisioned a series of dam and power plants above Florence Lake on the south fork. Another dam woud be built at Blayney Meadows. At the highest level, it was proposed to dam the outlet of Evolution Lake, raising the level high enough to divert the water into a penstock, which would lead to a powerhouse located in Maclure Meadow below

However, their plans were thwarted when the courts ruled that the utility did not have the right to condemn key parcels of private property in Blayney Meadows. As it developed, land that passed into private ownership under the often-abused Swamp and Overflow Act, served as a barrier to further development in the south fork. In 1950, the Evolution Valley area—the centerpiece of this upper drainage—was incorporated into Kings Canyon National Park, closing the door to commercial development. Today much of the surrounding basin lies within wilderness area, precluding similar development.[15]

To complete the proposed dam on the south fork, the construction firm of Stone and Webster utilized

Southern California Edison Company's Powerhouse No. 8 stands at the junction of Big Creek and the San Joaquin River. Southern California Edison Co.

another Eastwood creation, the multiple arch dam. Eastwood had pioneered this technique back in 1906 with the Hume Lake dam, located in the rugged area east of 9,300-foot Kaiser Pass, realizing that the construction costs of a conventional gravity dam would be prohibitive. Utilizing a series of interlocking, concrete, half-cylinders, Stone and Webster were able to build the Florence Lake dam with only a fraction of the concrete needed for more conventional construction, saving the company the staggering transportation costs of hauling the added material over narrow mountain trails. Completed in 1926, the dam impounded the water that would service

the famed Ward Tunnel, a thirteen-mile conduit carrying the south fork water to Huntington Lake. So successful was the multiple-arch dam that over the years dozens were built around the world, usually in remote locations.

In the 1920s, the persistent Eastwood turned his energies to the neighboring Kings River watershed and began planning another vast hydroelectric project there. But it was not to be. On August 12, 1924, at the age of sixty-seven, Eastwood died in the Kings River—perhaps of a heart attack—while trying to save a woman swimmer, bringing an end to the life of yet another of the great men of the San Joaquin River. Somehow, Eastwood fell through the cracks of history. His biographer saw Eastwood not as the father of hydroelectrical power generation, but as the man who designed and engineered "The Ultimate Dam."

John Eastwood's concepts were unique, the scale almost boundless. They were fitted to the environment in which he was placed, the great land masses of the western United States. Everything he successfully accomplished, either personally or by others following his plans, foreran the times in dimension. This list is long, extending from the multi-phase high voltage transmission line to the first high dam built in Canada.[16]

In the period after World War I, SCE realized how imperative it was to know the amount of water that would be available each year. While Eastwood had measured the stream flows, the company needed to better know the amount of snowmelt that would be available for power generation, recognizing the fickle nature of Sierra winters. Indeed, water was money. SCE then hired a team of hydrographers and stream gaugers to make field measurements during the winter and spring months. At their heyday in the 1920s, twenty men were stationed at nine primitive camps in the San Joaquin River headwaters, below the Minarets, measuring the snow depths and calculating the stream flows.

One of these pioneers, Edward P. Steen of Fresno, spent several long winters at the Iron Creek gauging station on the north fork, working with two other hydrologists to measure the snowfall and runoff. Snowbound from November through May, the gaugers led isolated lives of hardship and privation, making bimonthly surveys of distant snow courses and stream gauging stations in the upper basin. Years later, Steen recalled:

We faced life and death situations almost every day; it was difficult and demanding work,

often under most trying conditions. Somehow we were never caught up in an avalanche.[17]

One of their ranks, Orland Bartholomew of Big Creek, achieved a small measure of greatness during the winter of 1928-29 when he spent ninety-two days, alone and unaided, skiing the crest of the Sierra from Cottonwood Pass on the south to Yosemite Valley, a journey mountaineers have described as the greatest ski adventure of all times.[18]

Eventually other dams were added to the Big Creek system. In 1925, work was begun on a new Shaver Lake dam, inundating one of the largest sawmills in the Sierra. More tunnels and powerhouses were added. After World War II, Mammoth Pool and Lake Thomas A. Edison were added to the system, providing even more generating capacity. When completed in 1929, the system had a total generating capacity of 4,218,000 kilowatts, the largest in the world. It was a hydroelectric system of superlatives that powered the spectacular growth and development of Southern California. With its integrated network of reservoirs, tunnels and powerhouses, the recycled or reused waters of the Big Creek project sustained the slogan that the San Joaquin River waters were, indeed, the "hardest working waters in the world."

Through the years, power development within the great chasm has continued to grow. In the wake of the 1973 Arab oil embargo, the Jackass, Chiquito and Granite creek projects reemerged on the west side of the river, but have not yet been built. The Balsam Meadow project was completed in 1988. Today a combined SCE and PG&E network of nineteen dams and twenty-seven power plants crank out approximately thirteen hundred megawatts— enough electricity to power more than a million California homes. Within the San Joaquin River basin, that is, from the Mokelumne River south, approximately sixty dams and numerous power houses, including the vast Hetch Hetchy system, add even more power. It's the kind of power only John Eastwood could dream about— and only the San Joaquin River could produce.

CHAPTER ELEVEN

The River Betrayed

On August 8, 1951, the Friant-Kern Canal came to life as San Joaquin River water from Millerton Lake was diverted into the man-made canal, marking the completion of the ambitious Central Valley Project. A ten-day celebration accompanied the first diversion.

The *Fresno Bee* reported:

The largest crowd of any which has yet gathered along the 500-mile stretch of the CVP viewed the proceedings last night as the 153-mile Kern Canal formally was dedicated as part of the massive Valley reclamation project.

Thousands of persons lined Millerton Lake behind Friant Dam as the southernmost link in the engineering miracle, which the CVP is integrating into its overall operation, amidst fireworks, fanfare and speech making.[1]

Although water from the project had begun moving into the canal several weeks prior to the official dedication, enthusiastic crowds hailed the flow of water as it moved down the canal. Many saw the diversion as a new day—a new age of enlightenment and opportunity. At Orange Cove, for example, city fathers predicted arid sections would blossom with the arrival of water. At Lindsay, the high school band sounded an upbeat note as a long line of community leaders and politicians pontificated about the wonders and wealth the new water would bring. The following day in Bakersfield, at the end of the canal, Governor Earl Warren, a home town boy

who had made good, gushed on about the great things the transplanted water would bring.

For many of those who cheered the opening of the canal and the arrival of transported water, it was a day of celebration. But for the San Joaquin River, it was the beginning of the end; it was the day the river died. From that day on, 98 percent of the river would be diverted to distant lands that never had any water. By some convoluted way, it was death by strangulation. Yet few of those involved mourned the river's passing, nor could they foresee the environmental disaster that the project would bring.

In some respects, the river's demise had been ordained; the river's requiem is inextricably tied to California's unending but consistently controversial quest for more and still more water. Ever since the first European man arrived on its banks, the San Joaquin River had given of itself—sparingly at first—but then more and more. The Indians, the Spanish explorers and conquerors—like Gabriel Moraga—posed no serious threat to the river; they seldom took more than they or their horses could drink. And while the early trappers devastated the beaver populations, therefore altering the ecosystem, they left the river alone. The next wave of newcomers, the Mexican land grant settlers, also used the river to sustain their free-ranging cattle, but otherwise left the waterway to itself. However, the gold miners and the early loggers were something else; they silted and fouled the river. Then came the first farmers, dry-land farming at the onset, but turning gradually to irrigation, with one

California Governor Culbert Olsen and Interior Secretary Harold Ickes spoke at the onset of construction of Friant Dam, November 9, 1939. Fresno Bee

ditch following another. The likes of Henry Miller and his "digs me a ditch" refrain was repeated over and over.[2]

As irrigators and extractors, the early settlers brought an inordinate thirst to the scene. Some, such as Henry Miller, soon recognized that those who control the water also control the wealth. Water represented life and livelihood, vital to all. Shortly after statehood, and not long after California adopted the controversial riparian doctrine, the legislature attempted to face the larger problem, that is, the feast-or-famine dimension of its water supplies. To that end, a new surveyor general was ordered to prepare plans "for improving navigation, drainage and irrigation water" on the major rivers of California.

With the fledgling state struggling for legitimacy and credibility in that formative period, little was done. However, during the winter of 1861-62, the Great Flood year, the problem restated itself in very devastating ways. A few years later, the Great Drought of 1864 underscored the other side of the equation. Over the years, the continuing feast-or-famine scenario was played out again and again. The flood of 1867 was eclipsed only by the back-to-back drought years of 1868 and 1869. Once again, the legislature was deluged with pleas for assistance, not only from farmers and settlers, but also from riverboat operators who found it increasingly difficult to move up either the San Joaquin or the Sacramento Rivers without hitting a sandbar or other obstructions.

By 1940, work on Friant Dam was well underway, with only a handful of people aware of the dam's ultimate impact on the future of the San Joaquin River. United States Bureau of Reclamation

By the end of the 1860s, California water problems had assumed such proportions that even the federal government was forced to take notice. Farmers expressed concerns over irrigation supplies and emphasized the need for better, wiser and more efficient use of the state's limited water resources. President Grant's 1874 report brought other forces to bear. A subsequent study, authored by Lieutenant Colonel B. S. Alexander, outlined a comprehensive system of irrigation canals for better utilization of the water coming out of the Sierra.[3] While the plan was never implemented, it helped sow the seed of an even bolder plan, which some water historians

claim was the evolution of the Central Valley Project. It also signaled the first federal intervention in the water problems of California.

The 1870s were highlighted by several major controversies, including the siltation caused by hydraulic mining, along with a growing number of lawsuits over riparian water rights. Other forces were also at work. In 1878, William H. Hall, the first state engineer, ordered yet another study in an attempt to find ways of improving irrigation, drainage and navigation on the Sacramento and San Joaquin rivers.[4] Fresh from his involvement with the West Side Irrigation District, Hall had developed an

A large crowd turned out in June 1944 to witness the first diversion of Friant Dam water into the Madera Canal. Fresno Bee

intimate knowledge of the valley water problems and began looking at projects that would help meet the needs of a growing valley.

The passage of the Wright Irrigation Act and the floods of 1881 and 1889-90 also kept the water issue center stage. The passage of the Reclamation Act of 1902 brought even more national attention to the water problems of the West. During the dry years, the competition for water often became heated. Water law came to mean something other than riparian doctrine. Reported one Fresno newspaper in 1896:

The shortage of water this season has left some of the canals dry; and a number of shotgun guards, it is said, are required to protect the headgates and dams of the companies that are getting water.[5]

While irrigation represented a growing concern, the thrust of the larger water management scene emphasized flood protection, navigation and then irrigation. But it was not until after World War I that the state finally got back to taking a serious look at the problem. By that time, orchards, vineyards and farmlands had fanned out across the land, further solidifying the valley's reputation as "the food and fruit basket of the nation"—but also underscoring a growing dependence on irrigation and the need for assured water supplies. Yet the up-and-down San Joaquin River and the other major rivers continued to flow their fickle way.

Finally, in 1919, Colonel Robert Bradford Marshall, the chief hydrographer of the United States Geological Survey, submitted a "Marshall Plan" to the governor of California.[6] It was an ambitious plan, centered around moving surplus waters from the northern Sacramento Valley to the water deficient areas of the San Joaquin Valley. His plan envisioned a series of storage reservoirs on the major tributaries, linked by an integrated system of canals that would line the rim of the valley and even out the cyclic flows.[7]

The dry years following World War I again accentuated the problem. In the San Joaquin Valley, an estimated twenty thousand acres of crop lands were withdrawn from production.[8] Downstream in the Delta, the reduced flow devastated the water quality of Suisun Bay. At Pittsburg, for instance, salinity soared to 65 percent; by 1926, both Pittsburg and Antioch had to cease using the bay for the domestic water supply. Delta farmers, who had been pumping from the adjoining sloughs and waterways, soon realized they were irrigating with poor quality water, thereby threatening the future productivity of their lands.

The problem only prompted more reports and studies. A solution was needed. In the decade following 1925, no less than a dozen major studies were made of the valley's water problems, each one pushing the project forward. Foremost of these, the Central Valley Project report by State Engineer Edward Hyatt, evolved as a legislative act which was approved and signed by Governor James Rolph, Jr. on August 5, 1933.[9] Among other things, it established a state Water Project Authority, consisting of the directors of public works and finance, the attorney general, the state controller and treasurer. The thrust of their proposal was to move surplus water from the northern part of the valley to the water deficient areas in the southern part of the valley. Their collective charge was "to construct, operate the

Riparian landowner Everett B. Rank led the epic Rank vs. Krug *lawsuit, trying to stop the diversion of San Joaquin River water to distant lands.* Everett B. "Bud" Rank, Jr.

system of works for the development and distribution and sale of water and electric energy."

The $170 million price tag of the project was to be met by revenue bonds, along with some ill-defined participation from the federal government. However, the proposed hydroelectric generation from the project soon generated its own fireworks. The prospect of government generated electrical power triggered a storm of protest, orchestrated in no small way by Pacific Gas and Electric Company. The giant utility, along with other opponents, railed against the bill, raising the specter of socialism or something abhorrent to the American way of life. Long before the first shovel had been turned toward construction, the project was generating megawatts of rhetoric.

There were many other high voltage forces at work in the 1930s, none of which was more jolting than the economic fallout from the Great Depression. In California the nightmare was exacerbated by the storm of refugees from the Dust Bowl of Oklahoma and Arkansas. Economic malaise ruled the land. Any public works project that would pump money into the economy was viewed as inherently good and a true measure of progress. "Good-ole-boy" politics also ruled the statehouse. Boosterism became the byword of the day. Notwithstanding, a referendum was invoked against the bill, forcing a special election. By a narrow margin of only thirty thousand votes—439,368 to 409,977—the state water project was approved in December 1933.[10]

Governor Rolph, who had pushed the project, ordered an immediate effort to sell bonds and get the project underway as soon as possible:

California has voted and tells the nation that after 50 years of hard effort and an expenditure of $1,500,000 of the people's money it declares that it favors the mighty water and hydroelectric project that will bring the lands of California to normalcy and place the surplus winter water on the lands instead of permitting it to flow to the sea.

The great Central Valley Water Project has been approved despite the unfortunate short-sighted and bitter antagonism of interests and persons who have not hesitated to distort the facts regarding this 'great prosperity project.'

Now we shall go to Washington as a united state and push the application for $170 million to harness the winter waters of our state and restore prosperity to parched lands which have become barren and are reverting to nature on account of receding water tables.[11]

However, the state's effort to sell the bonds at the height of the Depression was to no avail. But with both President Roosevelt and Congress seeking measures that would provide some relief to the economic havoc of the day, the federal government soon picked up on the project. On April 8, 1935, Congress hesitantly accepted the CVP project by approving a $4.2 million Emergency Relief Appropriation Act. Roosevelt regard the CVP as a jobs program and signed it in short order. A few months later, the U.S. Bureau of Reclamation adopted the development and within a few months bureau engineers began the staggering task of reexamining the state plans, preparing preliminary designs and then detailed plans for the massive water plan. Along the way, the proposed Friant Dam grew to embrace a reservoir with 520,500 acre-feet, more than 25 percent larger than the original state facility.[12]

Among other things, the Emergency Relief Appropriation Act called for the construction of Shasta Dam on the upper Sacramento River, the Delta-Mendota Canal, a Contra Costa Canal, Friant Dam and the Madera and Friant-Kern canals. As the plans for the project unfolded, most of the major newspapers of California jumped aboard the bandwagon and fueled the fires of enthusiasm; along the way they left their professional responsibilities in the ditch. None of the newspapers questioned the issue of water rights when water was diverted from one watershed to another. No hard questions were asked. Those who questioned the impact of the project on fish and wildlife were often maligned or defamed. Nor did any of the journals address the enrichment of a few at the expense of the many, the endless litigation, or the agricultural wastewater problem and, perhaps, the ecological demise of the valley itself that would result from the death of the river.

Of all the state's major newspapers, only the *San Francisco Examiner* looked closely enough to see that as designed the project would kill the San Joaquin River. Newspapers were not the only ones to shirk their public trust responsibilities. The Department of Fish and Game blithely ignored the prospects of what the CVP would do to the fish and wildlife in the affected area. And no one considered the potential environmental impacts from the project to the bay itself. Yet the journalistic hyperbole

Friant Dam and Millerton Lake, along with the Friant-Kern and Madera canals, sealed the fate of the free-flowing San Joaquin River. Author's collection

---

continued to flow, with proponents dangling the carrot of twenty-five thousand new jobs and a new era of prosperity for the valley.

The news columns of the *Sacramento Bee,* the flagship of the McClatchy Newspapers, gushed:

> **A new era of prosperity dawns for the San Joaquin Valley for with the completion of the Central Valley Project the fondest dreams of man will be realized. Already the initial steps have been taken on this $170,000,000 irrigation and**

> **power project, which is destined to play so big a part in the future growth and development of this section of California.**[13]

Whenever a dissenting voice appeared on the scene it was quickly denounced by the press and other project proponents. For example, when W. A. Beard of Marysville, a former official with the Sacramento Valley Development Association, described the CVP as an "stupendous land speculation" he was quickly denounced and chastised.[14]

On February 19, 1937, the first shovel of dirt was turned at Friant as workers took the initial steps toward constructing the giant dam twenty miles northeast of Fresno, under the guidance of the Bureau of Reclamation. Construction of the largest irrigation system ever to be envisioned by man was underway. Seven months later, four hundred miles to the north on the upper Sacramento River, work was also begun on Shasta Dam, Friant's big sister and the "northern arch" of the massive CVP.

Thousands of workers flocked to California looking for work. As work progressed, word of a "revised" or modified bureau plan began filtering down. One of the early deletions was the power generation from Friant Dam. Fears of socialism and other perceived threats forced the government to drop plans for power generation from the dam. But a more ominous rumor surfaced over the bureau's plan to divert the river flows into the two canals that would come out of the dam. In early 1938, two hundred affected property owners between Friant and Gravelly Ford gathered to protest the rumored "closing of the San Joaquin River" under the bureau's revised plan for the Friant unit.[15] Organizing at Kerman, the group raised the first major objection to the Friant unit of the CVP by unanimously adopting a notice of protest which stated:

Those who originally bought lands on the river did so with the twofold idea of assuring themselves an adequate supply of water for any emergency and having the privilege and pleasure of living and raising their families in a homestead along a river. This deep-seated sentiment for a river has been noted in all of man's recorded history.

The original Central Valley Water Plan, as passed by the state, legislated and approved by the people, provided for a hydroelectric generating plant at Friant and the passage of sufficient water through the plant to maintain a regular flow of water in the San Joaquin River, as well as supplying electric energy for the Valley. We believe this plan should not be changed to permit the grabbing of all the water in the San Joaquin River by people who purchased land that did not have an adequate water supply. This is manifestly unwarranted and unfair to those who through foresight bought land with adequate water.[16]

Gradually, the bureau was besieged with letters of concern from a growing number of water users and their elected officials. In response, a long line of bureau officials began making their way to the area, trying to address those concerns.

On February 27, 1942, before a Fresno audience, Walker R. Young, the bureau's assistant chief, tried to allay the fears of the downstream water users. He responded by repeating what was to become a familiar refrain:

A negotiation committee has been appointed to deal with each of the 215 landlords on both sides of the river from Friant to Gravelly Ford. These lands will be affected in varying degrees by project operations. The San Joaquin River is to be maintained as a live stream wherever water is to be taken from it. All the river people will be treated fairly and squarely. It is gratifying that is has not been necessary so far to litigate water rights for the project, and I sincerely hope we can continue to reach amicable agreements in all our negotiations.[17]

In less than a decade, however, nearly all of Young's predictions and promises were proven wrong, if not deliberately false. Despite some delay from material shortages caused by World War II, Friant Dam was completed in 1947, about three years ahead of either the Friant-Kern or Madera canals. As the bureau began storing water behind the dam—even before the diversions were made into the canals—the lawsuits got underway.

In September 1947, Everett G. Rank of north Fresno

and a dozen of his neighbors brought suit in the Fresno County Superior Court against Secretary of the Interior Julius Krug, seeking to halt the diversion of the water to areas not riparian to the river.[18] The farmers organized as the San Joaquin River Riparian Owners Association and secured the legal counsel of Claude L. Rowe, a Fresno attorney and former city attorney. In time, they were joined by a thousand other downstream landowners and the City of Fresno. The suit was soon transferred from the Fresno County Superior Court to federal court—on its way to becoming the longest running lawsuit in the history of the federal court system, embracing sixteen years of litigation.

Rowe argued that the federal government had no right to divert the state's water without a permit, even though the federal government had paid the one major riparian landowner, the Miller and Lux estate, nearly $2.5 million for its water rights. In April 1950, Federal Judge Person M. Hall issued a temporary injunction against the bureau's diversions. The bureau then defied the injunction and began reducing the flow into the downstream channel as they began the first water diversions into the Madera Canal. Within a year, the downstream farmers and water users saw the river drop and then heard their pumps sucking air as diversions into the Friant-Kern Canal got underway. The San Joaquin River had been strangled and diverted from its natural course.

As the lawsuit proceeded, the experts finally got around to taking a more critical look at the CVP. What started as a trickle became a torrent as a long line of experts began surfacing, pouring out the failures of the Friant unit of the CVP. In 1952, Dr. George E. P. Smith, a consulting engineer from the University of Arizona, levied the most critical charge. He testified that almost everything was wrong with Friant Dam, which he described as the "keystone of the arch" of the CVP—but "an arch which failed." Foremost of his criticism was that the dam was too small, that is, its storage capacity at 520,000 acre feet was insufficient to accommodate the erratic flows of the San Joaquin River. Furthermore—

and most damning—the dam had also been built at the wrong location. If it had been built six miles upstream, it would have been able to provide sufficient carry-over storage for years, rather than a few months—and provide some minimum downstream flows below Gravelly Ford. As Smith put it:

> **The Friant Dam itself should never have been built. The Temperance Flat dam site and reservoir site with storage capacity of an excess of 1,800,000 acre feet located only six miles farther upstream are much better. Allowing for damage to (PG&E's) Kerckhoff Power House which could be rebuilt nearby, and a small loss in power output, more than compensated for by the new dam, the Temperance Flat project's cost would be quite comparable to that of Friant Dam.[19]**

But in February of 1956, in a decision that shocked the Bureau of Reclamation, Hall ruled that the federal government was illegally storing water behind the dam for which it had no title. In effect, the bureau had stolen the state's water. The district court's decision involved 263 separate rulings, the greatest number ever decided in a single federal case to that time. The judge's ruling came at time when the bureau was planning to reduce the downstream flows even more; Hall ordered the agency to construct a series of small impoundment dams that would provide water for agricultural pumping to the adjacent farmlands.[20] But the case did not stop there. In the other related lawsuits, the court ordered various kinds of relief or compensation for those downstream landowners, including the ranchers and duck hunters who had lost their beneficial uses of the river. In an out of court settlement involving the Hollister Land and Cattle Company, which held that they had lost their groundwater due to construction of the dam, the bureau was ordered to deliver annually 50,000 acre feet of CVP water to their grasslands.[21] This became the water supply for the Grasslands Water District, a 50,000-acre duck club.

Soon after Hall's ruling in *Rank vs. Krug*, the bureau

not only appealed the decision to the Ninth Circuit Court, but also applied to the state for the necessary water rights permit—with the point of diversion at Friant Dam. However, there the water plot thickens. By then the California Department of Fish and Game finally realized what had happened to the fishery—its mandated responsibility. Hurriedly the department protested the bureau's application, hoping to gain some leverage for the devastated downstream fishery. Instead, the department ran into an earlier 1951 opinion by then state Attorney General Edmund G. Brown, which held that the federal government was not required to preserve the fishery below the dam, because the primary purpose of the dam was not for fish but rather for irrigation.[22]

In a controversial 1959 decision, that has become known as D-935, the state water board denied the DFG protest, thereby legalizing the bureau's claim to 2.1 million acre feet of the San Joaquin River, more than the river's average annual production. However, DFG again protested that decision, claiming the board had been influenced by the irrigation lobby. When DFG Director James C. Fraser attempted to obtain legal assistance from the attorney general's office, he found numerous obstacles and objections coming from the governor's office—then occupied by the same Edmund G. Brown. Working on his own, Fraser managed to locate a retired San Francisco lawyer, Wilmer Morse, who though inexperienced in water law, agreed to handle the case at a minimal fee.[23] As Fraser related:

> **Unfortunately our intent to file the appeal leaked out and the water interests became concerned. A few days before the deadline for filing it we became aware of some rumblings in the U.S. Bureau of Reclamation and the irrigation lobby. We completed mimeographing the appeal document the day before the deadline and all systems were 'go.' It was either the evening before or early the morning of the deadline, when the Governor's office called our attorney at his home and ordered him not to file the appeal. He called**

> **me on the telephone the morning of the deadline day. I was furious as well as heart broken.[24]**

In effect, the felony against the river had been compounded.

Finally, in 1989, Felix E. Smith, a biologist with the U.S. Fish and Wildlife Service, concluded that "in essence the Bureau had stolen the entire flow and the many beneficial uses of the waters of the San Joaquin River for sale for essentially private uses, profit and benefit." In his subsequent effort to get the government to do its duty, Smith was harassed and threatened with a transfer from his Sacramento post. Now retired, Smith believes the water issues of the San Joaquin River and Friant Dam are fraught with "prejudice, legal abuse, tampering with quasi-judicial proceedings and outright fraud." [25]

Smith pointed out that when the CVP was "reauthorized" in 1954 to bring it into compliance with federal law, the U.S. Fish and Wildlife Service wanted to support the DFG before the state water board. However, a gag order was placed on the service by the Bureau of Reclamation, which felt such releases "would be catastrophic" for the CVP. Once again, the system—the government—had failed the river.[26]

In 1962, the Ninth Circuit Court of Appeals, which had been hearing the bureau's appeal of *Rank vs. Krug*, ruled that the issue was an administrative one and not subject to a judicial determination. At that stage both the city and the federal government asked the U.S. Supreme Court to hear the case. The final blow to the river came in December 1963 when the high tribunal refused to hear the case, ruling that the sovereign federal government had never given its permission to be sued. After enduring sixteen years of courtroom arguments, including some in the federal court, Rank and the downstream water users had been denied their day in court. After making the long trip to Washington, D.C. to hear the expected deliberations, Rank returned home empty-handed—and devastated at the high court's deferral. Within a couple of days he sustained a heart attack.[27]

The San Joaquin River—in the form of the Friant-Kern Canal—begins its 152-mile journey to the distant lands of Kern County.

Little did the Supreme Court realize the implications of their decision. Was justice served? By not addressing the case on its merits, they had, in effect, undermined the basic concept of a nation governed by the rule of law. Their decision could be construed as one where the federal government could do anything it wanted with state's water rights and not be held accountable.

In hindsight, the role of then Chief Justice Earl Warren in the deliberations comes into question. The former California governor and Kern County landowner, Warren had excused himself from the *Rank v. Krug* proceedings. On the surface, such an action on the part of the chief justice would appear proper, based on his Kern County holdings. But why would Warren excuse himself if the court had already decided not to hear the case? Was Warren culpable? By not ruling on *Rank vs. Krug* (by then *Rank vs. Dugan*), the court, in effect, had maintained the status quo as it concerned CVP water deliveries to Kern County, with the direct effect of enhancing property values for all Kern County landowners obtaining CVP water.

The San Joaquin River's fate was sealed. The river had been placed on the block of expediency, only to be denied its day in court. Eventually, the bureau was required to release five cubic feet a second, barely enough to wet the sand into the channel. The hydraulic brotherhood's kingdom was intact.

Other aspects of government failure still dog the Friant project. Efforts to obtain records of the bureau's early decision to take all the flows from the river, as opposed to just the flood flows as in the original state plan, have been unsuccessful. The state's plans to protect the Chinook salmon with minimum stream flows and other facilities were not incorporated into the Bureau of Reclamation's plans for the Friant project. Today a growing number of conservationists look at the river as a tragic failure of government. The fish, they point out, were not the only ones to be denied their day in court; they represent only one portion of a larger ecosystem that has been denied its basic rights. Every living organism from the simplest to the more complex fish and wildlife were impacted by the dewatering of the river. Today, hydrologists and other resource managers generally agree than any diversions larger than 25 percent will inalterably change the environment of any river. In the case of the San Joaquin that figure was essentially 98 percent.

J. Martin Winton, a long-time Fresno conservationist who once headed up the Grasslands Water District, said the San Joaquin River element of the CVP ranks as one of the greatest tragedies to beset California. Just before his death in 1990, Winton warned:

> **Obviously there was a need for flood protection. Certainly there was a need for more water and for better use of that water. But what the Bureau of Reclamation did is a disaster that threatens the future of the entire San Joaquin Valley.**
>
> **The original state plan said they were to divert only the surplus or flood waters. Instead the bureau took all the water from the county of origin and diverted the San Joaquin River waters to lands that never had water. In the process they killed the river. As it is, there are no flushing flows; the channel and the adjacent lands can no longer sustain itself. The water coming through the Delta-Mendota Canal is of such poor quality that it is poisoning the land. If they don't put some water back in the river, we will lose the whole thing.[28]**

Other problems tied to the dewatering of the channel began to appear. Since the construction of Friant Dam, vegetation has invaded the dewatered channel below the dam. Similarly, silt has also accumulated in the relicted riverbed to the point where the stream can no longer accommodate an occasional flow of 7,000 c.f.s. or more, let alone any major runoff. For instance, in the heavy winters of 1986, flood releases from Friant Dam spread out over land, forcing the evacuation of some residents downstream. Recognizing the river's inability to handle high water, the Corps of Engineers went to the Congressional till again and asked for $5 million for snagging and clearing. By the time the project went through the draft environmental review, the cost had escalated to $15 million, with the controversy over the proposed work increasing even more. As a result, the project is now on hold.

The legacy and tragedy of the San Joaquin River goes on. In many ways what happened represents an indictment of government, the failure of elected and appointed representatives to enforce and carry out their assigned duties and protect the public trust.

CHAPTER TWELVE

The River Rearranged

While the vaunted Central Valley Project was rearranging the hydrology of the entire Central Valley, another mammoth project was unfolding in the Delta where the shakers and movers of Stockton were re-plumbing the lower river to create a deepwater channel. From the very beginning of river transportation, the town fathers had recognized the need for improved navigation between Stockton and the upper San Francisco Bay. A deep water channel was imperative, they figured, if Stockton were ever to compete with Sacramento as an inland port. Just as the sand bars and obstructions had limited upstream navigation, the great oxbow turns and meandering nature of the lower San Joaquin River added significantly to the time and distance needed to travel the crooked channel between the Stockton and Suisun Bay, the uppermost inlet of San Francisco Bay.

Much like the CVP, the deep channel dream had an early genesis. Stockton's founding father, Captain Weber, had recognized the need for an improved shipping channel after he had to clear the abandoned ships out of the channel during the Gold Rush. The big hurdle to a dredged channel centered around the mind-boggling costs. As a result, very little was done until 1871, when a group of community leaders got together and founded the Stockton Ship Canal Company. Their collective goal was to improve navigation in the lower river.[1] Even when the first survey for dredging a channel to Venice Island was made in the early 1870s, the cost estimates nearly scuttled the dream. For the initial fifteen miles, the projected cost reached $3 million, stalling any progress for several years.

Nevertheless, Stockton's continued emergence as a marine and mercantile center only spurred additional interest in an improved shipping channel. Boatbuilding has long been part of Stockton's history. In 1870s, the California Steam Navigation gained control over the lower river. In that same decade, the company launched the 823-ton sternwheelers, *City of Stockton* and *Mary Garret*. Down the years other great boats were built along the river, including the famed *Delta King* and *Delta Queen*—boats that have been forced onto other waterways.[2]

Again and again ways were sought to develop a improved shipping channel that would link the city to the sea. During all those initial years, the prospect of deep-drafted, oceangoing vessels steaming their way to Stockton was little more than a dream, clouded by the continuing specter of impossible costs. Much like Sacramento to the north, Stockton had to settle for shallow-drafted barges and paddle wheelers. Shortly after the turn of the century, however, it was proposed that the channel be dredged to a depth of fifteen feet. But by the time World War I had come and gone—along with even larger ships—proponents were left calling for a twenty-four-foot-deep channel.

Finally, in 1925, after more than a half century of talking, the citizens of Stockton overwhelmingly approved a deepwater bond. The measure provided over $1.3 million for acquiring rights of way, dredging and a terminal site. A year later, state and federal support for the project emerged, calling for the improvement of the San

Delta marinas, such as this one, line the Stockton Deep Water Channel, offering a way of life far removed from the original channel. Author's collection

Joaquin River and Stockton. Under the joint financing package, the $8.2 million cost was to be shared by the city, state and federal governments.[3]

At the same time, the townfolks also became aware that they would need an administrative agency—some type of district—to maintain and operate the port. Working with the state legislators, they were able to establish a port district, headed by a five-man board of commissioners appointed by the city and county. Finally in 1928, the first dirt was excavated. In April 1930, the newly organized port district awarded the first dredging contracts, and work on the channel soon got underway. In an age before environmental impact reports, public involvement or dredging permits, the initial work was completed less than three years later. The new channel measured one hundred feet wide and twenty-six feet deep, cutting through eight large oxbow turns. The new alignment trimmed nearly four miles off the natural route, creating the Mandeville Cut and the Venice Cut.

On February 2, 1933, the oceangoing steamer *Daisy Gray* became the first deepwater ship to arrive at Stockton. A week later, the *Peter Helms* made its way to Stockton and off-loaded a mountain of lumber, building even

more support and enthusiasm for the channel. By the end of the year, 166 deep-drafted vessels had visited the inland harbor; the port of Stockton was underway, indeed. Before the channel work was finished, however, the proponents realized that a twenty-six-foot deep channel would be inadequate for larger, deeper-drafted ships coming onto the marine scene. Casting about, the community turned to the federal government once more, asking the U.S. Army Corps of Engineers to deepen the channel to thirty feet. By now, the continuing appearance of ocean-going vessels moving up the river channel only reinforced the port dream. Caught up in the wake of the Great Depression and seeking additional public works projects, the corps responded favorably. During the decade of the 1930s, much of the emphasis was focused on the development of a terminal area, including the first grain terminal, but it wasn't until 1937 that the port turned its first profit.

When the war clouds of World War II cast their shadow over the port, Stockton residents rallied around the man-made inland terminal once more. Most of the port, as well as nearly three hundred acres of surrounding land, were converted to a depository for the Benicia

Efforts to maintain a navigable channel in the lower river began early, utilizing a wide array of dredging and earthmoving equipment.
Newman Museum

Arsenal. Stockton's shipyards also flexed their military muscles, building an armada of minesweepers and smaller craft, further sustaining the area's reputation as an inland maritime center.

In the postwar era, the port added more and more cargo and warehouse facilities and gradually began expanding its operation from agricultural products to the warehousing and distribution of manufactured goods, with the capability of handling dry and liquid bulk materials. As the port's tonnage increased and as the ships kept getting larger, it became evident that a thirty-six-foot-deep channel was needed to accommodate the larger vessels. In 1965, Congress authorized the additional deepening; however, the project did not get underway

until 1968, when it soon ran into the National Environmental Policy Act of 1970. For the first time in over a century, someone had contested the corruption of the river. After considerable delay, the Corps of Engineers let the contract for the additional work in September of 1982, and the dredging of the channel to thirty-six feet began. Again, the river gave way.

Now, 150 years after Captain Sutter became lost in the maze of sloughs and channels, a well-defined Stockton deepwater channel stands in marked contrast. Instead of small sailing crafts, such as Captain Weber's original *Maria*, giant oceangoing vessels now loom above the landscape. Today, Stockton reigns as the largest inland port of California, transshipping some four million tons of freight a year. And instead of taking days—or even a week—the modern mariner can make the Suisun Bay to Stockton segment in about seven hours, adding yet another Orwellian dimension to America's infamous river.

It would be unfair to say that the deepwater channel was not without its costs or its benefits. Down the years, the construction of the channel has also encouraged other developments. Throughout the Delta, the river network provides a vast array of recreation opportunities reaching far beyond the comprehension of the early aborigines. The delta provides over seven hundred miles

What remains of the San Joaquin River enters the Stockton Deepwater Channel near Rough and Ready Island. Author's collection

The port of Stockton has brought new found prosperity to the port city, but the environmental costs of the deepwater channel have not yet been totaled. Author's collection

of navigable waterway in both the channel and the bypassed oxbow turns. Dozens of marinas or resorts have been developed, providing rest and recreation for the inland mariner and sportsmen. However, the deepwater channel has bypassed some of the river's rich and colorful past. Hal Schell of Stockton, an expert on the Delta, believes much of the river's heritage has been either lost or forgotten in the transformation:

The river, the delta have lost much of their identity. It's tragic what so-called progress can do to our history. Very few people have any idea of what has happened along the river.[4]

Despite the ongoing deep channel work in the lower river and the completion of the Friant unit of the CVP, the water brokers were not yet finished. In 1950s, the farmers between Firebaugh and Newman, having seen their riparian lands inundated about three or four times since the construction of Friant Dam, began complaining about the occasional flooding. Even though the Bureau of Reclamation had warned that the construction of Friant Dam would not control all incidents of downstream flooding, the riparian landowners concluded that it was wrong—perhaps "unnatural"—to see these historic swamp and overflow lands covered with flood waters.

Some type of flood channel or bypass was needed, they argued. Pointing to a December 1944 act, Congress had authorized "local interests" to construct levees and channel improvements, at their own expense, to prevent downstream flooding, subject to the approval from the Corps of Engineers, who had the responsibility of maintaining a clear channel.[5] After several unsuccessful appeals to obtain federal funds, the farmers turned to the state. Eventually, through the reclamation board, the state authorized the construction of the Eastside and Chowchilla Bypass System.

Consisting of about one hundred eighty miles of levees and control structures, the huge bypass system runs northward, east of the main channel. At a point about three miles east of Mendota Pool the diversion point was established. Construction began in 1959 and was completed seven years later, terminating just above the confluence with the Merced River. Most of the time the barrier stands high and dry, a monument to man's manipulative ways. During periods of heavy runoff, it is designed so that the control gates can be opened to allow some 5,500 c.f.s to be diverted from the main channel into the upper section, known as the Chowchilla Canal Bypass. Farther down, the bypass has increased capacity, its name changed to the Eastside Bypass, accepting additional floodwaters from the Brenda and Ash sloughs.

The 1944 act also called for federal construction of one hundred miles of levees and flood control work between the Merced River and the Tuolumne River. Again and again the natural hydrology was ignored or corrupted. Greed and ignorance prevailed once more. When asked about the dollar costs of the various projects, both state and federal agencies are hard put to come up with figures. Weighing the benefits of man's intervention against the destruction and degradation of the river is difficult to measure. Various critics from the conservation arena, such as the Audubon Society, Sierra Club and the Bay Guardian, point out that the full costs of these many diversions cannot be calculated. Those answers are hidden in the future and the San Joaquin Valley's ability to sustain its position as the breadbasket of the world. Today that position is in doubt.

CHAPTER THIRTEEN

Fish, Fowl & Fun Along the San Joaquin

When the likes of Jedediah Smith first arrived in the valley in the late 1820s, they were met by a wilderness landscape of unexpected dimensions. The broad valley rolled out to infinity—an endless prairie that seemed more barren and hostile than inviting. It was a primitive land, a wild and wondrous land, alive with fish and wildlife.

In the skies over the valley the waterfowl presented yet another picture of the San Joaquin primeval with huge flocks of birds often eclipsing the very sun. For untold centuries the Pacific flyway had brought in fantastic flights of waterfowl. During the ritual migration up and down the corridor, huge flights of ducks, geese, swans and coots would cloud the sky as they lifted off from the sloughs and ponds of the valley. There were millions of birds.

Even after the first settlers arrived, elk and antelope continued to roam the valley, although they had to avoid the free ranging cattle that moved over the land. Until the 1860s, the common black bear and even a few grizzly bears still clung to remote areas of the ancestral home.[1] A profusion of smaller mammals, coyotes, foxes and badgers, held on, struggling against the human onslaught that was moving across the land.

In the river and riparian areas, the fish and wildlife abounded well into modern times. The river was alive with fish: salmon, sturgeon, and perch, contributing to the fabric of biotic diversity that thrived for many years after man's arrival. From the very beginning, the fish and wildlife provided a measure of sustenance to the pioneers.

For example, fish could be caught with ease. One early Dos Palos settler boasted that his family had lived on fish for the first six months after its arrival in the valley; he boasted that he could catch one hundred pounds of perch in a hour—any time.[2]

By that time, of course, most of the original hunters and fishermen, the Indians and their small tule reed boats, had disappeared from the river. Those who had survived in some kind of symbiotic harmony for hundreds of years were, for all comparative purposes, gone also. Only in the upper reaches of the river, above Millerton, did the remnant bands of foothill Indians still turn to the river, fishing and swimming as their predecessors had done for ages unknown. In their place came newcomers who soon changed the face of the landscape, extracting here and there, often looking to the river for life as well as liquid. As the *Fresno Weekly Expositor* reported in 1878:

The San Joaquin River is now running twice the quantity of water than it did at this time last year...The river is full of fish—salmon, trout, suckers, perch, etc... Now is the time for fishing excursions. War is made on the finny tribe with brooms, pitch-forks, hoes and rakes, and a fishing excursion may therefore be said to present a very motley appearance.[3]

From the very beginning, the abundance of wildfowl had not gone unrecognized. In the 1870s, the

In the pre-Friant Dam days, when the San Joaquin River flowed as a live river, salmon fishing reigned as a major recreation and sports activity. Fresno Bee photo

availability of ducks and geese gave rise to market hunting, that is, commercial hunting. Tom Mott, a native of Los Banos and the son of a Miller and Lux official observed,

> In the years from 1870 to 1910, and in some instances as late as 1920, there was a group of men on the west side of the San Joaquin Valley who roamed between Tulare Lake and Newman during the winter and spring months hunting ducks for a living. These men killed large numbers of ducks and geese which were sold mostly on the San Francisco market[4]

According to another early Los Banos resident related to Mott:

> Hunting with animals, especially trained steers that served as blinds, was practiced for years in the Los Banos area. Several of the locals hunted geese from horses or wagon...or hid behind a steer, using the animal as a blind.

In the winter months when the cattle business was slow, the cowboys—many from Miller and Lux ranches—would often join the hunt. Being familiar with the valley, the cowboys knew the spots where ducks and geese would set down. They were also acquainted with the hills west of Los Banos where huge coveys of quail could be hunted.

Some of the hunters in their haste to harvest the birds used large double-barreled shotguns of 6- and 8-gauge. A few blunderbusses of 2- and 4-gauge could also be heard. All of the big guns were muzzle loaders. It was like hunting with a cannon, Mott observed. One hunter boasted that he had killed 191 geese with one shot from a giant shotgun. The slaughter took on various dimensions. In 1878, Perry McDowell, Elisa Manning and S. B. Roundtree of Los Banos hunted quail for the commercial market in the hills west of the valley. In one season the three shipped 950 dozen, or 11,400 quail, to San Francisco. It was a common event until the first game wardens began arriving on the scene in the early 1900s.[5] Another Los Banos hunter, Levy Smith, reportedly killed 147 geese with two shots. During a five month period he had also killed and shipped to San Francisco over nine thousand head of geese and ducks.[6]

One early hunter observed:

There were no game wardens and no hunting law in those days. The ducks and geese were so plentiful that it seemed there was no limit to the number that could be killed. It was slaughter more than sport; for many, the idea was to get as many as you wanted.[7]

Even Miller and Lux got into the hunt. Miller's employees helped the hunters get their bags of ducks to market by hauling great numbers of birds to Merced to be shipped to the restaurants and butcher shops in the Bay Area. The ducks were so numerous that they were destroying great quantities of feed on the company's lands, Henry Miller complained. Wildlife, both feather and fin, posed direct competition to his operations. Waterfowl were not the only targets of the market hunters. Rabbits and squirrels were slaughtered for hog feed. Miller and Lux paid three cents a pound for rabbits and provided the ammunition. The rabbits were hunted in the alfalfa fields and on the levees. The hunters would throw the dead rabbits into rows on the sides of the levees, where a wagon would come through and pick them up. The rabbits would then be taken to the farm where they were thrown into a kettle and cooked with grain, so they could be fed to the hogs. Squirrels fetched seventy-five

cents a dozen plus a bounty of two cents for the tails. "Chippy" birds, meadowlarks, brought twenty-five cents a dozen in San Francisco, while Billy owls fetched a nickel apiece. Except for domestic livestock—which rustlers often took—anything else that ate grass or grain was fair game.

There were lots of antelope in the early days. Sixty or 70 would come to the canal for water. If a hunter shot and dropped one, the rest of the antelope would remain in place. If the wounded antelope got up, then all would take off.[8]

Fishing saw another kind of threat. During the great salmon runs, the fishing was so good that a worried Henry Miller once confided to his workers that he didn't know how he was going to sell beef "when fish could be caught for free." On other occasions, Miller would invite his friends and even strangers onto his land to hunt, hoping they could control the vast number of geese that were eating *his* grass, grass which he rightfully felt belonged to his cattle.[9]

Many of the early ranchers felt that wildlife had no place in the settlement of the valley, and they made sure of it. It wasn't just the big game that disappeared. The badger didn't give up without a fight, but they soon disappeared in the wake of settlement. Many of the other "native residents" lost the battle also, including the once numerous rattlesnake. Flushed from their dens onto the levees with the first irrigation, rattlesnakes posed a major concern for any farmer or worker until they too were eliminated.

In the early days, some of the settlers even put fish on the local landscape as place names. While generic names such as Salmon Slough, Sturgeon Bend and Fish Slough never appeared on the official maps, they remained as popular fishing spots to many of the locals, nevertheless.

Years ago, when the river was a "real river," it served not only as an artery of transportation and irrigation but also as a way of leisure time activity. Just as it had been for the vanquished Indians, the river was the gathering spot

In 1921, Elzy Benson of Fowler thought the San Joaquin River was the best salmon fishery in the world. Benson collection

for many of those early settlers, providing some of the first opportunities for recreation. In the bucolic or comparatively innocent ways of the late 1800s, the river provided escape and enjoyment from the often harsh and hot days of summer. For many, the river banks became the local park—the "R&R" place of the day. During the warm days of July and August, as the river settled down from the spring runoff, it often became a magnet for many residents as they sought relaxation from the long work weeks of the times. At dozens of locations between Antioch and Millerton, families would often gather along the river to picnic, party or do a little fishing. Sunday

afternoons often represented one of the few times when the early pioneers escaped the hardships of the times, and many took advantage of the opportunity. For those youngsters who could escape the never-ending farm chores, the river and the nearby irrigation ditch became the favorite "swimming hole."

In the lower river between Antioch and Stockton, recreational boating came onto the scene in the early 1880s, led at first by small rowboats, but gradually joined by a growing fleet of sailboats. The old timers around Suisun Bay talk about some of the first "houseboats," which emerged in the late 1890s, towed behind small sailboats or square-rigged scows. With such conveniences, sportsmen and their families would often spend several days afloat on the bay or nearby waterways, as the recreational opportunities of the Delta became known. Gradually, Antioch emerged as a retreat for Oakland and San Francisco residents. For several years, Mark Hopkins of railroading's "Big Four," maintained a luxurious yacht at Antioch.[10]

Through the decades, the boating scene continued to change and grow, ushering in powerboating, and, ultimately, the giant marinas and landings that today identify the Delta's multimillion dollar fishing and recreation industry.

Hundreds of miles upstream in the headwaters of the river, another chronology with a recreation bent was unfolding. There, amid the towering peaks and deep canyons of the High Sierra, the river had begun attracting a growing number of hardy tourists and hikers. By 1892, John Muir had helped found the Sierra Club; its early members began seeking the lakes and streams of the Yosemite high country and beyond. That same summer, Theodore S. Solomons and a companion began a five-month odyssey of adventure and exploration in the high country, gradually moving down the spine of the Sierra, pursuing the dream of a high country hiking trail. Thus, twenty-two years after Muir had made his harrowing ascent of Mount Ritter, the two ascended numerous summits in the upper basin, ushering in a new era of recreation and recreation.

A proud fisherman poses with giant sturgeon in the early 1900s. The San Joaquin River once boasted a large and diverse fishery, but water diversions destroyed the river and that priceless asset. Patterson Historical Society

The view from Ritter is not greatly superior to that obtained from the summit of Mount Lyell, but it is different. The southern Sierra is near. The Fresno mountains are spread out as a vast panorama. Ten or fifteen miles to the south is the great trough of the San Joaquin, its irregularities of topography nearly indiscernible on account of the distance; and the country for miles seems a great, rolling Valley. The junction of the main and south forks with the "Balloon Dome" of Professor Brewer seem quite near. Farther to the southwest, through the great depression, the course of the river may be traced upon until lost in the purple obscurity of the foothills; and on a clear day the haze of the San Joaquin plain is a long, yellow spot of the western horizon.[11]

By 1890, the valley itself had changed. While the overflow areas remained grasslands for livestock, much of

the open range was converted to grain fields, orchards and vineyards. In the process, the valley lost much of its wildness and woodlands. At the same time, Miller and Lux officials, having seen their makeshift diversion dams swept away by repeated floods, constructed a timber dam at Mendota, further controlling the river, making the first major impact on the upstream fishery. As progress moved out across the valley in the form of roads, ranches and irrigation canals, a handful of sportsmen began seeing the decline of fish and waterfowl. As the century came to a close, a few observant individuals began speaking out. As one Fresno sportsman lamented in 1898:

The present deplorable conditions of our game fish is due to the failure to prosecute those who disregard these laws. Ten years ago the San Joaquin River was full of salmon, while today not one can be found in that river above the Miller and Lux dam.[12]

State and federal laws were passed banning market hunting and setting game limits. In 1901 a three month duck season was imposed with a daily limit of fifty birds.[13]

But the illegal hunting did not cease overnight. For years, there had been guerrilla warfare between the market hunters on one side and the game wardens on the other. There was talk at the time to "get any man who enforced the law there," Mott added. The market hunting took on lethal proportions April 12, 1910, when the *Los Banos Enterprise* reported a double killing involving a market hunter and a game warden.

By the 1920s, sport hunting had overtaken market hunting. Hundreds and thousands of hunters began sighting in on the waterfowl areas of the valley. Duck clubs emerged. On weekends, the railroad ran special "hunter trains" for Bay Area hunters. Come Sunday evening, the hunters would drift back to the railroad line where they would build bonfires as signals for the train to stop and pick them up. On the return trip, the shooters would pluck their birds, and the success of their efforts could be measured by the depth of the feathers on the floor of the train cars.[14]

For Los Banos, Gustine and the other "flyway" communities, hunting became a major enterprise and commercial venture, trailing right behind ranching. Gradually, the economic benefits of sport hunting encouraged these communities to shy away from market hunting and support waterfowl conservation. Despite the decline in waterfowl in the dry years of the 1920s, duck hunting continued to gain in popularity. By some estimates there were ninety-five large duck clubs in the area during the 1920s, with some having as many as a hundred members. Furthermore, the clubs developed considerable political clout, forcing the state to clamp down on illegal hunting.

Years later, one of the early wardens recalled:

> The limit was 25 and all were able to get limits, and there were also thousands of ducks killed by the unattached hunters, who then numbered more than the club members. There is no doubt that there were more ducks killed in one week than there are now during an entire season. The limit of 25 was easier to get than to get five at the present time.[15]

Duck hunting was out of this world with nine species, the mallard, brown tree duck, pintails, green-winged teal, red breasted teal spoonbill, gadwall, widgeon and wood ducks.[16] Duck hunting wasn't the only aspect of fun and games. In the period between the two wars, recreational use of the river rose steadily. From Suisun Bay to the foothills, the river was a magnet for fishermen and fun-seekers. Dozens of waterfront spots emerged along the river's course. Antioch had its "Bare-Ass Beach." At Stockton, "Malibu Beach," a popular gathering site along the Stockton Channel, turned into the local "swimming hole." On an oxbow along the river near Patterson, John Reis created "Ramona Lake," a fun spot for visitors from Patterson, Newman and Gustine; the small resort offered dancing, fishing and motorboat rentals.[17] The Patterson newspaper reported:

> Local farmers need rest and recreation away from the daily rigors. Hayrides, camping, fishing and boating on the river were popular pastimes.
>
> If the kids could sneak away, the river supplied terrain for frolic and adventure. At the river you could fish, swim, hunt rabbit and other game, or duck through trails which disappeared into the tree line. Of course the children were warned against unsupervised river excursions because at least once a year, someone got sucked under the clear-running stream. The San Joaquin River was a popular swimming hole. The irrigation canals and reservoirs were safer places to swim.
>
> Salmon traveled the San Joaquin, and at low water the town and country folks gathered to spear and club the trapped fish and cart them home in wagons.[18]

Pleasure craft, such as the sleek Patricia, *often piled the river as recreation boomed in the post World War I period.* Newman Museum

Other changes touched the river recreation scene. The internal combustion engine began showing up in power boats in the years before World War I. One of the first pleasure boats to show its motorized wake appeared in the river near Hill's Ferry in about 1910, providing another dimension to river recreation.[19]

In an age before air-conditioning, a shaded spot along the river was the only escape from the oppressive heat of the interior valley—and that's where the people went. At Firebaugh, dozens of family groups often lined the river bank-retreats. At Mendota, the "new" dam completed in 1921 only added to the popularity of that "watering hole." Upstream at Skaggs Bridge Beach, the popularity of the river gave rise to a county park.

North of Fresno, the Fresno Beach emerged as one of the favorite spots, and a trolley line was extended some nine miles from downtown to make the area accessible. To the northeast, Lane's Bridge and Fort Washington Beach emerged as other popular swimming and fishing spots. Farther east and into the foothill canyon, the river continued to draw a growing number of new Californians who came looking for fish and fun.

The first major impact on the San Joaquin River fishery came with the construction of the first diversion dams at Mendota, the so-called "brush dams." This was followed by Miller and Lux's so-called sack dam at Temple Slough, both of which devastated the fall salmon run.[20] The permanent dam at Mendota tightened the noose even more, interfering with the biannual migrations. Until the construction of Friant Dam in the late 1930s, the fishing on the San Joaquin and its maze of sloughs and tributaries had been good. During the spring salmon runs, hundreds of valley residents would be out along the river, trying to gig a salmon. A few more expedient—and illegal—individuals took to using dynamite to blast the deep holes of the river, killing hundreds of fish in the process. [21]

Early Los Banos hunters pose with a day's hunt, 131 geese, a measure of the historic populations of wildfowl. J. Martin Winton collection

Tony Imperatice, a native of Fresno who knew the river long before it was dammed, reminisced:

> The salmon fishing in the San Joaquin River was out of this world. It was one of the finest spawning rivers for salmon. I think the better part of the spawning areas was from about Rouillard's Riffle to where Friant Dam is today. There were hundreds and hundreds of salmon coming up the river. We used to get up on Lane's Bridge and see groups of five, six and seven fish forcing their way up the river.
>
> We also had a boat specially set for salmon spearing. It was equipped with gas lights and reflectors that shined down into the water. Some of the boats had motors, but we put ours in the river and drifted down at night, spearing salmon that were making their way up to the spawning areas.
>
> The salmon looked like silver torpedoes coming up the river. When you first saw them

they were not wild or moving fast. But as they came into the light from the boat, they really took off. If the water was 4 to 6 feet deep, you wanted to have your spear about halfway down, because the salmon came up from the bottom. Of course, when you gigged one, it was quite a task of trying to land it. Often we got into a scrape or some kind of a problem getting them into the boat, particularly if we were in a swift current.[22]

Imperatrice remembered the river as a "special place before it was strangled by man" at Friant Dam. In the shallower stretches of the river, sportsmen and others could often hear the salmon fighting over the boulders and obstruction as they fought their way upstream.

> Up and down the river, the salmon fishing was popular. The people would turn out for the salmon runs. They would go out and camp by the river, and they would picnic and fish. It was a lot of fun, and nobody bothered you. Occasionally, a big striped bass would come up the river—there were very few of them—some were very big fish, often weighing 30 pounds or more—but the salmon were even bigger.
>
> Even in the 1930s, the wildlife along the river was something to behold. In the flood plain there was every type of small animal—cottontails, badgers, coons, coyotes, deer and skunks. Occasionally a mountain lion would even stalk by. All the birds in the world that you could possibly mention, like orioles, blackbirds, killdeers, and quail. In late winter, the geese would come in, I would say by the thousands; they would land on the sandbars and spend the night.

At the onset of the Central Valley Project and the proposed construction of Friant Dam, a long line of expert witnesses, including professionals from the California Department of Fish and Game and the U.S. Fish and Wildlife Service, warned of the dangers to fish and wildlife posed by the huge dam.[23]

The old fishing bridge at Mendota gave rise to many fish stories in the early 1900s. A lot of them were true. J. Martin Winton collection

In its 1949 report to Congress, the U.S. Fish and Wildlife Service warned:

> **If the dam construction proceeds without consideration for such a self-perpetuating natural resource, the state and nation as a whole will suffer a heavy irreplaceable loss.**
>
> **It is essential that a comprehensive program of study be undertaken with respect to the fishery so that a minimum of harm may result, and so that these resources may not be destroyed.**

The USFWS estimated that the salmon harvest on the upper river was approximately 21,000 fish annually, worth thousands of dollars to both sport and commercial fishermen. Even by Depression day dollars of the 1930s, the spring and fall salmon runs were seen as vital to the state's fishery, affecting many of the tributary rivers. Downstream, the counts were placed in excess of 80,000 salmon. In addition, there were other prized fish, including striped bass, large and small mouthed bass, sturgeon, catfish, crappie, sunfish and steelhead. [24]

Dave Selleck, a retired central regional manager for the California Department of Fish and Game, estimated that had the fishery been preserved, it would be a multimillion dollar industry today. In the mind-set of the Depression era, the issue emerged as one of farmers versus fishermen. There was little or no concern for biological diversity and ecology.

According to Selleck:

> **The San Joaquin was probably the finest salmon spawning area in the state. It was a tragedy that we lost it. Back then people didn't care about fisheries, wildlife habitat or conservation. There was no conspiracy. They didn't see the CVP as a problem; but the diversion of the water was a tragic loss.** [25]

To preserve the fishery, the USFWS recommended a minimum flow below Friant Dam of 350 cubic foot second. Despite earlier assurances from the U.S. Bureau of Reclamation that the San Joaquin River would be maintained as a live stream, it was systematically dammed, diverted and then dewatered to its ultimate demise.

Besides the fishery, millions of ducks and geese of the great Pacific Flyway were eventually affected by the project. In 1939, as one of the initial steps toward the construction of the Friant Dam, the Bureau of Reclamation paid Miller and Lux $2.5 million for the water rights to over 98,000 acres in the grasslands area of western Merced County—the heart of the valley's waterfowl area and a prime stopping spot on the Pacific Flyway. While the company continued to provide water to some of its growers within the area, the water available for waterfowl dropped dramatically. From 100,000 acre feet annually before the dam, to 30,000 acre feet in 1951; 20,000 in 1952; 10,000 in 1953; none was provided for the years after. Efforts to get replacement water for the grasslands were unsuccessful. Besides the loss of waterfowl habitat, the depredation to neighboring crops exploded as hungry birds looked to the farmer's fields. However, unlike the fish, the ducks and geese had a few friends—and duck hunters—in powerful positions. In 1944, the Grasslands Mutual Water Association was formed, embracing some 110,000 acres, with about half of

For many valley residents, the San Joaquin River was one long swimming hole—and a source of relief in the days before air-conditioning. Don Cobb photo

that acreage controlled or owned by 139 different duck clubs or livestock companies. Again and again the landowners complaints were voiced. In a 1944 letter to Congress, the association stated:

> **We believe every drop of water in the San Joaquin River should be conserved, but to physically take a river out of one area—killing an untold salmon run, destroying waterfowl… habitat and thereby reducing wild waterfowl populations which belong to all the people of North and South America and driving farmers out of business by removing the water which produced pasture and for cattle—is a program that many of us fail to comprehend.[26]**

The inevitable government studies and hearings followed, but to little avail. In the late 1940s, the Hollister Land and Yellow Jack Land and Cattle companies brought suit against the federal government for the loss of their riparian water uses resulting from the continued diversions. In the settlement which followed, Public Law 674 came onto the books and set up a defined schedule of water transfers, guaranteeing the delivery of 50,000 acre feet of water. About that time, Congress "reauthorized" the CVP to bring the project into compliance with federal law; it specified that water from the project could be used for fish and wildlife once other priorities had been met. After years of neglect and indifference to the beleaguered river, a small victory had been achieved.

Down through the ensuing years, recreation on the river has taken many forms—often going to extremes. In the period after World War II, the Department of the Interior, the administrative parent for the Bureau of Reclamation, Fish and Wildlife Service and the National Park Service, must have recognized the impending tragedy. Millerton Lake gained National Park Service status, only to be "delisted" a few years later, before being picked up by the state Department of Parks and Recreation. Today, the reservoirs in the upper watershed provide a variety of recreational opportunities to a state exploding in growth. In the upper river above Mammoth Pool, a handful of rugged anglers still force their way into the often sheer upper canyon, where the fishing remains out of this world and largely unaffected by the forces of growth.

In 1980, a trio of adventurers led by Royal Robbins of Modesto made the first known passage through the gorge, traversing a canyon that had been touched only at selected locations by a handful of explorers or entrepreneurs. Using kayaks and mountain climbing gear, the three men spent six days fighting their way down the main fork from Devils Postpile to Mammoth Pool Reservoir. Where sheer cliffs prevented progress, they resorted to "big wall" climbing techniques, trailing their kayaks through cataracts and over waterfalls. In all the trio covered thirty-two miles, descending nearly five thousand feet along the way. As Robbins related:

It was a fantastic trip. It made all of the other gorges we have visited look insignificant, including some of those in South America. The grandeur and beauty were unexcelled.[27]

While recreational boating has exploded in the lower river and throughout the Delta, the environmental costs from farm drainage waters have been exceptionally high and will only become higher in the future. Today, health experts warn that eating fish or wildfowl from the lower river may be hazardous to the consumer's health. Not surprisingly, swimming is no longer recommended

in other reaches of the river: there is, in some sections, no water for swimming let alone wading. Nor do people drink from the river anymore. The change that has come over the river basin goes far beyond recreation; it is but one page in the river's demise. The loss fans out over woodlands and farmlands with abuses that signal a far greater tragedy. [28]

According to Imperatrice:

It was a beautiful river than ran clear and cold. In those days it even had a smell of its own; it was a fresh and inviting smell. While something had to be done to control the flooding, it's a damn shame that they had to kill the river in the process.[29]

Forty years after the Fish and Wildlife Service made its initial report, the agency described the river as

A classic case of extreme over exploitation. The San Joaquin River mainstream and all the major tributaries have been dammed, their flows captured, stored and diverted. Stream flows have been greatly diminished—in some cases even eliminated. Much of what is left has been degraded with toxic substances. Stream channels have been straightened, leveed and riprapped. Natural floodplains have been greatly reduced and the lands converted to other, often incompatible, uses. The once vast wetland complex that was nurtured by out-of-bank flows has virtually disappeared in the face of these alterations. Fish and wildlife populations have suffered tremendously as a result.

The San Joaquin basin is host to no fewer than 17 federally listed threatened or endangered species, virtually all of which owe their precarious status to habitat alterations. Many other species have been eliminated from the basin entirely.[30]

Today, conservationists look at the river—the heartland river of the Golden State—and ask why. "How could this happen?" they ask. In the place of a wild or natural river, they see one of the most—if not the most— abused and misused rivers in the nation. It is a river described variously as an "agricultural drain," a "dead river," the "lower colon of California," or, as in the case of the Delta, "where the sewer meets the sea."

CHAPTER FOURTEEN

Selenium, Salts and the San Joaquin River

In the summer of 1980, Gary Zahm, manager of the San Luis National Wildlife Area at the time, knew something was wrong in the sprawling wildlife complex located in the heart of the San Joaquin Valley. As a trained wildlife biologist, he had a premonition that all was not right. Then one of his friends started talking about the disappearance of fish in the San Luis Drain. As Zahm related it:

> For some time he had been catching striped and black bass out of the drain. All of a sudden there weren't fish anymore; that was the first thing. Then I noticed that for a permanent woodlands, there wasn't the diversity of wildlife that one would expect. There weren't any muskrats, bullfrogs or snakes. Those two things convinced me something was wrong.[1]

Subsequent inspection at the nearby Kesterson National Wildlife Refuge added to those concerns; things just didn't seem right. The algae looked different. There wasn't as much waterfowl on the ponds, which had been built at the refuge to store agricultural drainage water from the Westlands Water District. When Zahm looked into the murky water, he couldn't see any fish. Even the ubiquitous cattails appeared sick.

But it was the silence that told of the looming tragedy at Kesterson, Zahm observed. The birds and wildlife were avoiding the national wildlife area. Subsequent and closer inspections in 1982 confirmed his fears, revealing an even more ominous threat. Scientists summoned to Kesterson found dead and deformed embryos in the nests of ducks and waterfowl. Tests of the birds indicated inordinately high levels of selenium. The silence manifested itself in other ways: with the exception of the tiny mosquito fish, there were no fish. It was that gathering evidence of a scenario that would impress the name Kesterson on the national environmental scene. The first day of reckoning had arrived.

Selenium constitutes one of those unique elements. vital to life in small quantities, it can cause toxicity, mutations and even death at higher levels. Its role in human and animal diets is extremely complex and poorly understood. Compounds of selenium find their way into a wide range of industrial and scientific uses. But the presence of high levels of selenium at Kesterson signaled a major turning point in the life of the San Joaquin Valley and modern-day agriculture—a turning point many growers, agricultural and irrigation experts have still not fully comprehended.[2]

The selenium story goes way back. Even before the government built the Central Valley Project, the United States Bureau of Reclamation had recognized that drainage would be a massive problem. For years the early settlers and growers had painted a rather bleak picture for agriculture in the west side of the San Joaquin Valley, compounded by the presence of certain elements or compounds. Selenium, for example, was prevalent in many areas along the western slope of the valley. Furthermore, they also knew irrigation and the existing

The San Luis Drain led to Kesterson Reservoir, known also as the Kesterson National Wildlife Area—and the scene of the 1983 environmental and selenium crisis. United States Bureau of Reclamation

growing practices would leach out huge amounts of heavy metals and other toxins, all of which would accumulate in the agricultural wastewater.

If this were not sufficient warning, history could have been another teacher. The failures of irrigated societies in early Mesopotamia, Syria and the Roman Empire should have served as a warning. Salt and mineral accumulations on irrigated lands have been a recurring problem throughout human history. Egypt did not have drainage problems until the Aswan High Dam was built in 1960s.

Yet the bureau pushed ahead with its West Side expansion phase of the CVP, expanding its project even before the first phase was completed—and without any significant studies toward the drainage problem. Then in the mid-1950s, the bureau eventually recognized that some kind of master drain would be necessary to prevent

additional irrigation water from turning the lower valley into a wet, boggy marsh. Finally, with its 1956 feasibility report, the bureau recommended the construction of a 197-mile-long drain, the San Luis Drain, running from Kettleman City to a discharge point at Dutch Slough, near Antioch in the Delta. A year later the San Joaquin Valley Master Drain evolved as a joint state and federal project, which eventually became the San Luis Drain.

But several things happened along the way. In 1966, Ronald Reagan displaced Edmund G. "Pat" Brown as governor, bringing a sharp turn to state politics and effectively shutting off the tap for state-funded water projects. For several years Brown had been pushing both the CVP and his own State Water Project, going to extremes to avoid controversy—and sidestepping some of his administrative responsibilities along the way. Concurrently, the citizens around Antioch, who had been on the receiving end of river dumping for years, concluded that they didn't want any wastewater deposited in their backyard, and they began telling their state and federal legislators so. In addition, the blooming of the environmental movement of the late 1960s brought additional concerns to the fray. In the larger Bay Area, for example, a host of environmental organizations had emerged and began questioning the wisdom of the drain. As a result, alternate discharge points were proposed, including pumping the wastewater over the Diablo Range to Monterey Bay.

Against this background of events, the state officially withdrew from the San Luis Drain project in 1967. Among the reasons given, Reagan cited the refusal of farmers of the Tulare Basin and the eastside of the valley to go along with a proposed five-dollars-an acre drain assessment; farmers in those areas claimed they didn't have a wastewater problem and didn't need or want a drain.

Despite the state's action—and without an apparent second thought—the Bureau of Reclamation responded by announcing its intentions to push on, without understanding the chemistry of the drain water or a defined discharge point. In 1968 the bureau began construction of the drain, followed by work on Kesterson Reservoir. Located just two miles west of the San Joaquin River in Merced County, the $10 million reservoir was intended to serve as a staging or regulating area for the drain. As designed, the reservoir consisted of twelve interconnected ponds, each four feet deep, covering 1,200 acres of former wetlands adjacent to the river. With work underway, a joint agreement was hammered out between the bureau and the United States Fish and Wildlife Service to operate the reservoir as a federal waterfowl management area, on the premise that the drainage would be good for wildlife. The first flows of freshwater came in 1971, using CVP water from the Delta Mendota service area, enabling a limited bass fishery to become established. But then came the wastewater. Finally, in the late 1970s, monitoring of the wastewater began; these tests were limited to four trace elements—but not for

The selenium debate continues to swirl over the waters of the San Joaquin River. Deformities have appeared in a variety of marine and birdlife.
U.S. Fish and Wildlife Service photo

selenium. At about the same time the funding for the drain dried up, halting construction of the drain north of Kesterson.

The first act of the impending tragedy was just beginning. As far back as 1976, farmers from the neighboring Westlands Water District had been installing drainage tile on 42,000 acres in the northeast section of the district, recognizing that a drainage problem existed. As the wastewater began moving northward, it soon became evident that without a discharge point, the drain was, essentially, a "closed" system. Even earlier, in 1967, conservationist J. Martin Winton of Fresno had warned the government that Kesterson could become a "death trap" for wildlife unless drainage was provided. By 1981, the inflows into Kesterson were exclusively from Westlands drainage water. Then the dead ducks and deformed embryos were discovered. When selenium was identified as the cause, the bureau's initial reaction was one of denial, or of questioning the competency of its sister agency, the United States Fish and Wildlife Service to test for selenium. While some variability in the testing was uncovered, the bottom line came out the same: samples of wildfowl taken from the area revealed significant levels of selenium, posing a health risk.

For nearly twenty-two miles between Gravelly Ford and Mendota Pool, the San Joaquin is a dead river, the site for littering and illegal dumping. Author's collection

Only then did the bureau get around to establishing testing standards for selenium and for other trace elements. Finally, in November 1983, after the state Health Department issued a warning about eating Kesterson ducks, the wildlife service acted, closing the wildlife area to public entry. [3]

By then, the controversy had become so severe that the discharge point and completion of the drain had all but been forgotten. The bureau found its credibility at an all-time low and its public scrutiny at an all-time high. In February, 1985, pressured by mounting complaints, the state Water Resources Control Board jumped into the fray, ordering an abatement and cleanup program at Kesterson. Within a few weeks, the Department of the Interior announced it would close Kesterson. Then a year later, Westlands growers started plugging the drains,

while waging a last minute appeal to the top officials of the Department of the Interior.

As Lloyd Carter, a veteran California activist who has specialized in valley water problems, explained:

The whole thing was a disaster waiting to happen. The more the bureau pushed the project, the deeper it got bogged down.

Kesterson was just the tip of the iceberg. When you look back on what has happened with the various water projects, it represents the failure and corruption of government...It is a tragedy, one that was brought about by ignorance and greed. [4]

Even before Kesterson became a hot spot, the federal irrigation projects had been drawing increased criticism.

In particular, eastern Congressional delegations had grown weary of western water projects which always cost more and which never quite got around to repaying but a fraction of their costs. The vaunted CVP, they noted, had only repaid 5 percent of its nearly $1 billion cost; at the current repayment schedule, it would take two hundred years to pay back the amount invested. And, the repayment rate for building the drain would take about 270 years to repay.[5] Opposition even arose from the members of the farm community which had often been in lockstep with the growers. Now, the more observant farmers realized that a majority of California's growers received no subsidies. The emerging perception of the water lobby as embodied in the "Hydraulic Brotherhood" or the "water mafia" further eroded both Congressional and public support of the irrigation scene.

Another protracted battle also muddied the bureau's reputation, reaching all the way back to the Reclamation Act of 1902. Under the terms of that enabling legislation, a farmer could own 160 acres or less and receive federally subsidized irrigation water. With the arrival of Central Valley Project water, many big landowners experienced a massive windfall. Some, as former refugees from the Dust Bowl disaster of the 1930s, had arrived in California during the height of the Great Depression and managed to acquire unwanted "desert land" at depressed prices, only to see the value soar with the arrival of federal water. While most of the land was controlled by the railroad and giant agricultural corporations, all landowners profited from the delivery of public water to desert lands. Over the years, many of these operators had formed so-called "paper farms"—acquiring leases to thousands of acres— but still receiving subsidized water. Where many other California farmers were paying twenty to thirty dollars an acre foot for irrigation water, those at the end of the CVP pipe were paying only seven and a half dollars an acre foot, up to 1990. It was a sweetheart deal, considering the price was far below the true cost of the water to the taxpayer, with estimates from some conservationists and water experts going to fifty dollars an acre foot.[6] On top of that, the farmers were using the subsidized water to grow

crops that were also subsidized—a "double-dipping" kind of arrangement.

Efforts to redress the situation had begun as a voice in the wilderness, reaching back to the 1950s. At that juncture, a grassroots organization, National Land For People, saw the subsidies as a national disgrace and as corporate welfare. With a dozen members from around the Fresno area, the organization sought to do something almost radical: it wanted the government to follow its own laws concerning the 160-acre limitation or require the large landowners to pay the full, true cost of the water for irrigating lands in excess of 160 acres. By adhering to the law, they argued, it would encourage single family farmers, perhaps the most efficient and environmentally sensitive of all growers.

One of the organizers of National Land For People, George Ballis, a journalist-turned-activist, described the violations of the reclamation law as "water welfare for the rich," enabling large farmers to grow subsidized crops with subsidized water.

Against this background, the 600,000-acre Westlands Water District found itself in the eye of the growing storm over the reclamation law acreage limitations. Under growing pressure from various sectors, Congress began grappling with the issue in the late 1970s; at that point, Westlands began bringing in its heavy guns including paid lobbyists and lawyers and their champion, Congressman, Tony Coelho, D-Merced.

In time, Congress hammered out a new law. Under the terms of the 1982 Reclamation Reform Act, the growers could obtain subsidized water for up to 960 acres, but above that acreage they were to pay the full cost of federal irrigation water. No sooner was the law passed than the process became corrupted. The water brokers went back to their paid congressmen and the Bureau of Reclamation to amend or administratively modify the law. The controversial leasing loophole, which enabled big growers to continue to receive cheap water for lands in excess of the 960 acre limitations, was not closed. It was back to business as usual. In the end, the National Land For People organization lost; the taxpayers lost; the environment lost. Almost everyone lost but the big corporate farmers. George Ballis stated:

> **The intent of the 1982 law was totally corrupted by the Southern Pacific Railroad and the big land owners. We lost to economic and political pressure. The new measure killed the reclamation reform, free enterprise and the river.[7]**

The results prompted Rep. George Miller, D-Martinez, to note, "They made legal what we made illegal in the reforms of 1982."[8] Even the bureau acknowledged that the intent of the law had been subverted and that a good attorney could still draft lease agreements whereby large acreage could still receive subsidized water.

While the battle may have been lost, the tide of the water wars had begun to swing, however slowly. The turning point had come even earlier, perhaps unnoticed, in the greening of the environment during the early 1970s. Focused in Central California, this effort was marked by the battle to build the New Melones Dam on the tributary Stanislaus River. Initially perceived as a battle of farmers versus white-water rafters, the struggle drew in sportsmen and conservationists, which spurred several environmental organizations to further efforts to save a handful of remaining wild rivers in California.[9]

While New Melones was eventually built, the water brokers were served notice that Californians were not going to take it anymore. Out of that battle emerged a vanguard of environmental activists led by Jerry Meral, Mark Dubois and Patricia Schifferle, who would help swing the pendulum of protection. In the late 1970s, the battle to save Mono Lake was launched. In 1982, the proposed Peripheral Canal was defeated. In 1986, freshman Congressman Rick Lehman of the 17th District—in the heart of agribusiness—opposed the construction of the proposed Rodgers Crossing Dam on the upper Kings River and, even more surprisingly, was reelected.

About the same time Kesterson was coming into the farming vernacular, two other buzzwords were creeping into the language of farming: "organic" and "sustainability." Across the agricultural scene the conventional wisdom, if that were the operative word, was under siege. A growing number of people began questioning the future of American agriculture. In some areas, the yields per acre were beginning to drop from their record highs. Others charged that current practices were not sustainable. Still others complained that the continued reliance on pesticides, irrigating with salt-laden, subsidized water, and accelerating crop rotation was not only shortsighted but was ruining the land. In 1983, for instance, scientists calculated that the brackish, salt-laden waters of the Delta-Mendota Canal were depositing 1.6 million tons of various salt compounds a year, or about three hundred pounds an acre a year.[10]

"It's a salt cycle that comes down the canal and drains out through the bay—again and again," explained Alex Hildebrand, a Manteca-area farmer and engineer.

More recently, concerns over the future of valley agriculture have come from the American Farmland Trust, whose recent studies have concluded that urban encroachment, air pollution, drainage and water supplies pose a critical problem.[11] A 1987 public television special, aptly entitled "Further Down the Drain," cast a bleak picture for the future of San Joaquin Valley agriculture. Some experts have suggested that over a million acres of valley farmland will become unproductive unless the drainage problem is addressed.[12]

Along the way, critics of the bureau began identifying the agency as the "Bureau of Wreck-a-nation"—often failing to identify the main villain: the pork-barreling, water brokers of the United States Congress.[13]

On a national scale, the National Academy of Sciences has a clearer focus, urging a fundamental reassessment of American farming practices.

> **The political setting has played a critical role in creating situations conducive to irrigation-related problems. The decision to irrigate the West was, of course, primarily a political one.**

Policy makers chose to promote social goals—the settlement of the West—through the Reclamation Act of 1902. This occurred at a time when there was great belief in the ability of technology and engineering to overcome almost any natural obstacle. The importance of political, economic and social factors cannot be overstated. In short, the institutional setting in the West created many of the problems now being faced, it created a structure that prevented the problem from being addressed effectively early on, and it will ultimately determine what solutions will be implemented. [14]

Experts such as Jan van Schilfgaarde, associate director of the United States Agricultural Research Service, has warned that if further catastrophes like Kesterson are to be avoided, a new water ethic or policy must be created which balances environmental, agricultural, and other factors more effectively than in the past. New ideas and new approaches are needed which would reexamine other dimensions of contemporary agriculture.[15]

For this purpose, C. Peter Timmer, a professor of development studies at Harvard University, has urged an end to federal farm policies that subsidize unsustainable agricultural practices. These extravagant subsidies to farmers cost American taxpayers $26 billion a year during the mid-1980s. This sum is spent on an industry that employs only 2 percent of the nation's work force. Even worse, most of the monies go not to family farms but to large agribusiness corporations that could operate profitably without backing up to the public treasury.[16]

The corruption and the concern went well beyond the river and delta into San Francisco Bay, where scientists have been investigating the impact of the waste-water on the natural ecosystems. There, organizations such as the Bay Institute of San Francisco have begun documenting the relationship between the excessive agriculture pollution from the San Joaquin Valley with areas known for birth defects, cancer clusters and other

health problems. The organization is also looking at the contamination of shell and fish life in the bay, suggesting that the spinoff from Kesterson reaches all the way to the bay.[17]

Controversy continues to swirl over California's heartland river, now regarded by some as the river of death. During the last few years the only water in the San Joaquin River between Kesterson and the Merced River has been agricultural wastewater, and runoff from one or two particularly wet winters. Recent tests of downstream samples reveal even higher levels of selenium. Other trace elements such as boron and arsenic present additional health concerns. The growing premise that the drain may never be complete further clouds the future of irrigation in the West.

The water tragedy, the Kesterson scenario, suggests that availability of cheap irrigation water encouraged the farming of marginal land that should never have been irrigated. The abundance of subsidized water also encouraged over-irrigation or, at least, excessive deep percolation of farmlands, which may have exacerbated the drainage situation, an allegation some farmers dispute. However, a 1991 Westlands Water District study acknowledged that 30 percent of the water applied to the lands served no prudent use or benefit.[18]

The corruption of the river hydrology continues to this day. In late 1989, then Secretary of the Interior Manuel Lujan, Jr. redefined the word "compromise." As the forty-year water contracts for millions of acre feet of subsidized water of the Friant-Kern and Madera canals came up for renewal, river advocates began pressing the government for an environmental review of those contracts. Perhaps one day, they reasoned, some of the river's water could be returned to its rightful course, the San Joaquin River. As it turned out, the environmentalists were putting hope before reality—and politics. The secretary, knowing some fifteen different environmental groups would go to court if such a review were not ordered, came up with a "compromise."[19]

Lujan ordered an environmental impact statement, but then assured the growers that the results of that study would not affect their right to a contract renewal or the quantity of water that would be delivered under those contracts. In other words, the status quo remained. Once again the "Hydraulic Brotherhood" had its way.

Representative Miller was outraged by the decision:

This is like studying the sinking of the Titanic without examining the significance of icebergs. Secretary Lujan's decision is an exercise in duplicity,

Other observers to the scene, such as Lloyd Carter, believe the future of San Joaquin Valley agriculture is bleak. Rising groundwater from the irrigation projects now threatens the lower areas of the basin. The wastewater problem, increasing urbanization and air pollution, exacerbated by both the quality and quantity of the water, underscore the gravity of the situation. According to Carter:

The San Joaquin River has been killed by man's greed and ignorance. It has either been diverted to the point of exhaustion, or it has become contaminated to the point where it is little more than a public sewer.

Agriculture as we know it in the Valley today is doomed. The problems at Kesterson are just the tip of the iceberg.[20]

CHAPTER FIFTEEN

Hard Choices

It would be easy to blame the problems of the San Joaquin River on those who came before us—the so-called "Sins of Our Fathers" syndrome. But the problems facing the heartland river of California are more complex than that.

Over the past century, Californians have developed the largest, most extensive water storage and distribution facilities in history. Yet today those facilities are unable to meet the perceived needs of an ever expanding California.

These contradictions and incongruities speak to only part of the problem. In a so-called average year, California receives approximately 200 million acre feet of rain or snowmelt—but there are few so-called average years. Despite the fickle nature of this supply, we have placed demands on our water resources that transcend reason. The urban residents and environmentalists point to the statistics, noting that agriculture takes approximately 80 percent of the available supply. Industry and municipalities take most of the remainder, leaving little for all the other plants and wildlife that make up our world.

Farmers, municipalities, industrial users all want their place at the drinking fountain. Agriculture calls for new water supplies—more dams—more bricks and mortar—claiming that the farmers need a dependable source of water.

As the agricultural interests point out, only half of available supply of surface and groundwater is "developed," ignoring those creatures large and small who have no voice in the debate.

Municipalities seek more. Sportsmen and commercial fishermen demand some minimal stream flows and riparian restoration. Conservationists plead for more judicious use of the existing supply, while environmental leaders demand more water be left in the rivers for fish and wildlife. Elsewhere along the line, water users from industry to the environmentalists seek more of the magic molecule.

Every human being and every living organism requires water, enough to survive, to thrive and sustain the magic web of life—the biotic diversity that enhances our lives and our planet. It is the quintessential ingredient of life. But today that fragile web is increasingly threatened by the same greed and ignorance that defined the practices of yesteryear. Whether by design or default, our present approach to responsible water use and allocation is flawed. Today, after a century of controversy marked by rancorous debate and lengthy litigation, California's water crisis continues to escalate.

What is needed is a reality check, recognizing the finite resources that are available. Today almost every major California river is oversubscribed; that is, there are more demands for its water than it can provide. In many areas of the state, the water table continues to drop, as does water quality. The natural hydrology of the major rivers has been altered or destroyed. The litany of abuses and misuses of our water resources goes on.

The real culprit is not the farmer or irrigator, nor the homeowners or the manufacturers. Least of all, the malefactor is not the altruistic environmentalist, whose ultimate goal is the preservation of biotic diversity, with some semblance of balance between man and nature. The real culprits are those who believe the problem could be solved by yet another reservoir or deeper well. They are those who build up to the available capacity of any service or resource—and then expect more. California represents a classic case of this "build-up syndrome"—whether it is a water project, freeway, airport or school.

For years, both state and federal politicians have shied away from touchy water or growth controls issues. In particular, state government has failed to address the mounting water crisis, ignoring the need for some kind of balance between water supply and demand. It has failed to establish firm water quality standards and enforce them. State government continues to waffle on the need for underground water controls, and so the pumps drone on. In the so-called dry years, underground pumping is accelerated, as the water table and water quality drop lower. The mining of water suggests a grim scenario where only those with the biggest pumps and deepest pocketbooks will survive. The state refuses to rewrite its ambiguous, litigious-prone, dual-system water law. Such issues are often too volatile or too hot to handle.

For the past hundred years, almost everyone thought new supplies of the precious molecule would be found. Even in the late 1800s, water-hungry Californians sought additional supplies. One promoter called for a tunnel through the Sierra that would tap into Lake Tahoe and provide vast amounts of water to the Bay Area. The idea went forward until irate Nevada residents threatened a lawsuit, pointing out that the lake's water also belongs to them. Some of today's water wishes have even more outlandish proportions. Some futurists call for desalinization; harvesting of icebergs from Alaska; diverting rivers of the Pacific Northwest; or some other far-reaching effort. Others look to technology, genetic engineering of crops or other advanced approaches to squeezing even more out of a drop of irrigation water.

Before any corrective action can take place, however modest, Californians must confront the growth issue. Every year, the state slips farther behind the growth curve.

In a state where rain and snowmelt are often out of sync with the water needs of 34 million people and 10 million acres of farmland, the future is anything but promising. Over the past twenty years, domestic water use has doubled. The outlook is further clouded by California's rocketing population projections. The state is expected to grow to more than 40 million within the next twenty years, yet water allocated to farms, cities and the environment is decreasing. It should come as no great surprise that more people are taking their place at the drinking fountain, also.

There can be little hope of addressing the critical water issue until state leaders face up to the growth issue. Growth only compounds the situation, making competing interests more defensive and intractable. California's great Central Valley cannot remain the breadbasket of nation if it continues to divert water to population growth. As it is, prime farmland is being turned into shopping centers and subdivisions. We see a 400-mile-long strip city unfolding along Freeway 99 between Bakersfield and Redding, bereft of any planning or effective controls, and with even less concern for water supplies. Against this horizon, a growing number of farmers see their final or ultimate crop as houses—accepting the fact that an acre of subdivision requires approximately the same amount of water as an acre of farmland.

To address the vexing water dilemma, it will be necessary to recognize growth and seek some kind of consensus among the various stakeholders—business, environment, agriculture and urban interests. Each one needs to understand that without some addressing of the problem, the situation will only deteriorate, taking on draconian dimensions.

An optimist might hope that a new century would bring new insights and wisdom to the water scene—a new world perspective. Americans, particularly Californians, need to redefine growth and development, away from the consumptive and destructive to quality growth. A wise man once observed that Western man—and woman— are "desert makers." That is, in the quest for ever more, they will develop or utilize any available resource until there is nothing left—a wasteland—even at the expense of their own descendants. We should recognize the real water culprits: they are all of us.

The problem besetting California water politics and the San Joaquin River and Bay-Delta in particular, will require a new mind-set, using an approach bordering on the radical. There is no panacea or magic bullet that will address all the competing interests against the reality of ever-increasing demands for water deliveries. Nor should it be a doomsday scenario for California agriculture. Any reasonable answer will require a new and higher level of stewardship and sacrifice from all Californians—one that recognizes the realities of the twenty-first century.

Without such fundamental changes toward balancing demand with supply, the future of the Golden State will be anything but bright. Without drastic changes in California's arcane water law and recognition of its finite water resources—and balancing those supplies to all of the needs of all Californians, including fish, fowl and native plant life—the golden web of California life will gradually unravel.

The key to restoring the San Joaquin River is to make fewer demands upon the river itself, accompanied by major environmental restoration. From a real-world perspective, restoring the lower San Joaquin River to a "pre-Friant" scenario is impossible. Restoration of the anadromous fishery is admirable but likewise highly improbable. But it should be possible to restore some viability and natural dynamics to the river and its riparian areas. Nature exhibits remarkable recuperative powers when given the opportunity. With time, the health of the river could be improved.

How would one define some acceptable level of restoration?

One starting point is to put some water back in the river. Some agonizingly slow efforts are being made. In January 1998, the U.S. District Court in Sacramento ruled in favor of the Natural Resources Defense Council, directing the Bureau of Reclamation and the Friant Water Users Association to renegotiate water contracts and make releases into the downstream channel. Yet most recently,

in October 1999, the court granted an eighteen-month stay to develop a plan for those releases into the channel below Friant Dam.

Mendota and Mendota Pool cry out for relief, too. The water-beleaguered residents of Mendota should bring suit against the state and federal government over the destruction of their riparian and underground water supplies. There can be no statute of limitation for an ongoing wrong. Through the combined actions of the state and federal government, the water quality in Mendota has deteriorated to the point where it cannot meet present-day standards under the Clean Water Drinking Act.

Downstream, the water quality of the Bay-Delta needs to be improved. If the runoff called a river is killing fish and other aquatic life, it may also be harmful to humans. One possible approach would be to idle some Westland farmlands that contributed to the pollution of the river below Mendota. Recent court rulings have ordered the federal government to solve the drainage problem on the West Side of the San Joaquin Valley. In all likelihood, however, the proposed San Luis Drain will never be built. The court was not specific as to how the problem would be solved. By idling some of that West Side farmland, the runoff of waste ag water and other naturally occurring elements such as selenium could be reduced. Without those chemicals going into the lower river, the health of the Delta could be enhanced measurably.

The lower San Joaquin River, from Mendota to the Delta, could be designated a Superfund site. This is another one of the nation's numerous polluted or contaminated areas that needs to be cleared and restored. Much of the contamination has been created as a result of actions by the federal government. Now it is their responsibility to clean up.

It will take Friant water to restore the San Joaquin River. Some of this water should come from those distant lands in Kern County that now receive San Joaquin River water via the Friant-Kern Canal. The 108-mile-long canal was never intended to serve as a prime source for irrigation. The Bureau of Reclamation contracts with those Friant water districts should be renegotiated to allow for phased reductions and gradual elimination of those most distant deliveries to places far removed from the San Joaquin River watershed.

Such cutbacks can be justified. Some of those water users, such as Arvin Edison Water District, are already selling some of their excess allotments for golf courses and subdivisions. It makes little sense to be irrigating new subdivisions and golf courses when that water could be part of the restoration process. The city of Fresno could reduce its contractual diversions.

These phased reductions should start at the southernmost end so as to minimize the impact on the affected growers. Those who bought into the bureau's massive water redistribution program, through no fault of their own, should be compensated. It would be patently unfair to expect today's farmers who entered into those contracts in good faith not to be compensated when they were, effectively, misled by the government. Any compensation should be modest, recognizing that restoration is a shared responsibility. The water allocated to Kern County should be returned to the river.

The California State Water Resource Control Board has the authority to implement change. It also needs to exercise its implied authority to regulate the underground system, recognizing that surface and underground supplies are inextricably linked together. The realities of water politics may preclude such corrective measures, however.

A decade has elapsed since the State of California was drawn into the controversy over the San Joaquin River. In signing Assembly Bill 3603, in 1990, then Governor George Deukmejian recognized the crisis threatening the river and designated it under "urgency status." So far, the proliferation of studies and other federal legislation has accomplished relatively little. The creation of CalFed, the consortium of state, federal agencies, scientists and other concerned individuals looking at water problems of the Bay-Delta, has left a mountain of studies but little results. The San Joaquin

River Riparian Habitat Restoration Program has also recognized the need for corrective action. After ten years the San Joaquin River Management Program has finally recognized the need for a mission statement. Collectively the results have been disappointing at best, abysmal at worst.

There is a glimmer of light at the end of the water tunnel. As the plight of the river has become known, an increasing number of people have responded. A new level of stewardship is beginning to emerge. The Central Valley Project Improvement Act of 1992 put the spotlight on the problem, requiring a doubling of fish populations in the Delta. The Natural Resource Defense Council has obtained a court order, requiring the Friant Water Users to put some water back into the river. The Bay Institute has rallied others to the front. California Save Our Streams has rescued a few threatened waterways. Concerned citizens of Fresno, Madera and Firebaugh called for the development of parkways along their respective stretches of the San Joaquin, where restoration of the riparian areas would be a prime concern. After fifty years, the State Water Resources Control Board has recognized the need to do its mandated job. Finally, last year, the state legislature began discussing legislation that would force new developments to identify their source of water, rather than simply tapping into an already overburdened existing delivery system.

Despite what some see as foot-dragging, Senator Jim Costa, D-Hanford, also believes there have been tremendous changes in addressing the problems hanging over the river: "We're continuing to make progress…the Central Valley Project Improvement Act, CalFed and last year's [1999] 'big flush' define some of the success we have had. Who ever thought we would have the NRDC and the Friant Water Users talking about restoration. It's not as fast as some would like, but we are making progress."

Much more needs to be done. Both state and federal water officials need to act decisively and boldly—without another decade of studies and endless hand-wringing. The task will not be easy. The issues are vast and complex.

Those visionaries and conservationists who seek to restore the river need to develop a clear and concise program that will not reward or punish any one group of water users.

Fifty years ago, the San Joaquin River was placed upon the block of expediency; it was dammed, diverted and destroyed. Call it greed, ignorance, arrogance or collusion; blame the problem on other human frailties.

The bell that sounded the death knell for the river cannot be "unrung." While history cannot hold today's Californians responsible for those earlier mistakes or misdeeds, it will hold them responsible if they fail to address the need to balance water consumption against available supplies. This is a charge and challenge for all Californians.

Central California
and the
San Joaquin River

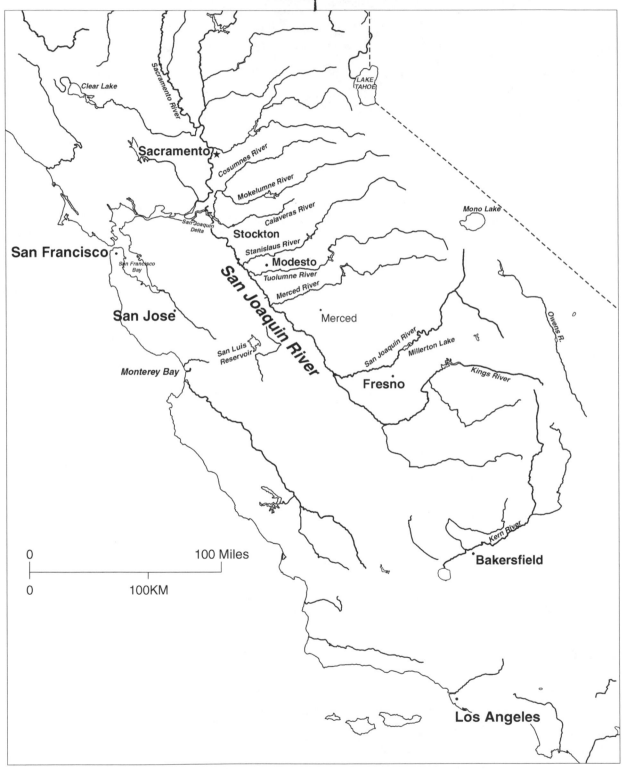

Clear Lake

Sacramento River

LAKE TAHOE

Sacramento

Cosumnes River

Mokelumne River

Mono Lake

Calaveras River

San Joaquin Delta

Stockton

Stanislaus River

San Francisco

Modesto

Tuolumne River

San Francisco Bay

Merced River

San José

Merced

San Joaquin River

Owens R.

San Joaquin River

Millerton Lake

San Luis Reservoir

Kings River

Monterey Bay

Fresno

Kern River

0   100 Miles

Bakersfield

0   100KM

Los Angeles

San Joaquin River—A Chronology

7000 B.C.(?)–The first Indians, forerunners of the Yokuts, arrive in the valley.

5000 B.C. (?)–Owens Valley Paiutes traverse Sierra crest and relocate in the Sierra foothills—as Mono or Monache Indians.

1543 A.D.–Explorer Juan Cabrillo passes the Golden Gate.

1769–Father Serra establishes the first mission at San Diego, followed by twenty others along the western flank of California.

1775–Frigate *San Carlos*, commanded by Lieutenant Juan Manuel de Ayala enters and explores uncharted San Francisco Bay.

1776–*San Carlos* carries Lieutenant Joaquin Moraga to the port of San Francisco; explorers then seek the source, "El Rio de San Francisco," the early name for rivers entering the Bay. Subsequent expeditions reach Calaveras River near today's Stockton.

1786–1808–Lieutenant Gabriel Moraga leads numerous Spanish expeditions into the valley, seeking mission sites and exploring valley, while naming the San Joaquin River and the major tributaries.

Late 1820s–French Canadian trappers under Michel LaFramboise enter valley, reaching today's French Camp. American trailblazer Jedediah Smith explores river basin, apparently discovering gold. Indian warfare increases.

1833–Joseph R. Walker makes first westerly crossing of High Sierra, fords San Joaquin River en route to Mission San Juan Bautista. Thirty Spanish land grants made for San Joaquin Valley cattlemen. Diseases introduced that decimate Indian popula-

tions. Dr. John Marsh establishes ranch near Mount Diablo.

1839–A lost and confused Captain John Sutter, of Sutter's Fort fame, rows up San Joaquin River for three days before finding his route on the Sacramento River.

1843–Captain John C. Fremont and Kit Carson begin an official survey of the Central Valley.

1845–Charles M. Weber establishes Stockton, known earlier as Tuleberg.

1846–Bear Flag Revolt and California's independence from Mexico. Treaty of Hildago signed 1848; California ceded from Mexico.

1848-49–Gold discovered at Coloma, triggering California's Gold Rush. Southern mining district booms around Mariposa and Columbia.

1850s–California statehood; San Joaquin, Mariposa and Contra Costa counties emerge as three of original twenty-seven counties. Steamers begin plying San Joaquin above Stockton, the gateway to the southern Mother Lode gold camps. San Joaquin City established upstream. Hill's Ferry river crossing established.

1851–Mariposa Indian War breaks out; Yosemite discovered. Fort Miller, Millerton established on upper San Joaquin. Newly formed legislature adopts riparian water doctrine.

1854–Stanislaus County formed. Firebaugh ferry begins service; 1855, Merced County carved out of Mariposa County; 1856, Fresno County established with county seat at Millerton.

1857–Steamer *Gipsey* forces its way upstream to

within three miles of Millerton—nine days above Stockton.

1858–Cattle barons Henry Miller and Charles Lux form Miller and Lux, acquiring vast land and cattle holdings.

1860s–Cattle and sheep raising dominate valley landscape. Loggers begin cutting the Sierra timberlands.

1861-62–Valley settlers introduced to the Great Flood—only to be followed three years later by the Great Drought.

1864–William Brewer and the California Geological Survey map upper San Joaquin River drainage. Livestock operators forced to take livestock to the upper drainage to find relief from extended droughts. Yosemite Valley and Mariposa Grove set aside as state preserve.

1867–Christmas flood devastates Millerton.

1868–Naturalist John Muir arrives in Yosemite.

1869–The Central Pacific Railroad completes the first bridge across the San Joaquin River at Mossdale.

1870s–Wheat growing spurred by arrival of irrigation. Central Pacific Railroad spans the length of the valley, leading to the decline of river traffic.

1871–Construction of San Joaquin and Kings River Canal begins; after sixty-three miles the firm runs out of money and is taken over by Henry Miller. Dredging of a Stockton channel proposed.

1874–Millerton abandoned; Fresno county seat moved to Fresno.

1877–Drought reduces San Joaquin River to a trickle, devastating valley's livestock industry.

1878–French Trail in the upper San Joaquin Canyon begun, linking Oakhurst to the Mammoth Lakes Mining District. State orders water study of Sacramento and San Joaquin rivers—for irrigation, flood control and navigation. Henry Miller completes first major canal.

1885–Fresno incorporated. Steamboats and barges begin disappearing from dewatered river.

1886–California Supreme Court decision on *Lux vs.*

Haggin reaffirms legal preeminence of riparian water rights.

1887–Legislature passes Wright Act, allowing the creation of public irrigation districts; eventually fifty-some districts created in San Joaquin River drainage.

1888–Newman station established—in the wake of Hill's Ferry. Railroad moves down the west side of the valley.

1890–Yosemite National Park established. Another major flood envelops Stockton and other valley communities.

1892–Challenge and subsequent appeal of *Lux vs. Haggin* challenge, leading to compromise and a dual system of water law in California.

1893–Madera County carved out of Fresno County. Sierra Forest Reserve organized under Department of Interior to control logging and grazing on public lands in the upper drainage of the San Joaquin River.

1895–San Joaquin Electric Company formed; John Eastwood's first hydroelectric plant established on Willow Creek tributary.

1898–First reserve rangers hired to patrol Sierra.

1902–Reclamation Act of 1902 passed, paving the way for massive federal water projects in the arid West.

1905–Yosemite Valley receded to federal protection.

1908–Minarets, upper middle fork, withdrawn from Yosemite National Park boundaries by mining interests.

1909–Community of Patterson founded by T. W. Patterson.

1910–Work begins on Eastwood's Big Creek Project, the largest hydroelectric project ever envisioned by one man.

1911–Steamboat *J.R. McDonald* makes last run from Stockton to Skaggs Bridge, in last ditch effort to restore commercial navigation on the river.

1913–President Wilson signs Raker Act, paving the way for dam building in Yosemite National Park.

1916–Henry Miller, the great irrigator and the man who

changed the river and the valley, dies in San Francisco.

1917–Stockton civic leaders propose channel dredging to twenty-four-foot depth. Southern California Edison Company acquires Pacific Light and Power Company's interest in Big Creek Project.

1919–Colonel Robert Bradford Marshall submits prototype state water project to governor—underscored by years of drought or flood on the San Joaquin River.

1920s–Continuing water problems force additional state and federal studies of the Central Valley rivers. Steamboating and barging on the river come to a close.

1921–The Mendota Dam rebuilt, replacing a series of wood and brush diversion dams.

1925–Stockton Deep Water Bond passes, sustaining the goal of a deepwater channel to the bay.

1926–Federal support for a Stockton channel emerges with passage of H.R. 5062. Riparian doctrine upheld again in *Herminghaus vs. Southern California Edison Company*.

1930–Dredging begins on Stockton deepwater channel.

1931–State version of the Central Valley Project approved by legislature and governor, but challenged by referendum, only to be narrowly approved by voters December 19, 1933.

1935–Congress passes Rivers and Harbor Act of 1935. President Franklin D. Roosevelt commits federal government to Central Valley Project.

1937–December flood ravages both San Joaquin and Sacramento drainage, causing $14,000,000 in damages.

1939–Work begins on Friant Dam; U.S. Bureau of Reclamation vows to maintain San Joaquin River as a "live stream." Federal government purchases Miller and Lux water rights for $2.45 million.

1941–First bids let for construction of Madera Canal.

1942–World War II temporarily halts construction of Friant canals; Stockton becomes a military port serving the war effort.

1944–Friant Dam completed; first water deliveries made in Madera Canal.

1944–Bid let for construction of Delta Mendota Canal; 1946, work begins on 153-mile Friant-Kern Canal.

1947–Downstream riverbottom owners launch epic *Rank vs. Krug* lawsuit over the dewatering of the river below Friant.

1959–Governor Edmund G. "Pat" Brown kills state lawsuit over San Joaquin River fishery, allowing U.S. Bureau of Reclamation to divert river flows.

1960s–Port of Stockton begins a major expansion, followed by the dredging of the river channel to depth of thirty-five feet.

1962–U.S. Supreme Court refuses to hear *Rank vs. Krug*, permitting Bureau of Reclamation to regulate release of water from Friant Dam.

1983–Selenium detected at Kesterson National Wildlife Refuge; San Luis Drain ordered plugged.

1985–Kesterson Reservoir closed.

1987–San Joaquin River Parkway proposed. Environmentalists challenge extension of Friant water contracts.

1989–Interior Secretary Manuel Lujan Jr. renews CVP water contracts.

1992–Central Valley Project Improvement Act approved by President George Bush.

1994–State and Federal task force launch CALFED, another attempt at resolving California's water problems.

1998–Natural Resources Defense Council and Friant Water Users Association agree to return 400,000 acre feet of water into relicted river channel.

2000–Calfed debate goes on. Courts order federal government to complete San Luis Drain. Water wars take new turn as Westlands Water District threatens to sue Friant Water Users Associaton over water diversions.

Chapter Notes

CHAPTER ONE: THE GENESIS OF THE SAN JOAQUIN RIVER

1. Clark, Lewis. Interview by author, Fresno, California, November 14, 1979.

2. Mott, Tom, Sr. Personal papers of Tom Mott Sr., Fresno, California.

3. Hill, Mary. *Geology of the Sierra Nevada*. University of California Press, 1975, pp. 18–21.

4. Huber, King N. "Amount and Timing of Late Cenozoic Uplift of the Central Sierra Nevada, California—Evidence from the Upper San Joaquin River Basin." Geological Survey Professional Paper 1197, U.S. Government Printing Office, 1981, pp. 1–27.

5. Eckhardt, Wymond. *Devils Postpile National Monument*. Sequoia Natural History Asssociation, 1977, pp. 3–7.

6. Matthes, Frances E. "Reconnaissance of the Geomorphology and Glacial Geology of the San Joaquin Basin, Sierra Nevada, California." Geological Survey Professional Paper 329, U.S. Government Printing Office, 1960, pp. 26–27.

7. Mederios, Dr. Joseph. "Valley Changes Staggering." *Fresno Bee*, Dec. 27,1981, p. B-1.

8. Winchell, L. A. *History of Fresno County*. Sierra Publishing Co., 1920, pp. 77–78.

9. Ibid., p. 80.

10. Mott, op. cit.

11. Stewart & Nuss Sand & Gravel Company employees. Interview by author, Fresno, California, June 17, 1987.

CHAPTER TWO: THE INDIANS AND THE RIVER OF MANY NAMES

1. Wooten, Clarence B. "Kerman, Its Inhabitants, Wildlife and Aborigines." *Kerman (California) News Print*, Aug. 7, 1964.

2. Swanton, John B. "Indian Tribes of North America." Smithsonian Institution, Bureau of Ethnology, Bulletin 145, 1952; and Sturtevant, William C. *Handbook of North American Indians*. Vol. 8 (California), Smithsonian Institute Press, 1978, frontpiece map.

3. *History of Merced, Stanislaus, Calaveras, Tuolumne, and Mariposa Counties,* 1973, p. 56. [Reproduction by McHenry Museum.]

4. Latta, Frank. Collected papers of Frank Latta, Box 17. Yosemite Research Library.

5. Morrato, Dr. Michael. "Chowchilla River Prehistory. *The Madera County Historian*, April 1972, p. 3.

6. Sanborn, Margaret. *Yosemite*. Random House, 1981, pp. 16–18.

7. Kientz, Louis. *Just Around Home at Auberry*. Private publication, 1983, p.36. [Published by Three Forests Interpretive Association, 2000.]

8. Ibid.

9. Watkins, T. H. *California*. American-West Publishing, 1973, pp. 35–36.

10. Gudde, Edwin G. *California Place Names*. University of California Press, 1969; and Hubbard, Harry. *Building the Heart of an Empire*, Meador Publishing Co., 1938, p. 22.

11. Wooten, op. cit.

12. Ibid.

13. Gilbert, Bill. *Westering Man*, Athenaeum, 1983, p. 137.

14. *History of Merced, Stanislaus, Calaveras, Tuolumne, and Mariposa Counties*, op. cit.

15. Segerstrom, Donald. *Calaveras—The Land of Skulls;* Mother Lode Press, 1955, pp. 2–11.

16. Mott, Tom, Sr. Personal papers of Tom Mott Sr., Fresno, California.

17. Coleman, Dr.Earl. Personal papers of Dr. Earl Coleman, Fresno, California.

CHAPTER THREE: STOCKTON TO MILLERTON—PORT TO FORT

1. Josephy, Alvin M. *The Great West*. American Heritage Publishers, 1969, p. 132.

2. Hubbard, Harry D. *Building the Heart of An Empire*, Meador Publishing Co., 1938, pp. 50–51.

3. *California Historical Quarterly*. Vol. 11, April 1923, pp. 35–36.

4. Josephy. op. cit., p. 180.

5. Gudde, Erwin G. *California Place Names*. University of California Press, 1969, pp. 313–14.

6. Hubbard, op. cit., pp. 55–56.

7. *Latter-day Biographical Encyclopedia*. Andrew Jenson History Co., 1920, pp. 606–7; and Gudde, op. cit., p. 115.

8. *Illustrated History of San Joaquin County*, Thompson & West, 1889, p. 17.

9. Ibid.

10. Hubbard, op, cit., p. 72.

11. Lewis, Donovan. *Pioneers of California*. Scottwal Associates Publishers, 1993, p. 464.

12. Ibid., p. 513.

13. *Illustrated History of San Joaquin County*, op. cit., p. 2.

14. Ibid.

15. Muir, Leo J. *A Century of Mormon Activities in California*. Vol.1. Desert News Press, 1957, pp. 36–37.

16. Patterson, W. K. "Major James Savage Monument." *Fresno Bee*, September 24, 1984, p. B-1.

17. Eccleston, Robert. *The Mariposa Indian War, 1850–51.* University of Utah Press, 1957, pp. 24–40.

18. Ibid., pp. 52–62.

19. *Millerton, Landmark of a Vanished Frontier*. California State Library, Historical Society of Southern California, Vol. III, 1893, pp. 22–25.

20. Bishop Kit. *A California Pilgrimage, 1855*. California State Library, 1921, p. 53.

21. Klette, William. "Miners Monument: Lonely Sierra Trail." *Fresno Bee*, September 8, 1968, p. B-2.

CHAPTER FOUR: THE SAN JOAQUIN BECKONS

1. *History of Stanislaus County*. San Francisco: Elliot & Moore Publishers, 1881, p. 169.

2. *Daily Union Democrat of Sonora*, reprinted in *Stanislaus Stepping Stones*, 1978, pp. 32, 34.

3. Brewer, William H. *Up and Down California, 1860–1864*. Yale University Press, 1930, pp. 508–9.

4. Woods, Dave. Interview by Tom Mott, 1924. Personal papers of Tom Mott, Sr., Fresno, California.

5. Rose, Gene. *Reflections of Shaver Lake*. Word Dancer Press, 1987, p. 17.

6. Blasingame, Morgan [of Millerton, California]. Interview by author, 1986.

7. Rose, op. cit., p. 7.

8. Brewer, op. cit., p. 244.

9. Ibid., pp. 378–379.

10. Ibid., p. 540.

11. Ibid., pp. 544–6.

12. Simpson, Jack [early Fresno-area cattle rancher]. Interview by author, Fresno, California, 1984.

13. Coleman, Dr. Earl. "The Diamond D Saga." *History of Blayney Meadows*. Private publication, 1959.

14. Solomons, Theodore S. "Among the Sources of the San Joaquin." *Sierra Club Bulletin*, January 1894, pp. 61–79.

CHAPTER FIVE: HENRY MILLER—THE MAN, THE MYTH AND THE RIVER

1. Smith, Joe. "The Death of Late Henry Miller." *Fresno Bee*, October 16, 1966, B-1.

2. Toscano, Joseph. Interview of Joseph Toscano by Tom Mott, 1918. Personal papers of Tom Mott, Sr., Fresno, California.

3. Tredwell, Edward E. *The Cattle King*. Panorama Publishing Co., 1954, pp. 11–13.

4. Ibid.

5. Thome, Joe. "Lux & Miller—Businessmen of the Los Banos." *Fresno Bee*, May 7, 1978, p. B-1.

6. Milliken, Ralph. Letter to Tom Mott, Sr., 1935. Personal papers of Tom Mott, Sr., Fresno, California.

7. *Fresno Bee*, October 16, 1966, p. B-1.

8. Smith, Joe. "Canals of Henry Miller." *Fresno Bee*, January 15, 1960, B-1; and Smith, Joe. "Tales of the San Joaquin." *Fresno Bee*, March 27, 1952, p. B-3.

9. *History of the Canal Companies under Miller and Lux*. Central California Irrigation Co. report, 1965; and *Fresno Bee*, January 15, 1950.

10. Pryor, Alton. "How the West Was Watered." *California Farmer*, November 18, 1988.

11. *Fresno Bee*, October 16, 1966.

12. Ibid.

13. Mott, Tom Sr. Personal papers of Tom Mott, Sr., Fresno, California.

14. *Fresno Bee*, October 16, 1966.

15. "Judge Orders Miller Estate Split." *Fresno Bee*, May 28, 1963. [The value of the estate varied over the years from $25 million to $40 million. By standards in the year 2000, the estate would range into the billions.]

CHAPTER SIX: WATER AND IRRIGATION—POWER AND POLITICS

1. Young, Walker R. *Fresno Bee*, February 27, 1942, pp. 1, 7.

2. *Fresno Bee*, November 14, 1962, p. 3.

3. "A Hundred Years Ago." *Sonora Union Democrat*, February 10, 1962.

4. Ibid.

5. Brewer, William H. *Up and Down California, 1860–1864*. University of California Press, p. 242.

6. *Water Conditions In California, Report 1*. California Department of Water Resources, February 1, 1989.

7. Brewer. op. cit., pp. 243–4, 283–4.

8. Mathews, Cheri. Biographical sketch of Silas Wilcox. *Modesto Bee*, July 10, 1984.

9. Patterson, William. "All Hail Father of Irrigation." *Fresno Bee*, October 3, 1978.

10. *Fresno Weekly Expositor*, July 13, 1870, p. 3.

11. *Fresno Bee*, July 10, 1949, p. B-1.

12. *Fresno Weekly Expositor*, July 30, 1873, p. 3.

13. Barnes, Dwight. *The Greening of Paradise Valley*. Modesto Irrigation District, 1987, p. 17.

14. Wilson, T. P. Document. T. P. Wilson file, special collections, Fresno State University, Madden Library, Woodward section.

15. Shallat, Todd A. *Water and The Rise of Public Ownership on the Fresno Plain, 1850–1978*. Fresno Public Works Department, pp. 18, 23–27.

16. Shallat. op. cit., p. 27.

17. Barnes. op. cit., p. 18.

18. Ibid., p. 19.

19. Mott, Tom Sr. Personal papers of Tom Mott, Sr., Fresno, California. [Observations regarding Henry Miller.]

20. Burns, Glenn [of Millerton, California]. Interview by Tom Mott, Sr., April, 1986.

21. Rose, Gene. Evelyn Rank article. *Fresno Bee*, March 18, 1988.

CHAPTER SEVEN: STEAMBOATS ON THE SAN JOAQUIN

1. Winchell, L. A. "San Joaquin River Valley Empire II." *Fresno Morning Republican*, June 26, 1923, p. 6-B.

2. *Fresno Bee*, May 7, 1952, p. B-1.

3. Smith, Joe. "Steamboat Days" (magazine supplement). *Fresno Bee*, February 14, 1943.

4. "Stockton." *California Historical Nugget*. California Historical Society, Vol. 7, No. 4, 1940.

5. MacMullen, Jerry. *Paddlewheel Days in California*. Stanford University Press, 1941.

6. Winchell, op. cit.

7. Josh. *San Joaquin (Stockton, California) Republican*, May, 1857. [The writer, identified only as "Josh" reported in the *San Joaquin Republican* of Stockton, May 1857. Also reprinted in the *Mariposa News*, June 8, 1857.]

8. Ibid.

9. Stockton, Billy [of Los Banos, California]. Interview by Tom Mott, Sr. Personal papers of Tom Mott, Sr., Fresno, California.

10. Hutchings, James. *Hutchings' California Magazine*, Vol. l, No.4, October, 1859.

11. "Steamers Plied the Valley Rivers." *Stanislaus Stepping Stones*, Summer, 1986, p. 35.

12. Winchell, op. cit.

13. "Firebaugh Became A City." *Fresno Bee*, April 16, 1956, p. B-1.

14. Mott, Tom Sr. Personal papers of Tom Mott, Sr., Fresno, California.

15. Mott, op. cit., Stockton interview.

16. *Canals of the San Joaquin River*. Report on Irrigation in California, Bulletin 100. U.S. Department of Agriculture, Government Printing Office, 1901, pp. 215–239.

17. "Steamboating on the San Joaquin River." *San Joaquin River News,* November/December, 1988, p. 8.

18. Harrison, Dorothy. "Crows Landing? What's That?" *Stanislaus Stepping Stones,* 1984, p.142.

19. Crow, John. Letter to Henry Miller. Personal papers of Tom Mott, Sr., Fresno, California.

20. Kahart, Jessie. "Hills Ferry Highlights." 1930 article, reprinted in *Newman 1888–1988*. Newman (California) Centennial Committee, 1988, p. 18.

21. Brotherton, Jack. "Hill's Ferry Offered Fun." *Stanislaus Stepping Stones,* September, 1987, p. 559.

22. Simon Newman profile. *Newman 1888–1988*. Newman (California) Centennial Committee, 1988.

23. Ibid.

24. Moody, Ralph. *Stagecoach West*. Thomas Y. Crowley Co., 1967, pp. 104–08.

25. Mott, op. cit.

26. Smith, Joe. "San Joaquin River Waterway." *Fresno Bee,* November 18, 1963, p. B-1.

27. *Fresno Morning Republican*, June 16, 1911. [Also reprinted in *The Madera County Historian*, Vol. XI, No. 1, January 1971, pp. 1–5.

28. "Historical Sketch of Upper San Joaquin River Navigation." Document 322, submitted to the 65th Congress, 1917; and Wood,

Raymund. Speech to E. Clampus Vitus, 1974.

    29. *Fresno Morning Republican*, op. cit.

    30. Ibid. [See also, Washburn, Edgar B. and Sean E. McCarthy. *San Joaquin River Navigability and Preliminary Ordinary High Water Line Study*. Report to the Assembly Committee on Water, Parks and Wildlife, October 24, 1989, p. 16.

CHAPTER EIGHT: JOHN MUIR AND THE HEADWATERS OF CONSERVATION

    1. Kimes, William, and Maymie Kimes. *John Muir, A Reading Bibliography*. Panorama West Books, 1986, p. 163.

    2. Ibid.

    3. Sanborn, Margaret. *Yosemite,* Random House, 1981, pp. 78–80.

    4.Williams, John H. *Yosemite and Its High Sierra*. Self-published, 1921, p. 50.

    5. Sargent, Shirley. *Yosemite, The First 100 Years, 1890–1990.* Yosemite Park and Curry Co., 1990, p. 34.

    6. Muir, John. *The Mountains of California, 1894*, pp. 52–73.

    7. Ibid., pp. 241–43.

    8. Wolfe, Linnie Marsh. *Son of the Wilderness: The Life of John Muir.* University of Wisconsin Press, 1945, p. 144.

    9. Clark, Lew and Ginny Clark. *Mammoth-Mono Country.* Western Trails Publication, 1981, p. 14.

    10. McCormick, Kevin G. and Jay Goldsmith. Correspondence. Sierra National Forest historical files. [The Sierra National Forest headquarters is located in Clovis, California.]

    11. Tully, Gene. Interview by Leon R. Thomas. Sierra National Forest historical files (Sierra history file), October 11, 1956.

    12. Rose, Gene. *Reflections of Shaver Lake.* Word Dancer Press, 1987, p. 107.

    13. Eckhardt, Wymond. *Devils Postpile National Monument.* Sequoia Natural History Association, 1977, pp. 20–22.

    14. Kimes and Kimes, op. cit., p. 92.

CHAPTER NINE: TOOLS TEMPERED IN THE RIVER

    1. "Letter from Millerton." *Fresno Weekly Expositor*, January 23, 1878, p. 3.

    2. Mott, Tom Sr. Personal papers of Tom Mott, Sr., Fresno, California.

    3. Paterson, Alan M. *The History of the Turlock Irrigation District.* Turlock Irrigation District, 1987, p. 107.

    4. "Fresno Scraper Helped Shape Farming." *Fresno Bee,* September 22, 1985, p. R-5.

    5. Ibid.

    6. Mott, op. cit.

    7. "Fresno Scraper Gave Its Birthplace Global Fame." *Fresno Bee*, February 22, 1981, p. J-16.

    8. *Fresno Bee,* September 22, 1985.

    9. Barnes, Dwight. *The Greening of Paradise Valley.* Modesto Irrigation District, 1987. p. 7.

    10. Wood, R. Coke, and Leonard Covello. *Stockton Memories.* Valley Publishers, 1977, p. 2.

    11. *Caterpillar World,* May 1984, pp. 3–39.

    12. Ibid.

    13. Wood and Covello, op. cit., p. 89.

    14. Ibid.

CHAPTER TEN: SAN JOAQUIN HYDROPOWER

    1. Whitney, Charles Allen. "John Eastwood: Unsung Genius of the Drawing Board." *Montana Magazine*, Summer, 1969, pp. 38–42.

    2. "Hydro Electric Development on the San Joaquin River." Incorporation documents of the San Joaquin Electrical Company, April 2, 1895. Pacific Gas & Electric Company, 1959.

    3. Welch, Marguerite Eastwood. Correspondence with author,

1981. Author files. [Marguerite Eastwood Welch of Oakland, California is John Eastwood's niece.]

    4. Coleman, Charles. *The History of PG&E.* Publication of Pacific Gas and Electric Company, 1952, p. 46.

    5. Fowler, D. *Hydro Development in the San Joaquin River Basin.* Fresno, California: [Publisher unknown.] 1923, p. 45.

    6. Ibid, p. 47.

    7. Lowe (article). *Journal of Electricity*, 1896. p. 80.

    8. Fowler, op. cit., p. 48.

    9. Walker, Roy. Private obervations. Southern California Edison Company correspondence files, Rosemead, California.

    10. Myers, William A. *Iron Men and Copper Wires.* Trans-Anglo Books, 1983, p. 101.

    11. Ibid.

    12. Johnston, Hank. *The Railroad That Lighted Southern California.* Trans-Anglo Books, 1965, p. 10.

    13. Miller, Catherine. "Herminghaus vs. Southern California Edison." *Pacific Historical Review*, Vol. LVIII, No. 1, February, 1989, p. 8.

    14. Rose, Gene. *Reflections of Shaver Lake.* Word Dancer Press, 1987, pp. 80–84.

    15. Ross, Fred. Conversation with author, Blayney Meadows, California, 1986. [Fred Ross was a longtime Sierra packer at Blayney Meadows, California.]

    16. Jackson, Donald Conrad. "A History of Water in the West: Johns Eastwood and the Ultimate Dam." Dissertation. University of Pennsylvania, 1984.

    17. Adams, Larry. "Stream Gaugers Recall Icy Mountain Hazards." *Fresno Bee*, February, 1966, p. F-3.

    18. Rose, Gene. *High Odyssey.* Howell-North, 1974 and Panorama West, 1988, pp. 17–29.

CHAPTER ELEVEN: THE RIVER BETRAYED

    1. Baker, George B. "Friant Ceremony Starts Southern CVP Fete Series." *Fresno Bee*, August 8, 1951, p. A-1.

    2. Mott, Tom Sr. Personal papers of Tom Mott, Sr., Fresno, California.

    3. "Irrigation of the San Joaquin, Tulare and Sacramento Valleys, California." President U. S. Grant Executive Document 290, March 23, 1874.

    4. "Central Valley Project." *Fresno Bee*, July 26, 1952, p. A-1.

    5. *Fresno Morning Republican*, April 6, 1896, p. 8.

    6. "History of the Central Valley Project." U.S. Department of the Interior, Bureau of Reclamation report, 1940, pp. 1–12.

    7. Young, Walker R. "Preserving the Central Valley—A Brief Sketch of the Reclamation Bureau's Vast Project in California, 1939," U.S. Bureau of Reclamation, 1939, p. 543. [Walker Young was the Assistant Chief of the Bureau of Reclamation.]

    8. Report on the San Joaquin Valley; U.S. Army Corps of Engineers, 1928.

    9. "Central Valley Project." *Sacramento Bee*, August 6, 1933, p. 1.

    10. Associated Press. "Rolph Orders Full Speed Ahead." *Fresno Bee*, December 21, 1933. p. 1.

    11. Ibid.

    12. "History of the Central Valley Project," op. cit.

    13. "Central Valleys (sic) Project." *Fresno Bee*, November 11, 1936, p. B-1.

    14. Associated Press. "Marysville Foe of Valley Plan Launches Attack." *Sacramento Bee*, May 13, 1936, pp. A-1, 8-B.

    15. "Kerman Group Protests Plan to Close River." *Fresno Bee*, February 7, 1938, p. 1-A.

    16. Ibid.

    17. "Bureau Official Sees Friant Progress." *Fresno Bee*, February 27, 1942, p. 1-A.

18. "Water Users File Suit to Settle Riparian Rights." *Fresno Bee*, September 26, 1947, p. 1-B.

19. Smith, Dr. G. E. P. *The Failure of the Keystone of the Arch of the Central Valley Project.* University of Arizona special paper, January 15, 1952.

20. "Judge Rules Against Bureau." *Fresno Bee,* February 8, 1956, p. A-1.

21. U.S. Department of the Interior document ("Proposed Contract with Grassland Water District"), 1954.

22. Smith, Felix. *A Sham—The San Joaquin River Give Away.* Private paper. Committee to Protect the Public Trust, 1989.

23. Carter, Lloyd. "30-Year-Old Water Battle Resurfaces." *Fresno Bee*, February 23, 1989.

24. Ibid.

25. Smith, Felix, op. cit.

26. U.S. Supreme Court, 2h3n 1963; petitions, 31, 51 and 115.

27. Rank, Everett Bud Jr. Telephone interview with author, January 17, 2000.

28. Winton, J. Martin. Interview by author, October 23, 1988.

CHAPTER TWELVE: THE RIVER REARRANGED

1. *Port of Stockton*, 50th Anniversary publication, Port of Stockton (California), 1983, p. 15.

2. Ibid., p. 7.

3. Ibid., p. 9

4. Schell, Hal. Telephone interview by author, Dec. 9, 1989.

5. "Lower San Joaquin River, California, Clearing and Snagging." Draft report, U.S. Army Corps of Engineers, April 1989, pp.1–4.

CHAPTER THIRTEEN: FISH, FOWL & FUN ALONG THE SAN JOAQUIN

1. Mott, Tom Sr. Personal papers of Tom Mott, Sr., Fresno, California.

2. Ibid.

3. *Fresno Weekly Expositor*, August 25, 1878. p. 3.

4. Mott, op. cit..

5. Ibid.

6. Black, H. E. "Duck Hunting in Past Years." Unpublished game warden's report, Madera, California, 1968.

7. J. Martin Winton, interview, Fresno, September 27, 1989.

8. Mott, op. cit.

9. Winton, J. Martin. Personal papers. San Joaquin College of Law, Clovis, California.

10. Holcomb, Earl H. Interview by author. Antioch Historial Society meeting, Antioch, California, September 17, 1989.

11. Solomons, Theodore S. "Among the Sources of the San Joaquin." *Sierra Club Bulletin*, January, 1894. pp. 61–80.

12. "To Protect Game." *Fresno Morning Republican*, August 25, 1898, p. 3.

13. Smith, Robert S. Personal papers, February 23, 1976.

14. "When Sport Became Slaughter." *Fresno Bee*, February 24, 1986, p. C-6.

15. Black, op. cit.

16. *A Great Variety of Game Birds, History of Merced County*, Elliott Pub. Co., 1919 (reprint), p. 146.

17. "The River Supplied Adventure." *The Patterson Irrigator*, May 31, 1984.

18. Ibid.

19. Newman Museum. Photographic collection (notation on back of photograph).

20. Winton, op. cit.

21. "Dynamiting Fish." *Fresno Daily Evening Expositor*, June 26, 1897, p. 1.

22. Imperatrice, Tony. Interview by author, Feburary 11, 1988.

23. "Central Valley Basin, A Comprehensive Report of the Development of Water and Related Resources of the Central Valley Basin for Irrigation, Power Production and other Beneficial Uses in California, and Comments by the State of California and Federal Agencies." U.S. Bureau of Reclamation, August, 1949, pp. 242–49.

24. Ibid.

25. Selleck, David. Interview by author, Fresno, California. Dec. 4, 1989. [Selleck is a retired regional director of the California Department of Fish and Game.]

26. "Grassland Water Summary." Report of the Grassland Water District, 1963, p. 13.

27. "Gorge Explorers Take A Trip Out of This World." *Fresno Bee*. September 13, 1980, p. B-1.

28. "Woodlands of California's Central Valley, Status and Trends, 1939-1980." U.S. Fish and Wildlife Service, June 1989, pp. ii, 7.

29. Imperatrice, op. cit.

30. "Woodlands of California's Central Valley," op. cit.

CHAPTER FOURTEEN: SELENIUM, SALTS AND THE SAN JOAQUIN RIVER

1. Zahm, Gary. Telephone interview by author. with Gary Zahm, January 29, 1990. [Zahm served as manager of the San Luis National Wildlife area for the U.S. Fish and Wildlife Service.]

2. "Selenium." *California Geology,* May, 1986, pp. 99–106.

3. Winton, J. Martin. "Grasslands Water, Kesterson." Personal papers of J. Martin Winton, 1989. San Joaquin College of Law.

4. Carter, Lloyd. Conversation with the author, February 17, 1988.

5. Winton, "Grasslands Water, Kesterson," op. cit., p. 8.

6. Shabecoff, Philip. "U.S. Issues Rules on Water for West." *New York Times,* April 9, 1987.

7. Ballis, George, National Land For People. Interview by author, January 8, 1990.

8. "New Water Rules Leaky." *Fresno Bee,* April 10 1987, p. B-1.

9. Palmer, Tim. *Stanislaus: The Struggle For a River.* University of California Press, 1982, pp. 46–51.

10. "Risks, Challenges and Opportunities: Agriculture, Resources and Growth in a Changing Central Valley." American Farmland Trust report, August 22, 1989.

11. "San Joaquin Drainage Program." Draft final report. American Farmland Trust, June, 1990, pp. 3-S.

12. Ulrich, Katherine. *Vital Statistics, A Factual Profile of California's Heartland,* November, 1989.

13. Warner, George. "Remembering the San Joaquin." *Bay on Trial.* Vol. 1, Spring, 1989, p. 3.

14. *Irrigation Induced Water Quality Problems.* National Academy Press, 1989, p. 5.

15. Schilfgaarde, Jan van. "Hurting Farming Practices." *Fresno Bee,* January 15, 1990.

16. "The Subsidy Monsters Cost $25 Billion a Year." *Selma Enterprise,* January 25, 1989, p. 10.

17. Davoren, William T. "San Joaquin Valley Health Project Proposal." The Bay Institute, November 27, 1989.

18. "Irrigation Efficiency Studies." Westlands Irrigation District, December, 1989.

19. "Lujan Renews Water Giveaway." *Headwaters*, January-February, 1990, p. 14.

20. Carter, op. cit.

Index

Index